The Ethics of Species

We are causing species to go extinct at extraordinary rates, altering existing species in unprecedented ways, and creating entirely new species. More than ever before, we require an ethic of species to guide our interactions with them. In this book, Ronald L. Sandler examines the value of species and the ethical significance of species boundaries, and discusses what these mean for species preservation in the light of global climate change, species engineering, and human enhancement. He argues that species possess several varieties of value, but they are not sacred. It is sometimes permissible to alter species, let them go extinct (even when we are a cause of the extinction), and invent new ones. Philosophically rigorous, accessible, and illustrated with examples drawn from contemporary science, this book will be of interest to students and researchers of philosophy, bioethics, environmental ethics, and conservation biology.

RONALD SANDLER is an Associate Professor of Philosophy and the Director of the Ethics Institute at Northeastern University. He is also a senior researcher in Northeastern's Environmental Justice Research Collaborative and its Nanotechnology and Society Research Group. Sandler is author of *Character and Environment: A Virtue-oriented Approach to Environmental Ethics* (2007) and *Nanotechnology: The Social and Ethical Issues* (2009). He is co-editor of *Environmental Virtue Ethics* (with Philip Cafaro, 2005) and of *Environmental Justice and Environmentalism: The Social Justice Challenge to the Environmental Movement* (with Phaedra C. Pezzullo, 2007).

Cambridge Applied Ethics

Titles published in this series:

The Ethics of Species

An Introduction

RONALD L. SANDLER

Northeastern University

CAMBRIDGE
UNIVERSITY PRESS

CAMBRIDGE
UNIVERSITY PRESS

University Printing House, Cambridge CB2 8BS, United Kingdom

Published in the United States of America by Cambridge University Press, New York

Cambridge University Press is part of the University of Cambridge.

It furthers the University's mission by disseminating knowledge in the pursuit of education, learning and research at the highest international levels of excellence.

www.cambridge.org
Information on this title: www.cambridge.org/9781107023468

First published 2012
Reprinted 2013

Printed in the United Kingdom by Clays, St Ives plc.

A catalogue record for this publication is available from the British Library

Library of Congress Cataloging in Publication data
Sandler, Ronald L.
The ethics of species / Ronald L. Sandler.
    p.   cm. – (Cambridge applied ethics)
Includes bibliographical references and index.
ISBN 978-1-107-02346-8 (hbk.)
1. Environmental ethics.   2. Bioethics.   3. Species.   4. Biodiversity.
5. Nature – Effect of human beings on – Moral and ethical aspects.   6. Human – animal
relationships – Moral and ethical aspects.   7. Conservation biology – Moral and ethical
aspects.   8. Mass extinctions – Moral and ethical aspects.   9. Genetic engineering – Moral
and ethical aspects.   10. Climatic changes – Moral and ethical aspects.   I. Title.
GE42.S263   2012
179′.1–dc23

                                                                                2012013413

ISBN 978-1-107-02346-8 Hardback
ISBN 978-1-107-65870-7 Paperback

To
Elijah Reed Sandler
and
Ruth Sydney Sandler

Contents

Preface

Our technology provides us with enormous and wide-ranging power with respect to species. We are causing species to go extinct at extraordinary rates, altering existing species in unprecedented ways, and creating entirely novel species. More than ever before, we require an ethic of species to guide our interactions with them and our choices regarding them. Central to an ethic of species are accounts of the value of species and the ethical significance of species boundaries. Developing these is the core theoretical project in this book. The core applied issues are what the value of species and ethical significance of species boundaries imply for species preservation under conditions of global climate change, modification of existing species (including ourselves), and engineering novel species. Species and the individuals that comprise them possess myriad varieties of value that need to be appreciated and considered in action, practice, and policy contexts. But species are not sacred. They do not have absolute or unconditional value, and they are not untouchable. It is sometimes permissible to alter them; it is sometimes permissible to let them go extinct (even when we are a cause of the extinction); and it is sometimes permissible to invent new ones. In fact, sometimes we ought to do these things, in just, caring, compassionate, and ecologically sensitive ways.

Acknowledgments

I am grateful to Northeastern University and the Department of Philosophy and Religion for a sabbatical from teaching during the fall 2010 semester to write the first draft of the manuscript for this book. I am fortunate to be a member of such a supportive and collegial department.

All or portions of the manuscript were read by John Basl, Jeremy Bendik-Keymer, Phil Cafaro, Katie McShane, Christopher Preston, Allen Thompson, two anonymous Cambridge University Press reviewers, and students in my spring 2010 Ethics and Emerging Technologies course, fall 2011 Environmental Ethics course, and fall 2011 Inquiry Seminar. I am grateful to them all for the many constructive comments, criticism, and suggestions that I received. The book is much improved as a result of their engagement with it.

Some of the material in this book draws from research that I have done with John Basl on artifacts and Judith Crane on species. I am deeply appreciative of the contributions they have made to my understanding of those topics. I am fortunate to have collaborators who are so philosophically astute and such good fun.

Jennifer Haskell, Carol Larson, Haden Quinlan, Luke Simon, and William Sisk provided valuable research assistance on this project. I am privileged to work with such motivated and capable students.

Most of all, I thank my family. Without the love and support of my wife, Emily, this book, like all good things in my life, would not have been possible. The book is dedicated to my children, Elijah and Ruth. Their wonder and enthusiasm toward the world make every day an unpredictable adventure. I love them everywhere and all the time.

1 Introduction

1.1 Why an ethic of species?

Humanity's relationship to other species has reached critical junctures. We are causing species to go extinct at an unprecedented rate in comparison with any other time in the last 65 million years.[1] The background or normal historical rate of extinctions is approximately one species per one million per year.[2] There is no precise data, and estimates vary, but many leading experts on biodiversity believe there are around ten million eukaryotic (or plant and animal) species.[3] Therefore, in normal times, there would be around ten species extinctions per year. However, as a result of human activity – for example, pollution, extraction, and habitat destruction – species extinctions already exceed one thousand species per million per year.[4] Moreover, the rate of extinction is expected to substantially increase due to global climate change, according to several scenarios surpassing 10,000 species extinctions per million per year,[5] over a quarter of species committed to extinction by 2050,[6] and one half of species extinct by 2100.[7] Even on optimistic (and increasingly unlikely) scenarios, in which the increase in the global mean surface air temperature of the planet is limited to around 2°C above pre-industrial temperatures, 20–30 percent of species are expected to be at increased risk of extinction by 2100.[8] The Earth's

---

[1] Magurran and Dornelas (2010).

[2] Baillie et al. (2004) calculates the historical rate of extinction as .1–1 E/MSY.

[3] Vié et al. (2009); Strain (2011).

[4] Baillie et al. (2004); IUCN (2011). For a review of the rates for vertebrates, see Hoffman et al. (2010).

[5] Wilson ([1999] 2010); IUCN (2011). Assuming 10 million species, this is approximately 275 species per day.

[6] Thomas et al. (2004).   [7] IPCC (2007a).   [8] IPCC (2007a).

next major extinction event appears to have begun, and this time it is anthropogenic.[9]

In addition to eliminating species, we are engineering them in unprecedented ways. Intentional manipulation of species has been occurring since at least the beginning of agriculture – through selective breeding, hybridization, and grafting – and recombinant DNA techniques have been used for decades to insert genes from one individual into another, including across species. However, advances in genetic engineering have substantially scaled up the precision, intensity, and comprehensiveness of these modifications.

One research group has engineered a yeast (*Saccharomyces cerevisiae*) that produces high concentrations of artemisinic acid – the precursor for artemisinin, an antimalarial drug – by transplanting genes from sweet wormwood (*Artemisia annua*), the traditional source of artemisinin, and several bacteria species, which code for the requisite metabolic pathway, into the yeast.[10] Another research group has chemically synthesized the entire genome of a *Mycoplasma mycoides* bacteria, inserted it into a non-*M. mycoides* host cell, and "booted it to life" – that is, started up the metabolic processes of the *M. mycoides*.[11] Engineering biology has become sufficiently accessible that there is now an annual genetically engineered machine competition in which high school and undergraduate teams use and contribute to "a continuously growing collection of genetic parts that can be mixed and matched to build synthetic biology devices and systems."[12]

While some researchers are intensively reengineering existing biological parts and systems, others are developing life forms that are not derived from prior organisms. One research team has created "self-replicating cells assembled from nonliving organic and inorganic matter."[13] These entities are approximately one million times smaller than bacteria and do not contain any biomolecules found in modern living cells. They are artificial, evolving life forms (or life-like forms) that are unrelated to any existing or prior life forms.

Technologies that are used to modify ourselves, members of the species *Homo sapiens*, are also increasingly powerful. People are eager to incorporate

---

[9] Barnosky et al. (2011).   [10] Ro et al. (2006).   [11] Gibson et al. (2010).
[12] Registry of Standard Biological Parts (2010).   [13] AAAS (2005).

technologies into their lives if they believe they will improve their abilities or health. The human growth hormone industry, although largely illegal, is estimated to be worth several billion dollars annually;[14] and 7 percent of college students[15] and 20 percent of research scientists use off-label pre-scription pharmaceuticals (e.g., methylphenidate [Ritalin] and modafinil [Provigil]) to increase alertness and productivity.[16] This is not a historical aberration. People have been enthusiastically ingesting natural and engi-neered chemical compounds to improve or repair biological functioning for millennia, and coffee, an effective stimulant, has long been among the most traded commodities in the world. The difference with emerging technolog-ical enhancements – such as genetic technologies, brain-machine interfac-ing, and nootropics ("smart drugs") – is the magnitude of augmentation that they will enable, as well as the extent to which they will do so by modifying or integrating with our biological systems. Already people are controlling computers with their brain states;[17] people have bionic arms that are spontaneously integrating with their nervous system;[18] researchers are successfully combining human and nonhuman genomic material;[19] and pharmaceuticals intended to increase longevity have gone into clinical trials.[20]

It is because we have the power to cause mass extinctions, substantially modify existing species, and create novel species that we require an ethic of species. Central to an ethic of species are an account of the value of species and an account of the ethical significance of species boundaries. The former concerns the sorts of value that species have and the bases for their having it. The latter concerns whether species boundaries carry normative significance, such that mixing species, modifying species, or intentionally creating individuals outside existing species boundaries is intrinsically problematic. These are the core theoretical issues of this book. The core applied issues are what the value of species and normative significance of species boundaries imply for species preservation under

---

[14] Olshansky and Perls (2008).

[15] McCabe et al. (2005). Others have suggested that the rate could be as high as 35 percent (University of Michigan Health System 2008).

[16] Maher (2008).   [17] Hochberg et al. (2006).   [18] McGrath (2007).

[19] Ourednick et al. (2001); Almeida-Porada et al. (2005); Jacobs et al. (2007).

[20] Keim (2008).

conditions of rapid climate change, modification of existing species (including ourselves), and engineering novel species.

In the remainder of this Introduction, I explicate the conception of species that is operative in the book and then provide an overview of the book's organization, central claims, and arguments.

1.2   Species as forms of life

There is no widely agreed upon definition of "species," but rather a host of competing species concepts. Species are sometimes conceived in terms of reproductive isolation: that is, as interbreeding (or potentially interbreeding) populations.[21] They are sometimes conceived phylogentically or evolutionarily: that is, as a lineage of ancestral descendant populations.[22] They are sometimes conceived ecologically: that is, as populations that occupy an ecological niche different from that of any other lineage in its range.[23] They are sometimes conceived genetically: that is, in terms of overall genotypic similarity distinct from that of other organisms.[24] And they are sometimes conceived morphologically: that is, in terms of shared anatomical features different from those of other groups of organisms.[25] That there are so many different conceptions of species has given rise to the issue of whether there is one correct account of species (*species monism*), or whether there is a plurality of legitimate species concepts (*species pluralism*). A related issue is whether species are real categories into which biological organisms are divided based on their features (*species realism*); or whether species are merely conventions (*species conventionalism*), that is, useful ways to organize the living world, but not reflective of the fundamental features of living things.[26] The status of species boundaries tracks that of species. If species are real, then so too are species boundaries; if species are conventions, then species boundaries are as well.

Part of the explanation for why there are myriad conceptions of species is that biologists with different concerns and research projects refer to

---

[21] Mayr and Ashlock (1991).   [22] Wiley (1978).   [23] van Valen (1976).

[24] Sokal and Crovello (1970).   [25] Cronquist (1978); Kitcher (1984); Stamos (2003).

[26] In addition to the monism/pluralism and real/conventional aspects of "the species problem," there is a metaphysical dimension, i.e., whether species are collections of individuals, abstract forms, or historical individuals distinct from the organisms that comprise them (Crane 2004).

different kinds of groups as "species." For instance, the ecological species concept is more useful for ecologists formulating and studying questions about ecological relationships and functions than is the phylogenetic species concept; whereas the phylogenetic species concept is better suited to the work of evolutionary biologists interested in ancestral relationships than is the ecological species concept. And while reproductive isolation is a useful approach to categorization when trying to distinguish groups of sexually reproducing organisms whose ranges overlap, it is less useful where populations do not overlap geographically, and it is not at all useful when studying populations of asexually reproducing organisms. That there is a multiplicity of species concepts that are used productively to study and explain the biological world provides support for species pluralism. It suggests that each of the various concepts picks out biologically significant features of organisms. The monistic idea that there is a single best way to divide organisms into species seems belied by productive biological practice.

Species pluralism garners additional support from the fact that no one species concept captures an aspect of organisms or the biological world that is more fundamental than all other aspects. For example, all natural (or nonengineered) organisms have ancestor relationships, so it is possible to categorize the natural world, including at the species level, phylogenetically. But all organisms are also inextricably ecologically situated, and this is crucial for understanding why organisms and populations have the characteristics they have and behave as they do. In fact, the ecological situatedness of populations turns out to be important for understanding phylogeny, since environmental changes are crucial in explaining evolutionary history, while phylogenetic information can be useful for understanding the functioning of ecological communities.[27] So it is not the case that either phylogenetic relationships or ecological ones are more explanatorily fundamental. Each captures something important about life in an evolved biological world, which is why they are powerful and influential species concepts.

Organisms have phylogenies, ecological niches, genetic features, and reproductive communities. These are all explanatorily important, and no one of them picks out the fundamental causal structure of the biological world. For these reasons, species pluralism is the more plausible view.

---

[27] Tan et al. (2011).

However, species pluralism does not imply full-blown relativism. Biological reality places constraints on what counts as a legitimate species concept, otherwise species divisions would be arbitrary and we would have to accept "the suggestions of the inexpert, the inane, and the insane."[28] At a minimum, a legitimate species concept needs to classify organisms into groups, since the point of a species concept is to divide and organize organisms. Moreover, it must do so by features that are biological properties of organisms or groups of organisms. These properties can be either internal (e.g., genetic) or relational (e.g., ancestral). A legitimate species concept must also be explanatorily useful. It must help make sense of the world by organizing it in ways that increase our understanding of it or increase our ability to make predictions regarding it.[29]

The conception of species that is primarily used in this book is that species are groups of biologically related organisms that are distinguished from other groups of organisms by virtue of their shared *form of life*. A species' form of life refers to how individuals of the biological group typically strive to make their way in the world. For example, it concerns what sorts of things they consume and how they acquire it; how they reproduce; how (and when and whether) they move; how they avoid predators; and how they repair themselves when damaged. It is straightforward to distinguish a group of organisms on this basis. The form of life of a cottonmouth snake (*Agkistrodon piscivorus*) is clearly different from that of a silver maple (*Acer saccharinum*), a black swallowtail butterfly (*Papilio polyxenes*), and an Arctic fox (*Alopex lagopus*). It is also quite different from that of eastern garter snakes (*Thamnophis sirtalis sirtalis*) and timber rattlers (*Crotalus horridus*). These species have distinct life cycles, behaviors, habitats, predators, prey, and protections. Of course, they do so largely because of differences in their biological parts and processes: that is, their phenotypes. These, in turn, are largely explained by their genetic differences: that is, their genotypes. It is for genetic reasons that individual grey wolves have a sufficiently common biological form and a sufficiently common set of behaviors (e.g., sociability and diet) under sufficiently common environmental conditions that they constitute a form of life (*Canis lupus*) that is distinct from that of coyotes (*Canis latrans*), zebra mussels (*Dreissena polymorpha*), and green herons (*Butorides virescens*).

---

[28] Kitcher (1987: 190).   [29] Crane and Sandler (2011).

Individual organisms express the form of life that they do because of the life form that they are: that is, their genotype and phenotype. Nevertheless, form of life descriptions track real biological features of organisms – red-winged blackbirds (*Agelaius phoeniceus*) really do migrate south for the winter, whereas ringed-neck pheasants (*Phasianus colchicus*) really do not. Moreover, while the way in which individuals go about the world is largely explained by their genotype and phenotype – for example, by their wing structure – the differences in their genotype and phenotype are also in part explained by how their ancestors went about the world – for example, whether or not they migrated for the winter. Thus, the form of life conception of species classifies organisms by something that is both biologically real and explanatorily useful. It is a legitimate species concept.[30]

In fact, the form of life conception of species is a familiar one. It is operative in zoology and botany when work in those fields involves describing what biologically related individuals do and how they go about doing it. It is the conception around which nature programs about species are organized when they focus on how they migrate, hunt, reproduce, survive the winter, and generally get on in the world. It is almost always the conception of species at work in the practice of professional and amateur naturalists. Moreover, it is the conception of species that picks out what captures many people's imagination about living things and what troubles them most when it comes to the specter of anthropogenic species extinctions: beautiful, amazing, and unique forms of life will cease to be instantiated. It is not the genotype that they primarily want to see preserved, or even the phenotype as it might be in a zoo or farm, but organisms going about the world in their distinctive ways: migrating wildebeest (*Connochaetes taurinus*); soaring condors (e.g., *Gymnogyps californianus*); roaming polar bears (*Ursus maritimus*); spawning salmon (e.g., *Oncorhynchus tshawytscha*); towering torreya (*Torreya taxifolia*); leaf-cutting ants (e.g., *Atta colombica*); dancing honey bees (e.g., *Apis mellifera*); and breaching humpbacks (*Megaptera novaeangliae*).[31]

---

[30] For further discussion of this species concept, see Crane and Sandler (2011).

[31] A similar conception of species has been suggested by Holmes Rolston III: "It is admittedly difficult to pinpoint precisely what a species is, and there may be no single, quintessential way to define species … All we need for this discussion, however, is that species be objectively there as living processes in the evolutionary ecosystem; the varied criteria for defining them (descent, reproductive isolation, morphology, gene pool) come together at least in providing evidence that species are really there … A

This conception of species also animates beliefs about the moral significance of species boundaries. The reason why many people are concerned about mixing genetic material across species boundaries is not to do with the sanctity of the genes themselves, but with the sanctity of natural forms of life and the ambiguity of engineered ones. It is thought to be unnatural to insert genes from one individual into the genome of another when the forms of life are not reproductively compatible. Part-human transgenics are thought to be objectionable because the resultant life forms might have some human and some nonhuman characteristics. Robust human enhancement is thought to be a threat to human dignity because it might result in changes to human nature and the human form of life. Creating *de novo* living things is thought to be hubristic and playing at God because it involves bringing novel forms of life into existence. It is crossing, altering, or creating species categories and boundaries, understood in terms of forms of life, not genes or lineages, which many people find unsettling.

The form of life species concept is imperfect. It does not divide every entity in the biological world into neat categories. But in an evolved biological world, there will be ambiguous and marginal cases on any conception of species.[32] There will be organisms that can be biologically grouped in more than one way or that do not fall neatly into a single species category. There also can be reasonable disagreement about whether a group of biologically related organisms have a sufficiently distinct form of life from another group of organisms such that they constitute a distinct species or are instead a variety or subspecies. This sort of ambiguity is also common to all species concepts, since for any species concept it is necessary to determine how much similarity and difference constitutes the species level.

The form of life species concept tracks how biologically related organisms typically strive to make their way in the world, but there is variation among individuals. For example, some Canadian geese (*Branta canadensis*) do not fly south for the winter, while others do. Moreover, many individuals, even if they strive in the ways characteristic of their species, will not

---

species is a coherent, ongoing form of life expressed in organisms, encoded in gene flow, and shaped by the environment" (1989: 210).

[32] The form of life conception of species used throughout this book is naturalistic in the sense that (nonengineered) species are the product of unguided evolutionary processes that have no goal or teleology. They are not established by intentional supernatural or nonnatural agency. This is as true of *Homo sapiens* as it is of any other naturally evolved species.

succeed in realizing their complete form of life. The primary reason for this is that many organisms die early in their life cycle. It is also important to note that the form of life species concept, like many other species concepts, allows for dynamic species. If the ways in which the individuals of a species population go about the world substantially changes, then the form of life of the species can change. (However, if the changes are robust and sudden enough, or if they occur throughout only part of the species population, then it might constitute the emergence of a new species.)

Unless otherwise specified, the conception of species used throughout this book is the form of life conception. Species categories are distinguished by the form of life that individual organisms of the species instantiate or express. Individual organisms are conspecific (or members of the same species) when they are biologically related organisms that share a form of life or express the same form of life. Throughout the book I will also distinguish between the biological grouping criteria for species and the form of life descriptions of species. The biological grouping criteria are the genetic or phylogenetic characteristics shared by members of a species. The form of life descriptions are the propositions that describe how members of the biological group typically go about the world.[33]

The value of species is often thought to be related to the value of biodiversity. This is particularly so in conservation biology, where a prominent justification for preserving species is that it maintains biodiversity. Therefore, an ethic of species, insofar as it concerns the value of species, necessarily involves discussing biodiversity and the value of collections or systems of diverse species.

As with "species," there is no single, universally employed conception of "biodiversity." There is instead a plurality of important varieties of biodiversity, and different conceptions of biological diversity are useful for different purposes. For example, intraspecific genetic diversity is useful when studying the viability of species populations and their capacity to respond to stressors. Generally, the less genetically diverse a population, the less robust and adaptable it is in comparison with a more genetically variable (and comparably sized) population of the species. However, intraspecific genetic diversity does not provide information regarding the importance of organism or population traits to the systems in which they are

---

[33] Crane and Sandler (2011).

located. For this reason, functional diversity often is more useful when studying the integrity and stability of systems, since it concerns the role of traits of organisms and populations in ecosystem processes. Because it concerns ecosystem processes, functional diversity is also crucial to the capacity of ecosystems to reliably provide ecosystems services. Another type of biological diversity, beta diversity, concerns the diversity between areas or ecosystems. The greater the beta diversity between two or more systems, the more species that are found in one, but not the other, system. Beta diversity is therefore useful for studying why species are distributed as they are, and it is crucial to protection designation decisions and management planning.

Each of these conceptions of biological diversity (and there are many others) is legitimate. They each capture something biologically and ecologically significant. However, because the focus here is on species, "biodiversity" will be used to refer to species-level diversity understood through the form of life conception of species, and not genetic diversity or phylogenetic diversity, for example. More specifically, biodiversity will be understood in terms of species richness – that is, the number of species in a geographic area or system (or what is referred to as alpha diversity) – informed by their relative abundance and uniqueness (or beta diversity). Biodiversity is thus a property of places and systems. One area or system is more biodiverse than another if it has a greater variety of species, less common species, or larger populations of species than the other.[34]

1.3   Overview

The first part of the book focuses on the value of species, particularly as it pertains to species preservation and ecosystem management under conditions of global climate change. In Chapter 2, I consider several different types of value that species have been thought to possess and, for each type, assess whether they do in fact have that value. The typology of value that is used includes a final value/instrumental value distinction and a subjective value/objective value distinction. I argue that species have instrumental value, as well as subjective final value. They are valuable as a means to

---

[34] For a more extensive discussion of the complexities involved in characterizing "biodiversity," see Sarkar (2005) and Maclaurin and Sterelny (2008).

sought ends and they are valued for what they are, not merely for what they can do for us. I also argue that species do not have objective final value. They do not have value in and of themselves or independent of people's attitudes with regard to them. In making this argument I reject the widespread commitment in environmental ethics to the objective value of natural historical relationships.[35] The chapter concludes with an argument for the view that, while species lack objective final value, individual organisms possess it. They have a good of their own or interests that we ought to care about for their own sake.

In Chapter 3, I discuss the species conservation dilemma that arises from global climate change. Given the increased rate of extinctions expected to be associated with global climate change, conservation biology – the discipline committed to the preservation of species and biodiversity – seems more important than ever. However, global climate change undermines conservation biology's predominant species conservation strategies, place-based preservation, and ecological restoration. Place-based preservation involves establishing protected areas where local stressors, such as pollution, extraction, and recreational use, on nonhuman species populations and their habitat are eliminated or reduced. However, populations cannot be prevented from going extinct by reducing local stressors if, as is the case with global climate change, the habitats themselves are coming apart and this is what is driving the extinctions. Ecological restoration aims to return a degraded space to what it was, or would have been, absent anthropogenic impacts. However, a distinctive feature of global climate change is an accelerated rate of ecological change. Therefore, past ecological systems and trajectories are, to the extent that global climate change occurs, increasingly poor proxies for ecological integrity in the future, and restoration is undermined as a species conservation strategy. An additional implication of the increased rate of ecological change is that the justification for native species prioritization in ecosystem management is diminished.

In response to the species conservation dilemma, many conservation biologists have begun to advocate for a new conservation strategy called assisted colonization (or assisted migration or managed relocation). Assisted colonization is intentionally moving individuals of a species to a location beyond their historic range, and establishing a viable independent

---

[35] Rolston (1986); Katz (1992); Preston (2008).

population in that location for the purpose of preventing the species from going extinct. In Chapter 4, I conduct a value analysis and assessment of assisted colonization as a species conservation strategy under conditions of global climate change. I argue that, except in quite rare cases, assisted colonization is not well justified. Only in respect to a small number of species – for example, those that are high in instrumental and subjective final value – is value preserved by a successful assisted colonization. But successful, responsible assisted colonizations are themselves likely to be quite rare, given the challenges and uncertainties associated with global climate change, the features of those species that are most likely to be in need of relocation, and the possibility that there will be significant stake-holders who will be resistant to relocations. Moreover, even in the rare cases of responsible, value-preserving, successful translocations, there are likely to be disvalues: the opportunity costs associated with the assisted coloniza-tion and the impacts on the individual organisms involved (both the relo-cated individuals and those in the recipient system). Therefore, by the conclusion of Chapter 4, I have argued that both traditional species preser-vation strategies, as well as the emerging alternative strategy, are under-mined by global climate change.

In Chapter 5, I defend a positive account of how to respond to the species losses associated with global climate change. Given the ecological chal-lenges posed by global climate change, it is not possible to accomplish traditional conservation goals with traditional conservation strategies. However, it does not follow that new strategies to accomplish traditional goals are always needed. It is also possible to revise the goals. I argue that for less impacted ecological spaces reserve-oriented ecosystem management remains well justified, even under conditions of global climate change. However, the goals for such places must shift away from preservation of particular species and assemblages (i.e., traditional preservationism) to promoting adaptive capacity, allowing for ecosystem reconfigurations, and maintaining ecosystem services. This, in turn, requires changing expectations for what the reserve-oriented approach can accomplish. It also involves revising management strategies. For example, it requires significantly less faithfulness to past systems, as well as refraining from propping up dwindling populations (when they are threatened by global climate change). I also argue that in already highly impacted and manipu-lated ecological systems, where subjective and instrumental values are predominant, intensive species preservation and ecosystem engineering projects can be well justified. The chapter (and first part of the book) concludes with a discussion of the implications of the value of species for ongoing debates regarding mitigation, adaptation, and geoengineering responses to global climate change. I argue that the value of species strongly favors mitigation over adaptation, but not by means of "hard" geoengineering, such as atmospheric aerosol injection and ocean fertilization.

The second part of the book concerns the ethical significance of species boundaries, particularly with respect to species modification and species creation. Chapter 6 concerns whether nonhuman species boundaries are normatively significant in a way that provides an intrinsic or nonoutcome-oriented reason not to create transgenic organisms. I discuss several arguments for the normative significance of species boundaries. I argue that each one fails, and conclude that there is no objective basis for the ethical significance of species boundaries. However, I also discuss several arguments against the normative significance of species boundaries, and show that each of these fails as well. That arguments both for and against the objective normative significance of species boundaries fail implies that the view that species boundaries are normatively significant can be part of reasonable comprehensive doctrines or worldviews. As a result, it needs to be respected in both political and nonpolitical domains. For example, people need to be informed with regard to whether products they use involve transgenics, so that they can act in accordance with their worldviews. However, respecting people's worldviews does not require refraining from researching, using, or benefiting from transgenic individuals. When there are good reasons for actively opposing or prohibiting particular transgenic research programs or applications, these flow primarily from nonintrinsic concerns – for example, concerns about justice or risks – which vary among research programs and applications. Therefore, differential assessment of the creation and use of nonhuman transgenics is necessary.

In Chapter 7, I consider whether *Homo sapiens* species boundaries are ethically significant in ways that other species boundaries are not. There are two respects in which the category *Homo sapiens* is taken to have special normative significance. The first, is that it defines a moral community for human beings or delineates individuals with a distinctive moral status. The second, is that human nature itself provides justification for or against altering it. Both these views are prominent in the discourse on human enhancement. Moreover, the first view, because it concerns the moral status of humans and nonhumans, has wide-ranging implications for issues in environmental ethics and bioethics. I consider several versions of the view that *Homo sapiens* delineates a special moral community or individuals with special moral standing. I argue that each one fails. In the course of doing so, I defend a capacities-based account of moral status on which an individual's moral status is determined by his or her capacities and relationships, and not how he or she is grouped biologically. I also argue that human nature cannot provide justification either for or against human enhancement, since it is not normative in the requisite ways. Therefore, I conclude that there is no special normativity to the species category or boundaries of *Homo sapiens*. As with nonhuman transgenics, there is nothing intrinsically, objectively wrong with creating part-human individuals. Whether to proceed with a particular transgenic or human enhancement research program or application depends primarily on extrinsic considerations – for example, those to do with compassion, prudence, and justice – and, to a lesser extent and only in some cases, on subjective final values.

Some engineered organisms may not fall even partially into preexisting species categories. This might be because they are not created from biological materials or because they are so thoroughly recombined and reengineered that they constitute a novel species. Such organisms would not be interspecific, so they could not be described as mixing species or charged with failure to respect species boundaries. Instead, they would constitute artificially selected, *de novo* species – or artifactual organisms and species. Chapter 8 concerns whether the artifactualness of such organisms and species has any (noninstrumental) value or normative significance. I argue that artifactualness is relevant to some forms of subjective final value, but that this is not a basis for opposing or prohibiting creation and use of them. I also argue that artifactualness is not relevant to the sort of objective final value possessed by individual organisms. The implication of these arguments is that creating novel organisms and species does not raise any unique intrinsic ethical concerns, and, just as was the case with transgenics and human enhancement, evaluation of them and public policy regarding them should focus primarily on extrinsic considerations.

In the Conclusion, I restate the main theoretical conclusions reached in this book regarding the value of species and the ethical significance of species boundaries, as well as their implications for the applied topics addressed throughout the book. I also put these conclusions in context by briefly indicating aspects of the applied topics that are incompletely addressed (or not addressed at all) in the book, such as the ethical dimensions of risk assessment and public engagement in policy making. The topics addressed here are central to an ethic of species, but they are not nearly the whole of it.

2   The value of species

It is widely agreed that species are valuable, and that this value justifies their protection. However, there are different views regarding what sorts of value they possess and the bases on which they possess it. In this chapter I consider several different types of value that species have been thought to have, and for each type assess whether it is reasonable to believe that they do, in fact, have that value. Because species conservation practices and policies are ultimately justified by their preserving the value of species or biodiversity, a clear understanding of the nature and basis of that value is necessary for evaluating them.

2.1   Types of value

Typologies divide and organize conceptual terrain. Most typologies are conventional and programmatic. This one is no different. It is *a* typology of value, not *the* typology.[1] The types are not mutually exclusive. An entity, including a species, might possess value of more than one type.

The broadest categories of value are *instrumental* and *final*.[2] Instrumental value is the value that something – an entity, experience, act, or state of affairs – has as a means to an end. It is usefulness value. The extent to which something has instrumental value is dependent upon the goals or ends of others, human or nonhuman. Thus, a thing's instrumental value can differ from individual to individual (or entity to entity). Yard sales, for example,

---

[1] The considerations that have guided its development are that it encompass the full range of possible values; the types are clear and distinguished by significant features; the types are neither too gross (and too few) nor too fine (and too many) to be helpful in organizing discourse on them; and it reflects ongoing discussions on value in environmental ethics and moral philosophy more generally.

[2] This distinction is adopted from Korsgaard (1983).

are predicated on the fact that something one person no longer needs can be of use to someone else; and acidic soil is conducive to the flourishing of blueberry bushes, but not to the flourishing of tetras.

That something is an effective means to some end does not itself result in its having instrumental value. The end must also be that of some entity or be valuable or worthwhile.[3] Thus, instrumental value is always derivative on the final (noninstrumental) value of something else. It is also always conditional. Something's instrumental value fluctuates based on changes in the value of the end to which it is a means, the circumstances that obtain, and whether alternative or more efficient means are available. For example, a fishing line has instrumental value just in case a person wants to catch fish; and its value might diminish if that person gains access to a much more effective fishing net or moves to a location where fishing opportunities are limited.

Instrumental value can be divided into *present value* and *option value*. Something possesses present value if it is currently useful as a means to a sought after end. Something possesses option value if it is potentially a useful means to a sought after end, as when we save something that we do not need now just in case we need it later (even, in some cases, when we have no idea as to why or how it might be useful later).

Final value is the value that something has for what it is.[4] An entity, experience, act, or state of affairs possesses final value if it has value in

---

[3] The efficacy of something as a means to an end is distinct from the ethical evaluation of the means. Something might be an effective means to a valuable end, but nevertheless unethical. For example, human subjects research conducted without informed consent might produce findings that promote human health overall, but it violates the autonomy of the research subjects. Thus, the fact that something is instrumentally valuable does not imply that it is ethically acceptable; and the fact that something is ethically unacceptable does not imply that it is not instrumentally valuable.

[4] It is common in environmental ethics to refer to noninstrumental value as "intrinsic value." However, the "intrinsic value" terminology can be ambiguous and misleading. In addition to being used to refer to noninstrumental value, "intrinsic value" is also often used to mean "objective value" and "nonrelational value." Yet, as is discussed later in this chapter, these are conceptually distinct. It is possible that there is noninstrumental value that is subjective rather than objective, in the sense of being dependent upon the evaluative attitudes of valuers. It is also possible that there is noninstrumental value (both subjective and objective) that is based on relational rather than nonrelational properties. Because it is possible to have noninstrumental value that is dependent upon evaluative attitudes and/or based on relational properties, it is misleading to refer to noninstrumental value as "intrinsic." In contrast, "final value" captures what is crucial

itself: that is, its value as a means to ends is not exhaustive of its value.[5] Human beings are typically considered to have final value. They are not mere means or tools to be used by others. Appropriate responsiveness to final value is often, but not always, to try to protect or promote it. Sometimes it involves appreciation, acknowledgment, or gratitude, for example.[6] For this reason, although final value is always noninstrumental value, it is not exhausted by the value of ends to be brought about.

Within final value, there is a distinction between the sources of the value. Something possesses *objective final value* (hereafter, just *objective value*) if its value is independent of any actual preferences, attitudes, judgments, emotions, or other evaluative states regarding it. Objective value is discovered by valuers; it is not created by them. If objective value exists, there are properties or sets of properties that, when they are instantiated in an entity, experience, act, or state of affairs, have (or confer) value. Moreover, valuers ought to recognize and respond to the value.

Something has *subjective final value* (hereafter, just *subjective value*) if its value is dependent upon valuers having some evaluative stance regarding it. Subjective value is created by valuers through their evaluative attitudes, judgments, and preferences. It does not exist prior to or independent from them. There are a wide variety of things that are valued noninstrumentally – for example, personal mementos, cultural and religious artifacts, ceremonies and rituals, accomplishments, performances, and historical sites. The bases for approval of such things are diverse. For example, the valuing might be for what the entity represents, for what it embodies, for its rarity, for what it expresses, or for its beauty. But in each

about noninstrumental value – that is, it is value that is not for the sake of anything further – without the ambiguities or misleadingness associated with "intrinsic value." It also enables a useful distinction between noninstrumental value that is based on intrinsic properties and noninstrumental value that is based on relational properties. This distinction is difficult to make when using "intrinsic value" to refer to all noninstrumental value. In addition, using "final value" to refer to noninstrumental value follows the terminology employed in moral philosophy generally (i.e., beyond environmental ethics) more closely than does using "intrinsic value."

[5] Some things possess final value – that is, value as an end – as a result of their having instrumental value (Kagan 1998). This occurs when people value them as an end or in themselves at least in part because they are taken to be a means to an end. Religious artifacts and ceremonies are often valued in this way, for example.

[6] Sandler (2007).

case, the valuing is for noninstrumental reasons, not for what the entity can bring about.[7]

The basis for final value could be internal (or intrinsic) properties, relational (or extrinsic) properties, or some combination of intrinsic and extrinsic properties. On some varieties of objective value, it is a thing's internal properties – such as its form or composition – that are taken to be the properties by virtue of which it possesses the value. For other varieties, it is a thing's relational properties – such as its history, uniqueness, or context – that are thought to be the basis for the value. On still other varieties, it is a combination of a thing's internal and relational properties. Similarly, something might be valued noninstrumentally by virtue of its internal properties, relational properties, or both. It is for this reason that the internal/relational property distinction does not coincide with the objective/subjective distinction[8] or the instrumental/final distinction,[9] but rather cuts across them.

Distinguishing these types and sources of value is necessary because for each variety there are people who argue that species possess it and that ecosystem management policies and practices are justified by it. Some people advocate managing biodiversity and particular species to maximally satisfy current economic, medical, material, and recreational needs and

---

[7] Objective/subjective distinctions within instrumental value are also possible. One way to make the distinction is means focused: something is objectively instrumentally valuable to the extent that it is an effective means to a valuable end; whereas something is subjectively instrumentally valuable to the extent that it is an effective and desired means to a valuable end. For example, a car may be objectively instrumentally valuable for a person's getting to work, but not subjectively valuable if the person abhors cars. Another way to make an objective/subjective distinction within instrumental value is end focused: something is objectively instrumentally valuable to the extent that it is an effective means to an objectively valuable end; whereas something is subjectively instrumentally valuable to the extent that it is an effective means to a subjectively valuable end. For example, clean drinking water is objectively instrumentally valuable to human health, whereas a (nontransferable) plane ticket to Fort Wayne, Indiana is subjectively instrumentally valuable, since its instrumental value is contingent upon its possessor's attitudes about traveling to Fort Wayne. (Even when instrumental value is objective in this way, it is still conditional. For example, clean drinking water is objectively instrumentally valuable when a person is dehydrated, but it has instrumental disvalue when a person has hyponatremia.) These objective/subjective distinctions within instrumental value, while useful in some contexts, are not crucial for present purposes. Therefore, in what follows, the objective/subjective distinction is restricted to final value.

[8] O'Neill (1993).   [9] Korsgaard (1983).

wants – that is, on the basis of their present instrumental value. Others advocate for preserving biodiversity on the grounds that some species might prove useful to us in the future in ways that we cannot now anticipate – that is, on the basis of their option value.[10] Still others argue that species and biodiversity have subjective final value by virtue of people's preferences[11] or value commitments[12] regarding them, and that these ought to guide environmental policy and practices. Yet others argue that species have final value in themselves, whether or not anyone values them – that is, that they have objective value. On one prominent objective final value view, species are thought to have interests or a good of their own that we ought to care about – that is, they have *inherent worth*.[13] On another prominent view, species are thought to have value by virtue of being wondrous forms of life arising from natural historical processes – that is, they have *natural historical value*.[14] In both cases, that species possess objective value is taken to have implications for our duties to them and how we ought to manage them.

In the following sections, I assess whether it is reasonable to believe that species have these types of values.

2.2   Instrumental value

One common justification for preserving species and maintaining biodiversity is that doing so is essential to maintaining ecological integrity. On this view, species are instrumental to the end of ecological integrity, which is itself valuable. On some accounts, ecosystem integrity is important because ecosystems have a good of their own or interests that we ought to care about – that is, they have inherent worth, a variety of objective final value.[15] On other accounts, ecosystem integrity is valuable because ecosystems provide a broad array of material goods (such as natural resources and services[16]) and self-realization goods (such as educational, developmental, and spiritual opportunities[17]) – that is, it has instrumental value to us. On still other accounts, ecosystem integrity has value because people have

---

[10] Pinchot (1914). This is often used as a justification for both *in situ* preservation (e.g., rainforest conservation) and *ex situ* preservation (e.g., seed banking).
[11] Baxter (1974).   [12] Callicott (2006).   [13] Johnson (1991, 2003); Sterba (1995, 2001).
[14] Rolston (1982, 1995, 2001); Soulé (1985); Preston (2008).   [15] Sterba (1995, 2001).
[16] Millennium Ecosystem Assessment (2005).   [17] Cafaro (2001a); Sarkar (2005).

preferences for or positive evaluative attitudes toward it. People like the idea of there being intact thriving wilderness, and it therefore has subjective value.[18] These values are not mutually exclusive. Ecosystems and ecological integrity might be valuable in more than one of these ways.[19]

I discuss whether ecosystems have inherent worth later in this chapter. I conclude that it is possible that some ecosystems have a good of their own, but that typically they do not. Therefore, most ecosystems do not have inherent worth. Whether maintaining or increasing biodiversity promotes ecosystem integrity and, thereby, associated instrumental goods is an empirical question.[20] Evidence suggests that in many cases it does. For example, plant species richness has been found to enhance ecosystem multifunctionality;[21] restoration of biodiversity has been found to increase ecosystem services and productivity;[22] and maintaining biodiversity appears to be

---

[18] Callicott (1989, 2006).

[19] For this reason, Aldo Leopold's land ethic – "a thing is right when it tends to preserve the integrity, stability, and beauty of the biotic community; it is wrong when it tends otherwise" ([1949] 1968: 224–225) – is appropriately open and inclusive regarding why ecosystem integrity matters.

[20] A classic analogy often presented in support of the view that biodiversity is instrumental to ecological integrity likens an ecosystem to an airplane and the species within the ecosystem to the rivets that hold the airplane together (Ehrlich and Ehrlich 1981). An airplane can lose some rivets without there being any systematic damage. However, eventually, once enough rivets are lost, the integrity of the airplane is compromised and it comes apart. Similarly, according to the analogy, an ecosystem can lose some species without there being any systematic damage to the ecosystem. But if enough species are lost, the system can no longer be sustained (or is less able to respond to destabilizing events) and it comes apart. On this view, there simply is not enough ecological redundancy (i.e., multiple species that can play a particular functional role) and role adaptability (i.e., capacity for species to develop into new roles) within ecosystems to compensate for sustained species losses significantly above normal historical rates. Even if, contrary to the analogy, the diminishment of biodiversity within an ecosystem does not result at some point in a rather sudden or dramatic coming apart of the system, it may well be that species losses significantly above standard rates degrade or diminish ecosystem processes and, in this way, reduce ecosystem health, stability, and resilience. Norton (1990) emphasizes that species extinctions within a system are frequently weakly dependent. The extinction of a population within a system often increases the likelihood of further extinctions, since the extinct population typically has instrumental value to some other species. However, this is not always the case. Under some circumstances elimination of a species within a system can forestall further extinctions (Sahasrabudhe and Motter 2011). For a comprehensive critique of the rivet-popping analogy, see Sarkar (2005).

[21] Maestra et al. (2012).   [22] Worm et al. (2006); Benayas et al. (2009).

associated with a lower prevalence of infectious disease transmission.[23] Whether people have preferences for or pro-attitudes toward good functioning and biodiverse ecosystems is also an empirical question. Sociological research and membership in and contributions to environmental organizations committed to these ends suggest that there is widespread valuing of ecosystem integrity and biodiversity, as well as widespread preferences for preserving them for noninstrumental reasons.[24] Thus, ecosystem integrity does appear to be valuable, and in more ways than one. Therefore, when a particular species or biodiversity more generally contributes to ecosystem integrity, it is instrumentally valuable to the extent that it does so.

In addition, all species have at least some independent instrumental value. Even when they are not beneficial for us, they are for the individuals of other species that predate or otherwise make use of them.[25] Moreover, all species possess some scientific value, since there are scientific questions about them that can be answered only by studying them.

However, it does not follow from the fact that biodiversity often has considerable instrumental value, or the fact that every species has some instrumental value, that every species is equally or highly instrumentally valuable.[26] Some species are keystone species (e.g., eastern hemlock [*Tsuga canadensis*] and African elephants [*Loxodonta africana*]); some are recreationally valuable (e.g., rainbow trout [*Oncorhynchus mykiss*] and sequoia redwoods [*Sequoia sempervirens*]); some are medicinally significant (e.g., horseshoe

---

[23] Keesing (2010). Maier (2012) argues that the evidence for the linkages between biodiversity, ecosystem integrity, and instrumental goods are not nearly as strong as conservation biologists and environmental ethicists often suppose. There are two primary reasons for this. First, in many cases it is particular species or sets of species, not biodiversity or ecological integrity as such, that are crucial to providing instrumental goods. It may be that the species and the functions they perform, such as water purification or soil stabilization, are more likely to be present if biodiversity is maintained. But it is nevertheless the species and not the biodiversity that provide the goods; and as long as the species (or some artificial alternative) are present, the goods could be provided with much less biodiversity. (This is not the case, however, with respect to option value, where it is the richness and novelty of species that is the source of the value.) Second, as discussed below, the value of species to ecosystem integrity varies widely. As a result, so too does their value for promoting the instrumental values associated with ecosystem integrity.

[24] Kempton et al. (1995). In 2007, the National Wildlife Federation had 4.4 million members, the Nature Conservancy had 1 million members, and the World Wildlife Fund had 1.2 million members in the United States alone (Bosso 2005).

[25] Hunter (2001).   [26] Sarkar (2005).

crabs [*Limulus polyphemus*] and sweet wormwood); and some are economically significant (e.g., honey bees and mahogany [*Swietenia mahagoni*]).
However, many species are none of these. Similarly, some species are
more scientifically valuable than others. Due to the uniqueness of its morphology and genetics, the platypus (*Ornithorhynchus anatinus*) is scientifically
interesting in ways and to a degree that a species which has phylogenetically close and morphologically and genetically similar relatives in existence is not (e.g., the snail darter [*Percina tanasi*]). In fact, only a small portion
of species are keystone or dominant species, economically significant,
scientifically crucial, or medicinally useful.[27]

Therefore, case-by-case assessment of the instrumental value of species is
needed. It is a mistake to believe that, because each species is unique and
contributes to biodiversity, each has significant instrumental value. While
all species are instrumentally valuable, they differ widely in the types and
amounts that they possess.

2.3   Subjective value

An entity has subjective value if people have preferences for it or value it for
what it is (or that it is), not merely for what it can bring about. Thus, species
have subjective value if they are valued for what they are. Many people
value species in this way. They find particular life forms (or the variety of life
forms) wonderful, beautiful, fascinating, inspiring, and symbolic, for example. Not all such valuing is the same, however, and it is useful to distinguish
between *preference value* and *integral value*.

Preference value is the value that something has because people have a
preference for it. Conservation biologists and economists often refer to the
existence value of species, which is the value that a species (or biodiversity)
has because people have a preference for its continued existence, independent of its use value (i.e., its instrumental value). Charismatic megafauna,
such as tigers (*Panthera tigris*), chimpanzees (*Pan troglodytes*), and polar
bears (*Ursus maritimus*), have more existence value than parasitic round-
worm species because people have a preference for the existence of the
former, but not the latter. Because existence value stems from personal
preferences, it is treated, particularly in economics, as expressible in

---

[27] Maclaurin and Sterelny (2008).

monetary metrics and, therefore, as commensurable and substitutable with other preferences. The strength of the preference can be measured in terms of a person's willingness to pay to satisfy it; and its relative importance among an individual's preferences can be determined by what other preferences that person will (and will not) allow to be frustrated or unfulfilled in order to try to satisfy it.

People's preferences regarding species can vary over time in response to factors ranging from changes in economic circumstances to media portrayals. In addition, there is considerable divergence among people's preferences regarding both biodiversity and particular species (e.g., *Canis lupus*). Moreover, people often care more about some species, particularly those that are furry, cute, large, and bizarre, than other species. As a result, the preference value of species is not a particularly stable or robust type of value.

Another type of subjective value is integral value, or the value that something possesses when it is valued in a way that flows from one's worldview or core value commitments. Baird Callicott has been a prominent proponent of the view that species have integral value.[28] According to Callicott, integral value is a distinct type of value from existence value because, in contrast to existence value, "to accord something [this sort of] value ... is to declare that it should not be subject to pricing of any kind."[29] Callicott's point about pricing captures something crucial to integral value. Things with integral value – for example, significant cultural and religious artifacts – often are priced in the market place. This is appropriate, since, in principle, there is no reason that ownership of them should not be transferred by purchase. However, their integral value distinguishes them from things that lack such value, such as toasters and light bulbs, in that the price

[28] "[Species] may not be valuable *in* themselves but they certainly may be valued *for* themselves. According to this ... account, value is, to be sure, humanly conferred, but not necessarily homocentric" (Callicott 1989: 151). Callicott refers to this type of value as "intrinsic value." For reasons discussed earlier, I am not employing the "intrinsic value" terminology here. Things can be (and often are) valued as ends on the basis of their relational (i.e., nonintrinsic) properties. For example, if something is valued for its rarity or history, then it has subjective final value at least in part by virtue of its nonintrinsic properties. Moreover, because subjective value is determined by how something is valued, it is appropriate that types of subjective value are distinguished by the type of valuing that gives rise to it – that is, whether it arises from deep, integrated beliefs and value commitments, or less stable, more transitory preferences.

[29] Callicott (2006: 43).

that is put on them in the market place does not fully capture or express their value. Their market value (or price) is not exhaustive of their value.

Some people value all species (or biodiversity) integrally. This is often expressed in assertions that species have the right to exist or a value that is incalculable. However, some species possess more integral value than others, since some species are valued more than others or by more people than others. Particular species may be valued because the individuals that comprise them are charismatic, beautiful, unusual, or rare, for example. They might also have distinctive cultural or spiritual significance. For instance, bald eagles (*Haliaeetus leucocephalus*) are valued as a symbol of freedom in the United States, and Chinook salmon (*Oncorhynchus tshawytscha*) have spiritual significance to some Pacific Northwest Native American tribes, such as the Winnemem Tribe.

Integral value is more stable and normatively significant than is preference value. As indicated above, personal preferences can be idiosyncratic, transitory, and superficial. They are often neither the product of reasoned justification nor well integrated into a person's belief system. In contrast, when something is integrally valued, its value is part of well-established aspects of an individual's worldview and often constitutes a person's ideals. Thus, integral value is generally more stable than existence value. Moreover, because it is not entirely substitutable, what integral value justifies is more normatively robust than what existence value justifies.

Nevertheless, not all integral valuing should be regarded as equal. Some integral valuing may be deeper, stronger, and more stable than other integral valuing. There are also several ways in which integral valuing can be misvaluing. It could be based on false information or a lack of information – for example, that something thought to be wild is really cultivated. It could be inconsistent with a person's other or deeper value commitments and beliefs – for example, regarding what constitutes a flourishing life. And a valuer could misidentify the object of his or her evaluative attitudes through transference, association, or conflation. For these reasons, integral valuing, and subjective valuing more generally, is not beyond critical evaluation.

Callicott argues, following Mark Sagoff, that integral value commitments are typically expressed in legislative contexts – that is, through appropriately public, informed, and democratic processes.[30] Callicott further argues

---

[30] Sagoff (1982, 1988).

that such valuing of species is expressed in this way, and so their integral value is established, through the United States Endangered Species Act 1973 (ESA). According to Callicott,[31] the ESA is interpreted, particularly in *Tennessee Valley Authority* v. *Hill*,[32] and operationalized in a way that treats species as valuable in themselves, as possessing a value that is "incalculable" or not "expressible in terms of a price."[33]

Although legislatively expressed integral valuing of species is more stable and robust than is the existence value of species, limitations remain. If something's integral value is established by how it is valued in democratic public discourse (and in the resultant legislation), then it can be revoked should the basis for its being so valued, the valuing itself, or the legislation change. Therefore, if there were sufficient reason-based support for revising, reinterpreting, or reoperationalizing the ESA so that species are not treated as incalculably valuable in themselves, and this were accomplished, then species would cease to possess integral value. Many people, including some involved in agriculture and industry, and property rights advocates, support such a revision, particularly because recognition of the integral (or final or intrinsic) value of species does not appear in the text of the ESA.[34] Moreover, they provide economic, legal, and moral (e.g., property rights) reasons that are well integrated into their belief systems in support of such revisions. This indicates that the justifications offered in favor of recognizing species as valuable in themselves continue to be strongly and widely contested, and that an informed and democratic process does not guarantee a legislative outcome that recognizes species as integrally valuable.

In addition, many species' habitat exists only, or primarily, in countries where there is no legislation recognizing the integral (or final) value of species. Moreover, international declarations on the environment are mixed on whether nature, including species, should be regarded as valuable

---

[31] Callicott (2006).

[32] *Tennessee Valley Authority* v. *Hill and Others*, 1978, 437 US 153, No. 76-1701.

[33] Callicott and Grove-Fanning (2009) argue that the ESA has been interpreted in ways that provide endangered species with legal rights as understood by Stone (1972) – that is, legal action can be taken on their behalf, on the basis of harms done to them, and with remedy directed at them.

[34] In fact, the value orientation of the ESA appears anthropocentric: "species of fish, wildlife, and plants are of esthetic, ecological, educational, historical, recreational, and scientific value to the Nation and its people": 1973, section 2(a)(3).

in itself. The United Nations Rio Declaration on the Environment (1992) begins with a strong and unambiguous anthropocentric statement: "Human beings are at the centre of concerns for sustainable development ... [and] States have, in accordance with the Charter of the United Nations and the principles of international law, the sovereign right to exploit their own resources pursuant to their own environmental and developmental policies."[35] In contrast, the United Nations Convention on Biological Diversity (1992) begins with an equally strong and unambiguous acknowledgment of the final value of species: "*Conscious* of the intrinsic value of biological diversity and of the ecological, genetic, social, economic, scientific, educational, cultural, recreational and aesthetic values of biological diversity and its components ..."[36]

For these reasons, the integral final value of species is contested, and so somewhat insecure and unstable, even on a reason-based and legislation-oriented approach to establishing such value. If people value a species or biodiversity integrally – for its beauty, complexity, diversity, spiritual significance, or wondrousness – then that is a reason to try to preserve it. However, many people do not value species in this way or do so for only some species. Moreover, people's valuations, as well as legislation and the justifications for it, can, and often do, differ and change.

2.4 Objective value

Something possesses objective final value when it is valuable by virtue of what it is, independent of whether anyone recognizes its value or actually values it. Holmes Rolston III, a prominent proponent of the objective value of species, has characterized it with respect to species as follows: "These things count, whether or not there is anybody to do the counting."[37] If species possess objective final value, their doing so is not contingent on people's actual attitudes, preferences, or value commitments.[38] There are

---

[35] United Nations (1992a).   [36] United Nations (1992b).

[37] Rolston (1982: 146). Also: "A simpler, less anthropically-based, more biocentric theory holds that some values are objectively there – discovered, not generated, by the valuer" (2003: 146).

[38] Because objective final value is not dependent on any actual evaluative attitudes or judgments it is sometimes described as being stance independent (e.g., Schafer-Landau 2003). This conception of objective value does not require that for value to be objective

two accounts of the objective value of species that are prominent within the environmental ethics literature: that species have *inherent worth* and that species have *natural historical value*.[39] The former bases the value of species on their having a good of their own or interests that we ought to care about. The latter bases the value of species on a cluster of interest-independent intrinsic and extrinsic properties, such that entities that lack interests may, nevertheless, have natural historical value. In what follows, I discuss natural historical value and then inherent worth.

2.4.1   Natural historical value

According to Rolston, each species is a distinctive historical form of life that is the product, process, and instrument of creative evolutionary processes. On his view, each species possesses objective value because it is a unique and potentially productive evolutionary trajectory.[40] Species are to be protected because a species extinction "shuts down the generative processes, a kind of superkilling. This kills forms (*species*) – not just individuals ... To kill a particular plant is to stop a life of a few years, while other lives of such kind continue unabated, and the possibilities for

it must exist in the world entirely independently from valuers. It requires only that the value is not contingent upon any actual evaluative judgments or attitudes. Fitting attitude theories of value, on which value is analyzed in terms of certain evaluative stances being called for or warranted, are objective in this sense. On them, value is not dependent upon valuers' actual evaluative attitudes or judgments, but rather on there being certain stances that are called for or appropriate for valuers to take up toward certain objects, actions, state of affairs, or traits. Moreover, the attitudes that are appropriate or fitting for valuers to take up can be informed by facts about the valuers. For example, the fact that human beings are social may make negative attitudes toward antisocial traits or behaviors appropriate that would not be fitting if human beings were not social. Thus, a theory of value can be objective, in the sense of being actual stance independent, without providing an analysis of value that makes no reference to valuers. In addition, something's value can be objective even if it is contingent on certain facts about valuers, such as their form of life, which are relevant to which attitudes are fitting for them to take up toward certain objects. Of course, strongly realist theories of value that analyze value in ways that do not reference valuers at all or on which value can exist completely independently of valuers are also objective, in the sense of being stance independent. In contrast, a thing's possessing subjective final value is contingent upon valuers' actual evaluative stances.

[39] Rolston (1986) calls this type of value "objective intrinsic value." For reasons discussed earlier, I am not employing the "intrinsic value" terminology here.

[40] Rolston (1989, 1995, 2001). See, also, Soulé (1985).

the future are unaffected; to superkill a particular species is to shut down a story of many millennia and leave no future possibilities."[41] Rolston's is the most prominent *natural historical account* of the value of species. However, there are other versions that emphasize different historical, evolutionary properties – for example, complexity, diversity, and genealogy through "deep time."[42]

The claim that species possess objective value by virtue of their ecological and evolutionary situatedness is highly contested.[43] One type of objection to the view arises from skepticism about objective value in general. It is sometimes argued that there are no objective facts at all or no way to know things as they are in themselves, independent of some human construction. Therefore, there are no objective facts about value. It is also sometimes argued that facts are in the domain of objective, empirical sciences, whereas values are in the domain of subjective attitudes. So, although there may be objective facts, there are not objective facts about value. In section 2.4.2, I argue in support of interest-based objective value (or inherent worth). I defend the view that there are objective facts regarding which entities have interests and what those interests are, as well as nonsubjective reasons for caring about or taking those interests into consideration. If this is correct, then global skepticism regarding objective value as such is misplaced. However, it is possible that there is an objective basis for interest-based value, but not for noninterest-based values, such as natural historical value. Therefore, a defense of inherent worth, even if successful, is not sufficient to establish the existence of noninterest-based objective value in general or natural historical value in particular.

The concept of noninterest-based objective value is coherent. There is nothing self-contradictory, unintelligible, or even confused about the claim that there are some (interest-independent) properties that are valuable or confer value when they are instantiated, independent of anyone's actual attitudes or judgments with regard to them. The claim that the natural historical properties of evolved forms of life are such a set of properties is also coherent and intelligible. However, this does not establish that these

---

[41] Rolston (1995: 523). If species possess objective natural-historical value, they do not do so equally, since not all species are equally distinctive forms of life or potentially productive evolutionary trajectories. Compare, for example, the platypus with the snail darter.

[42] Katz (2000); Cafaro (2001b); Preston (2008).   [43] Callicott (1992); Norton (1992).

properties do in fact confer such value. The claim that Chicago Cubs World Series wins and glasses of orange juice are objectively valuable is also coherent and intelligible. The interesting and difficult challenge is explicating why some claimed set of properties are in fact objectively valuable.

Species are ecologically and evolutionarily situated in the ways described by Rolston. As already discussed, it is in part because of this that they often possess instrumental and subjective value. But it is not clear why species being so situated, and possessing a wide variety of instrumental and subjective values, also confers on them an additional type of value, an objective natural historical value. The reason cannot be, as Rolston seems to suggest, that they generate and are generated from other species, which possess the value.[44] This would beg the question as to whether species are objectively valuable by virtue of their natural historical properties. Moreover, it cannot be, as Rolston also seems to suggest, that they are objectively valuable because evolutionary processes, which depend crucially on species, have generated objectively valuable human beings (or other objectively valuable entities).[45] This would commit a version of the genetic fallacy. One cannot conclude that something has a certain value because it is the progenitor of something that has that value. A Chicago Cubs World Series victory might bring about great joy (which is valuable), but it does not follow from this that the victory itself is great joy.[46] It also cannot be that species are objectively valuable by virtue of their being unique achievements of evolution or of wild nature. This response just asserts the conclusion that species are valuable because of how they are evolutionarily situated or produced. It does not explain why these properties are valuable or confer value.

One type of argument sometimes taken to support the claim that nature has noninterest-based objective value is the last person argument.[47] Suppose that there is one person left on earth who has the capacity, just as he or she dies, to destroy all life on earth. Would there be anything wrong with him or her doing so? Many people have the intuition that there would be. If this is correct, the argument continues, there must be some value in the world independent of valuers by virtue of which it is wrong. That is,

---

[44] Rolston (1986).   [45] Rolston (1986).

[46] Rolston (1986) is aware of the specter of the genetic fallacy, and attempts to address it.

[47] Last person arguments originally appeared in Sylvan (1973), though his use of them was not to support the conclusion that nature has noninterest-based objective value. For a discussion of last person arguments, see Carter (2004).

there must be objective value in the nonhuman world. It is possible to formulate a species-specific last person argument. Imagine that what would be destroyed is not the whole of nature, but only all existent species. If many people would find destroying them wrong, even though there are no valuers left in existence, then, the argument concludes, species must have objective value.[48] Should this argument be taken as reason to believe that species have objective natural historical value?

It should not, even supposing that many people would have the intuition that the last person destroying all species would be wrong. First, it is not clear why the intuition should be taken as veridical. After all, some people have the opposite intuition. Why should one set of intuitions take precedence over the other? One possible reason might be that the best explanation for why people have the intuition that it would be wrong to destroy all species in the last person case is that species have objective value. However, there are many other potential explanations for the intuition. For example, people might care now (i.e., while they are alive) about the condition and future of nonhuman species even after their death, as many people do regarding the future well-being of their great-grandchildren;[49] or people might be opposed to wanton destruction generally. In addition, an explanation would be needed for why those who do not share the intuition fail to see the objective value of species or the implications of their having that value.

Furthermore, even supposing that it would be wrong to destroy all existent species, there are explanations for this that do not depend upon species having natural historical value. All anthropogenic species extinctions, by definition, involve the death of the remaining living organisms of the species. It could be that the anthropogenic contribution to the deaths of the individual organisms is what makes destroying species wrong; or it could be that species themselves have value, but of a different sort than natural historical value – for example, subjective final value.[50] It also is possible to make sense of the wrongness of the species annihilation by focusing on the character of a person who would destroy them, particularly when that person has benefited from them in the past. It is an action that

---

[48] The thought experiment can also be restricted to species whose members are non-sentient, so that the intuitions are not sensitive to the cognitive or psychological interests of individual nonhuman organisms.

[49] O'Neill (1992).   [50] O'Neill (1992).

expresses a lack of appreciation, wonder, and gratitude, for example, and is wrong for that reason.[51] Therefore, even if people have the intuition that wantonly destroying species is wrong, and even granting that this intuition is veridical, it does not follow that there is reason to accept noninterest-based objective value in nature, let alone natural historical value.

Similar difficulties apply to another argument for the objective natural historical value of species: the replication argument.[52] Imagine that a pristine natural landscape, such as an old growth forest, is completely destroyed by anthropogenic activities and then exactly replicated in the same place by human efforts. Would the replication have the same value as the original? According to proponents of the replication argument, it would not. Many people have the intuition that the original forest possesses some value that the replication lacks. If this is correct, then there must be a type of value that is based on the natural historical properties of ecosystems (or entities within the system), since the original and restored forests are identical in every other respect: that is, there must be natural historical value.

As with the last person argument, the replication argument fails to establish that natural ecosystems and species have objective value by virtue of their natural historical properties. Even if most people do have the intuition that natural ecosystems have value that nonnatural systems lack, it does not follow that they do in fact have such value. Good reasons need to be provided as to why the intuitions should be regarded as veridical, particularly when at least some other people have contrary intuitions about the case. The replication argument does not provide such reasons; it only prompts intuitions. Proponents of the argument often emphasize how the two systems contrast. The old growth forest developed by spontaneous, autonomous, and unguided processes independent from humans, whereas the replication is an artifact, designed and engineered by humans.[53] But this is only to highlight the differences. It does not explain why one has value that the other lacks by virtue of those differences. Moreover, there are explanations for why people might view natural ecosystems as having more value than less natural ones that do not appeal to objective natural historical value. For example, many people value ecosystems on the basis of their natural historical properties, such that they have subjective final value

---

[51] Sandler (2007).   [52] Elliot (1982); Katz (2000).   [53] Katz (2000).

by virtue of those properties. Such valuing both explains why people have the intuitions that they do about the replication and accounts for the greater value of natural systems and the species populations that comprise them, without appeal to objective value.

It is true that many people find species valuable by virtue of their ecological and evolutionary situatedness. They have subjective final value for this reason (hereafter, *natural value*).[54] But for a person who does not value them in this way, despite understanding well the ecological and evolutionary facts, there do not appear to be objective considerations that show his or her view to be unjustified or unreasonable. The most that can be said is that it would be good for the person to cultivate appreciation and wonder toward the richness and complexity of biological diversity, as well as toward the beauty and uniqueness of individual forms of life. Such attitudes would open him or her to rewarding and enjoyable relationships and experiences.[55] A walk through the woods is much more engaging and pleasurable for a person who is interested in nature than it is for a person who is not. However, that such character traits and attitudes are beneficial to the person who has them does not warrant attributing objective final value to nature or species. After all, the same can be said of appreciation of music and sport, for example. Cultivating an appreciation of football can provide enjoyable and enriching experiences that are not open to those who do not understand the subtleties and challenges of the game. But it does not follow that football has objective final value.

The foregoing does not constitute an argument that species do not possess objective natural historical value. Rather, it shows that the standard considerations offered in support of the view are problematic and that, absent any others (and it is difficult to see what they would be), the claim that species have natural historical value is unjustified. This is as much as can be shown when trying to prove the nonexistence of something non-physical, after granting that it is conceptually coherent. Moreover, it is sufficient to justify the claim that species ought not be regarded as possessing objective natural historical value. In cases like this, the absence of reasons to believe is strong evidence not to believe.

---

[54] Callicott (1989, 2006); Elliot (1992).
[55] Carson (1956); O'Neill (1992, 1993); Cafaro (2001a); Sandler (2007); Sarkar (2005). "Though we travel the world over to find the beautiful, we must carry it with us, or we find it not" (Emerson 2000: 278).

2.4.2   Inherent worth

Inherent worth (or interest-based objective final value) is the value that some-thing has by virtue of its having a good of its own or interests that valuers ought to care about for its own sake. Human beings are typically thought to have inherent worth. They have an individual welfare that makes a claim on others. It grounds, at a minimum, responsibilities not to harm people with-out justification. It may also ground responsibilities to promote their good. This is thought to hold independently of people's actual evaluative attitudes or stances regarding the worth of others.

An entity has a good of its own or interests just in case it is possible to make sense of harm and benefit to the entity directly, without reference to the good of any other entity. It is because a coyote has a good of its own that getting its leg caught in a steel jaw trap is bad for or harmful to it, quite apart from how it affects others or is regarded by them. Similarly, acid rain is bad for silver maples (*Acer saccharinum*) and oak wilt (*Ceratocystis fagacearum*) is bad for oak trees (e.g., *Quercus rubra*), regardless of how people or other organisms are affected or feel about it.

Having a good of one's own is necessary, but not sufficient, for possessing inherent worth. There must also be some nonsubjective justification for why people ought to consider and be responsive to it.[56] It does not follow from the mere fact that oak trees and coyotes have a good of their own that we ought to take their good into consideration. Some nonsubjective reason why we should consider them needs to be provided as well. In section 2.4.3, I argue that the good of nonhuman organisms, sentient and nonsentient, ought to be taken into consideration: that is, nonhuman organisms have inherent worth. In this section, the focus is on species.

Some ethicists have argued that species possess inherent worth that is distinct from that of the organisms that comprise them.[57] That is, they believe that species have a good of their own or interests, and that there are objective justifications, not dependent on anyone's actual evaluative attitudes, for the claim that we ought to care about them for their own sake. Species can have inherent worth only if they have a good of their own or

---

[56] Taylor (1986).

[57] Johnson (1991); Rolston (1995); Sterba (1995, 2001). "But endangered species are objec-tively valuable kinds, good in themselves; they do have their own welfare. Respect for life ought to be directly based on this value" (Rolston 1995: 526).

interests, distinct from those of the individual organisms that comprise them. Species are not sentient (though in some cases the individual organisms that comprise them are), so their good or interests cannot be cognitively or psychologically based. It cannot be that they feel, care, desire, or aspire to something and that this constitutes their good. This does not imply that species do not have a good at all. It was suggested above that nonsentient organisms have a good of their own. Because such organisms are not conscious, their good cannot be based on their having cognitive or psychological states.

One objection to the claim that nonsentient living things have interests is that only conscious beings are able to care about their own good or have their lives go better or worse for them in an experiential sense.[58] However, one must distinguish taking an interest in one's good or being aware of how well one's life is going, which require being in a cognitive or psychological state, from something being in one's interest, which does not.[59] It is true that an elm tree (e.g., *Ulmus americana*) does not care in a psychological sense if it is killed by an Asian longhorned beetle (*Anoplophora glabripennis*) infestation, but it does not follow from this that the beetles boring into its trunk is not bad for it or not in its interests. Similarly, it is true that the elm is not aware in a psychological sense of the damage being done to it by the beetles, since it lacks such capacities, but it is nevertheless "aware" in a physiological sense, as is evidenced by the fact that it responds in defensive ways. Thus, the absence of psychological capacities does not by itself imply either that an entity lacks a good of its own or that it is inert with respect to its good.

Still, in order to establish that nonsentient living things have a good of their own it is necessary to provide a positive account of what grounds their good. That is, there must be an explanation for why Asian longhorned beetles are bad for elm trees, whereas sunlight is good for them. If there is no such explanation, then assertions about what is good or bad for them are arbitrary. Moreover, as already mentioned, since they lack cognitive capacities, the explanation cannot track back to their caring, wanting, or otherwise taking an interest in anything. It also cannot depend on the attitudes of

---

[58] Singer (1977, 1989).

[59] Taylor (1989) and Varner (1998) appeal to this distinction in their defense of the moral considerability of nonsentient organisms. Feinberg (1974) also recognizes that plants have a good, but believes they constitute interests only in an attenuated sense.

others – for example, that people like elm trees that are large and long-lived. If it does, then the good at issue will not be the elm's, but that of the valuers', since it is based on their preferences.

What grounds the good of nonsentient organisms is that they are goal-directed systems. Their parts and processes are internally organized in ways and for reasons to do with accomplishing things or bringing things about, such as resisting predators and reproducing. There are "in order that" explanations for why it is that individuals have the parts that they do, the processes that they do, and the life cycles that they do. Flowers produce nectar in order to attract pollinators; ivy has tendrils in order that it can climb; tree roots are skototropic in order that they grow deeper into the ground. That nonsentient organisms are end- or goal-directed systems means that it is possible to affect them in ways that are conducive or detrimental to their accomplishing their goals or ends.[60] Asian long-horned beetles are bad for an elm tree because they diminish the capacity of the tree to accomplish one of its ends – distributing water and nutrients throughout its living tissue – which is needed for the tree to survive and reproduce. Asian longhorned beetles are not bad for elm trees because they make elm trees ugly to us, since the parts and processes of elm trees do not have the end of being attractive to us.

The explanation for why the living tissue of elm trees has the end of nutrient distribution and not attractiveness to humans is that it was selected for because it performed this role in prior generations of elm trees. The trait has persisted, it exists in current elm trees, because it performs that function in the elm tree form of life. The tissue is not there because it makes the trees attractive to humans; it was not selected for that reason. Thus, in a nonsentient living thing, the goals or ends of the organism (and its parts and processes) are the result of the causal explanations for why it is that those parts and processes exist or persist in that life form. This is an etiological account of teleology. In the case of naturally evolved organisms, the selection etiology, or causal process by which the teleology of their parts and processes is determined, is natural selection.

Here, then, is a summary of the *etiological account* of the good of non-sentient entities. An entity has a good of its own only if it is possible to make sense of benefit and harm to it directly. It is possible to make sense of

---

[60] Sober (1986).

benefit and harm to an entity directly only if there is something the entity is striving for or aiming to accomplish, that is, it is teleologically organized or goal-directed. For nonsentient entities, it is not possible to make sense of their teleology by reference to psychological or cognitive states, or by appeal to the desires or goals of others. However, it is possible to ground claims about the teleology of their parts and processes etiologically, by appeal to "in order that" explanations as to why they persist in organisms of that life form. Nonsentient living things are genuinely goal-directed systems because the parts and processes of the organism were selected for in their ancestors, and therefore exist in the organisms, for the purpose of realizing certain ends. Since nonsentient living things are genuinely goal-directed, what is good and bad for them (what benefits and harms them) can be specified in terms of what resources, conditions, and treatments are conducive to, or detrimental to, the realization of their goals.[61]

It is difficult to see how there could be a nonetiological, yet naturalistic, approach to grounding the ends, and thus the good, of nonsentient organisms. It cannot be done by appeal to the psychological states of the individuals themselves or of others. Therefore, it must have to do with the parts and processes of the organisms, how they came to be how they are (i.e., an etiological account), or why they do what they do (i.e., a systemic account). However, a systems account of teleology, that a part or process has a particular end because of the role that it plays in the system, requires a prior account of the end (or goal) of the system.[62] For example, one might say of the live tissue of the elm tree that it has the role of distributing nutrients in order that the system is healthy. However, this explanation requires an account of the health of the tree – that is, it involves being in certain states and is accomplished in part by delivering these nutrients in these ways – which is just what the etiological account provides. In the absence of that prior account of the ends or goals of the system, there is no way to ground the claim that the goal of the tissues is to distribute nutrients rather than grow into habitat for longhorned beetles. In a system where there is no prior account of the end or goal of the system, all claims about what the parts or processes are supposed to do or what is good or bad for the system are arbitrary. This is an implication of systemic

[61] Cahen (1988) and Varner (1998) offer similar accounts of the good of nonsentient organisms.
[62] Wouters (2005).

accounts of teleology. It is not particular to living systems. Therefore, for any nonsentient entity, either it has a good grounded in the relevant selection etiologies or it does not have a good of its own.[63]

Species are nonsentient entities, even when the individual organisms that comprise them are sentient. Therefore, either species have a good of their own grounded in some selection etiology or else they do not have a good of their own, and thereby fail to satisfy a necessary condition for possessing inherent worth. What are the possible ends or goals of species? The most promising candidates are such things as persisting over time, maintaining (or increasing) population size, and adapting to changing environmental conditions (or being pliable). Yet, while these might be measures of the robustness of a species, they are only apparent ends or goals of a species. In fact, they are by-products of the organisms that comprise species pursuing their own individual ends. Conspecific individuals are not coordinated or organized in ways or for reasons pertaining to the continuation, adaptability, or population size of their species, and individual organisms do not function well by virtue of promoting these. The reason for this is that species are not themselves a unit of selection. There is not competition between species as such, but between organisms and, in some cases, non-species collections of organisms. The competition is both inter- and intra-specific, but it is not a competition between all the members of one species and all the members of another species, or between one form of life and another form of life. It is between organisms, some of which are different life forms, as well as between highly internally organized and cohesive collectives of organisms, such as ant colonies and beehives. Species are too diffuse and their individual members too uncoordinated and independent from each other for them to constitute an entity on which selection might operate.[64] As a result, the evolutionary explanations for why

---

[63] Basl and Sandler (In press).

[64] The key mistake in Rolston's argument for the inherent worth of species is the inversion of which entity – the species or the individual – is primary in survival and selection processes. In Rolston's view: "The species line is the more fundamental living system, the whole, of which individual organisms are the essential parts. The species too has its integrity, its individuality; and it is more important to protect this than to protect individual integrity. The appropriate survival unit is the appropriate level of moral concern" (Rolston 1995: 524). However, the "survival unit" is not species, but individual organisms. Individual organisms are what live, die, and reproduce (or fail to do so). Species are instantiated and persist by virtue of the survival and reproduction of

individual organisms do what they do, and have the form that they have, do not appeal to the good of the species. Instead, they refer to the fitness of individuals, and, in some cases, collectives of individuals (e.g., ant colonies) that are the product of selection etiologies and thereby, unlike species, have goals or ends distinct from the individuals that comprise them.[65]

Species fail to have a good of their own even when they are conceived of as individuals, rather than as collections of organisms grouped together on the basis of shared properties.[66] What is crucial to having interests is not being an individual, but being an internally organized goal-directed system, the product of some selection etiology. Individual organisms satisfy this condition. However, species, even if they are ontologically historically persistent individuals, do not satisfy the condition, for the reasons provided above. Species lack a good of their own on etiological, not ontological, grounds.[67] Therefore, although individual wolves, human beings, silver maples, and some internally organized collectives (such as ant colonies) have interests, *Canis lupus*, *Homo sapiens*, and *Acer saccharinum* do not.

Sometimes anthropogenic species extinctions are referred to as "super-killings," since they eliminate not just individual organisms but entire lineages or forms of life.[68] This language must be understood metaphorically. Species, unlike organisms, are not alive. So, species cannot be killed. Moreover, a form of life does not cease to exist upon a species extinction. It ceases to be instantiated. There is still the form of life of the passenger pigeon. There is a way in which passenger pigeons, when they exist, go

individual organisms. Moreover, species do not have their own integrity, since they are not internally organized or goal-directed systems. Nor are species living, except perhaps in a highly attenuated sense on which the Catholic Church and Red Sox Nation are living as well (Sandler and Crane 2006). Species, rather, are comprised of living individuals.

[65] It is possible that all the existing individuals of a species are part of one group or population that is internally organized (e.g., an ant colony). However, if the population were to split into two collectives, the species would no longer be coextensive with the interests of any single collective. Thus, even when a collective is coextensive with all the existent members of a species, the interests of the collective are not the species' (*qua* species), they are interests *qua* hive or colony.

[66] Hull (1976, 1978); Ghiselin (1997).

[67] If, ontologically, species are nonhistorical individuals (rather than historically persistent individuals or collections of organisms) – for example, forms, criteria, or categories – then they are not physically instantiated and, therefore, could not have a selection etiology. As a result, they could not have interests of their own.

[68] Rolston (1995).

about the world. However, there is no current instantiation of the passenger pigeon. This is tragic, for reasons to do with the deaths of the individual organisms, the subjective value of passenger pigeons, and the callousness and thoughtlessness that their extinction involved.[69] But, it is not a wrong to *Ectopistes migratorius*. *Ectopistes migratorius* does not have a good of its own distinct from individual passenger pigeons. As a result, it cannot be harmed or wronged directly and does not have inherent worth. It is bad that *E. migratorius* went extinct, but not because it was bad for *E. migratorius*.

Species do not have inherent worth, since they do not have a good of their own. This may seem an implausible claim, given the common parlance of some activity or policy being beneficial (or harmful) to a species. Nevertheless, species fail to satisfy a necessary condition for having interests, even as the organisms that comprise them do satisfy it.[70]

2.4.3   Individual organisms

I argued above that individual organisms have a good of their own. However, having a good of one's own is necessary, but not sufficient, for possessing inherent worth. Therefore, it does not follow immediately from nonhuman organisms having a good that they have inherent worth. It must also be shown that we ought to care about their good for their own sake.

That individual human beings have inherent worth is presumed in what follows. One's own well-being and the well-being of other people are something that we ought to care about. They make a claim on us, and we need to consider them in deliberations regarding action, practices, and policies. Is

[69] Passenger pigeons were the most numerous bird species in North America when European settlers arrived. It is estimated that there were between 3 and 5 billion passenger pigeons and that they constituted 25–40 percent of the total bird population in what is now the United States. There were reports of nesting areas that covered over 850 square miles containing over 100,000,000 birds (Smithsonian Institution 2001). The last known passenger pigeon died in the Cincinnati Zoological Garden in 1914. The passenger pigeon's extinction was caused primarily by habitat destruction and commercial hunting.

[70] An implication of this is that species cannot be afforded rights based on their possessing inherent worth. Nor, for reasons discussed in Section 2.4.1, can they be afforded rights based on the objective value of their existence. Therefore, any justification for attributing rights to species must be either subjective or instrumental, and the rights must be understood as legal rather than moral (Callicott and Grove-Fanning 2009).

there any reason that we ought to care about the good of human beings, but not the good of nonhuman living things? To assert that the reason is because human beings are humans – members of the species *Homo sapiens* – is to beg the question. What is at issue is whether that distinction is a morally relevant one: that is, whether the boundary of inherent worth should be at membership in the species *Homo sapiens* or located somewhere else. To just claim its moral significance, without providing justification for it, is bald speciesism.[71] It is for this reason that a species membership approach to determining inherent worth is problematic. An entity's moral standing, when it comes to inherent worth, is determined by the properties or capacities of the entity itself. It is not determined by how it can be grouped biologically. If being a member of the species *Homo sapiens* is a morally relevant distinction, it must be due to the capacities or features of members of the species. When it comes to inherent worth, a *capacities-oriented approach*, rather than a *species membership-based approach*, is needed.[72]

A capacity often cited in order to explain why it is that humans have inherent worth and nonhuman living things do not is moral agency. Moral agents are entities that can understand moral concepts (such as right and wrong, permissible and obligatory), formulate rules and principles using those concepts, deliberate about which rules should be followed, apply the rules to make evaluations and judgments in concrete situations, and act on the basis of those determinations. Only moral agents can be held morally responsible for their actions. Only they can be morally praiseworthy or blameworthy. Therefore, many have argued, morality applies only to moral agents. Remove all the moral agents from the world and there is no morality, just events that occur. Because only human beings have the sort of rationality requisite for moral agency (as far as we know), only human beings have inherent worth.[73]

There are several difficulties with the above line of reasoning, as well as with using moral agency as the basis for inherent worth. First, it excludes human beings, such as infants, the severely mentally disabled, and those with late-stage dementia, who lack the requisite cognitive and psychological

---

[71] Singer (1977, 1989).

[72] The distinction between capacities-based and species membership-based approaches to moral status is discussed in greater detail in Chapter 7. So, too, is the case in favor of a capacities-based approach.

[73] Baxter (1974); Kant (1997).

capacities for moral agency. Since they are not moral agents, they lack inherent worth on this view. Yet, because of their vulnerabilities and dependencies, it seems as if they are especially worthy of our concern and assistance. Second, if it is in fact the case that all existent moral agents are human beings, this is just a historical contingency. It could change through evolution or the innovation of robust artificial intelligences. Or it may turn out that there already are nonhuman species in existence (e.g., alien species) whose members are rational in the requisite ways. Therefore, this criterion not only does not include all human beings, it does not necessarily exclude all nonhuman beings from having inherent worth. However, the most fundamental difficulty with the moral agency criterion for inherent worth is that it conflates moral goodness with moral worth. Only moral agents can be morally good or morally bad (i.e., virtuous or vicious), and absent moral agents there is no moral action (i.e., actions that are right or wrong). However, it does not follow from this that when moral agents act they need to consider only the good of other moral agents. It is true that there is no moral behavior in a world absent moral agents, but this does not tell us what moral agents ought to value or care about when they are in the world.

The same problem applies to other attempts to ground inherent worth in capacities associated with rationality. For example, it has been argued that only rational beings have inherent worth because only they are capable of reciprocal concern and mutual obligation,[74] or only they are capable of participating in collective decision making.[75] It is correct that only sufficiently rational beings (or beings that are rational in certain ways) are capable of mutual concern and reciprocal obligations, but it does not follow from this that they cannot be concerned for those who lack those capacities – indeed, this occurs all the time in parenting and end-of-life care. The fact that some individuals with a good of their own are not able to enter into such reciprocal relations does not imply that their good is not morally relevant. Similarly, it is true that only sufficiently rational beings can participate in collective decision making, but it does not follow that the interests of those who are not rational cannot be represented and considered. It is done all the time in veterinarian offices and courts of law, for example. Again, the incapacity of nonrational living things to participate in the sort of activities that rational agents can does not itself imply that their

[74] Kant (1997, [1785] 1998).   [75] Baxter (1974).

good should not be considered by moral agents. If they can be harmed, why should their good not be taken into account? That nonhuman living things are not rational or moral agents does not settle this issue.

Peter Singer, an influential defender of the moral considerability of sentient nonhuman animals, argues that if a being has interests, then there is no morally justifiable reason not to take those interests into account.[76] He believes, as do other animal welfare and animal rights proponents, that being conscious, sentient, self-aware, or an experiencing-subject-of-a-life, is a necessary (and sufficient) condition for having interests.[77] However, as argued above, this view conflates taking an interest in one's good with having a good. The etiological account of interests demonstrates that neither psychological complexity nor consciousness is a necessary condition for having interests. Psychologically complex animals have interests that nonsentient organisms lack – for example, experiencing pleasure and the absence of pain – just as social animals have interests that nonsocial animals lack – for example, being part of a well-functioning social group. However, that psychologically complex entities have different interests, more interests, or more complex interests than nonsentient living things does not imply that nonsentient living things lack interests altogether or that their interests need not be considered.

A proponent of the sentientist view that psychological capacities are necessary for having inherent worth might respond that while nonsentient living things may have interests, they do not have the capacity to care about their interests. And if they are not able to care about their interests, if it does not matter to them how well their life goes, then why should we care about them? The difficulty with this response is that there is no way to substantively specify "mattering to oneself how one's life goes" or "caring about one's own interests" that is consistent with sentientism and excludes all nonsentient living things. One way to specify the idea of "mattering to oneself how one's life goes" or "caring about one's own interest" is by appeal to having some sort of self-conception that requires an individual to be cognizant of itself as a distinct individual with a good of its own. However, this understanding would exclude severely mentally disabled humans who lack such a self-conception. It would also exclude most sentient nonhuman animals, and thereby undercut the sentientist's own view.

---

[76] Singer (1977, 1989).   [77] Regan ([1983/1985] 2004).

Therefore, "mattering to oneself how one's life goes" or "caring about one's own interests" must be understood in a way that does not require a robust (or even modest) self-conception. But then why should nonsentient things be excluded? After all, they respond to stimuli and are active in protecting and promoting their own interests. Appeals to "caring about one's own interest" or "mattering to oneself how one's life goes" fail to justify denying the inherent worth of nonsentient entities, since they either exclude too much or else merely reassert that nonsentient living things do not psychologically experience their lives and do not have psychological interests. But that is just to point out that they are nonsentient. It is not to justify why their interests are not considerable.

The difficulty with trying to deny the inherent worth of nonsentient living things within a naturalistic framework, once it is granted that they have a good (or interests), is that any proffered distinction for why their interests should not matter, whereas the interests of other entities should matter, is arbitrary or question begging. This is precisely the point of Singer's claim that if an entity has interests there is no reason not to take them into account. Humans typically have capacities that members of other species lack, but members of other species have capacities that humans lack. We are excellent at mathematics, developing technology, and building complex social systems, but we are terrible photosynthesizers and have poor buoyancy control, in comparison with individuals of some other species. Our capacities are particularly important to our form of life, but other species' capacities are just as important to their forms of life, and there is no non-question-begging reason why the capacities that are crucial to our form of life (or the form of life of any other species, for that matter) should be the standard for whether members of other species have inherent worth.[78]

That we have more capacities, or a broader range of capacities, including the capacities that make for robust culture, implies that we have different and broader interests than do individuals of other species. For this reason, the worth of human beings requires different responsiveness by moral agents than does the worth of Australia magpies (*Gymnorhina tibicen*) and black bamboo (*Phyllostachys nigra*). That we can have reciprocal concern and obligations with other human beings matters to how we should relate to and treat them. But it does not follow from it that magpies and bamboo have

---

[78] Taylor (1986); Sandler (2007).

no worth at all. Respect (for autonomy) is appropriate to other humans, but it is not for magpies and bamboo, just as compassion is appropriate for magpies but not bamboo. Care, or aversion to causing needless harm, is appropriate to us and them. If we were to encounter individuals of a species that have interests still broader or more complex than ours, it would be wrong to conclude that we have no worth or less worth than them. Instead, we should recognize that the forms of responsiveness and consideration appropriate to them might be different or more diverse. That is, their worth in combination with their capacities might underwrite a different *moral status* for them than our worth in combination with our capacities does for us; just as our sentience underwrites a moral status for us that is different from the moral status of bamboo: that is, we are due compassion, whereas bamboo is not. That an entity has inherent worth implies that its good needs to be taken into account. However, the ways in which its good is to be taken into account – that is, its moral status – depend on its capacities and relationships.[79]

Thus, there appears to be no adequate justification for denying the inherent worth of nonsentient living things once it is recognized that they have a good of their own. But, as has been emphasized, it does not follow from the fact that all living things have inherent worth that their worth should be considered or responded to in the same way – that is, they have the same moral status. Therefore, it does not imply that trees have the same rights as do humans, or that we cannot use them for our own needs. Appropriate responsiveness to the worth of other beings is determined by the capacities that they have, their relational properties (e.g., whether we have benefited from them), as well as the facts about our form of life. For example, we must appropriate from the natural world to survive, and this needs to inform appropriate consideration of the worth of other living things. Not all appropriation is caring, compassionate, ecologically sensitive, grateful, and nonmaleficent, but neither is all appropriation inconsiderate, ecologically insensitive, or cruel.[80]

All naturally evolved living things have inherent worth – that is, they have objective final value.[81] So, too, do any other naturally evolved entities with an

---

[79] This conception of moral status is discussed in greater detail in Chapter 7.

[80] Evans (2005); Sandler (2007).

[81] Because nonhuman living things are a locus of objective value, denying that species have such value is not to be committed to either anthropocentrism or to the view that the final value of nonhumans is only subjective and so conditional on human valuing.

etiological history.[82] Given this, when selection occurs at the group or eco-system level – both of which appear to sometimes occur (though, as discussed in Section 2.4.2, not at the species level)[83] – then those groups and ecosystems have inherent worth.

2.5 Conclusion

I have argued that species ought not be regarded as having either interest-based or natural historical objective final value. It does not follow from this that no nonhuman or nonsentient entities possess such value. Nonhuman individual organisms, including nonsentient ones, and even some collectives, have inherent worth. I have also argued that some particular species, and biodiversity in general, have considerable preference and integral subjective final value, though many individual species do not. The same is true of instrumental value. Biodiversity generally is instrumentally valuable, some individual species have significant instrumental value, but many individual species do not. Therefore, with respect to both instrumental value and subjective final value, case-by-case evaluation is needed. In the chapters that follow, this understanding of the value of species, biodiversity, and organisms is used to evaluate species conservation and other ecosystem management goals and strategies under conditions of global climate change.

[82] Artificial selection etiologies are discussed in Chapter 8.
[83] Sober and Wilson (1999); Swenson et al. (2000); Wilson and Swenson (2003); Okasha (2007).

3   The conservation biology dilemma

Conservation biology is concerned with the viability of species and eco-systems that have been impacted by human activities. It is an applied discipline. Conservation biologists develop, evaluate, recommend, and implement ecosystem and species management strategies, practices, and policies. At the core of conservation biology, as well as many forms of environmentalism, is a commitment to the value of species and biodiversity. Here is a classic and representative statement of the "Normative Postulates" of conservation biology:

"Diversity of organisms is good."
"The untimely extinction of populations and species is bad."
"Ecological complexity is good."
"Evolution is good."
"Biotic diversity has intrinsic value."[1]

Several of these value claims were discussed and evaluated in Chapter 2. For now, what is crucial is that these are the commitments that inform the perspective of many (if not most) conservation biologists and environmentalists. As a result, conservation biology studies biodiversity, individual species, and ecosystems, as well as the human systems that impact them, toward the end of developing and implementing strategies to protect species and maintain biodiversity under anthropogenically threatened conditions. The goal of conservation biology is not to understand and document extinctions, but to prevent them.[2] In this chapter, I argue that macro-scale anthropogenic ecological change, and global climate change in particular, generates something of a dilemma for conservation biology. Its overarching

---

[1] Soulé (1985: 729–732).
[2] "Conservation biology differs from most other biological sciences in one important way: it is often a crisis discipline" (Soulé 1985: 727).

goal of species preservation is put into tension with some of its basic "Normative Postulates."

3.1 *In situ* preservation and ecological restoration

The normative commitments of conservation biology have strongly favored two ecosystem management approaches: place-based preservation and ecological restoration. Place-based preservation involves protecting species and systems where they are by reducing or eliminating local stressors on them, such as pollution, extraction, and recreational use. The designation of areas as parks and reserves is a paradigmatically place-based approach to ecosystem management. Ecological restoration involves actively assisting ecosystems and species populations to recover and reestablish themselves in places where they once were or would now be, if not for degradative human activities. Contamination remediation, habitat revitalization, and species reintroductions are examples of common ecological restoration practices.

The core reasoning that leads from the normative postulates to support for place-based preservation and restoration is straightforward: value is good and value loss is bad, so one should try to preserve value where it might be lost and reestablish it where it has been lost. As it applies to species, this basic reasoning is buttressed by the fact that, according to the normative postulates, the value of species is ecologically and evolutionarily contextualized. Species are valuable by virtue of their ecological and historical relationships. Given this, the value of species can be fully preserved only where they are, and it can be fully reestablished only where they once were or would now be – that is, in their evolved ecological context.

The case in favor of preservation and restoration is further strengthened by the fact that, on the normative postulates, independence from human control and design is value adding. Because of this, it is better if we do not impact (or minimize our impact) on species and ecosystems to begin with. However, when we have already altered or degraded a place, it is preferable to recreate, as far as possible, what would have been in that place absent our activities, rather than implement our own independent vision for it. Thus, a commitment to natural historical value – which is contained in the normative postulates – also favors place-based preservation and restoration as ecosystem management strategies.

The foregoing is a highly generalized description of the conservation biology justification for place-based preservation and restoration. However, most advocates of species preservation – and there are many of them among conservation biologists, environmentalists, and environmental philosophers – endorse some variation of it. The strength of the commitment to *in situ* species preservation through place-based and restoration-oriented ecosystem management strategies is manifest in the high priority that is given to creating protected areas, maintaining native species, and reintroducing lost species populations. *Ex situ* species conservation strategies, such as preserving species in zoos, botanical gardens, and seed banks, are never the first choice. They are often considered regrettably necessary last resorts.

In the remainder of this chapter, I argue that rapid and large-scale ecological change, and global climate change in particular, undermines both the efficacy and justification for place-based and restoration-oriented approaches to species preservation.

3.2   Global climate change

The global mean surface air temperature of the Earth has been increasing for the past 100 years, and since 1970 it has been doing so at a rate of 0.15–0.2°C each decade.[3] The mechanism by which this is occurring, the greenhouse effect, is well established. Energy from the sun enters the Earth's atmosphere as shortwave radiation. Some is absorbed, and some is reflected back out by the atmosphere and the Earth's surface. The energy that is absorbed heats the Earth and is then radiated as longwave (infrared) radiation. Some types of gas molecules in the atmosphere absorb the longwave radiation and re-emit part of it back toward the earth. In this way, heat is "trapped" by the atmosphere, thereby making the earth warmer than it would be if those gas molecules were not there.

The more heat-trapping molecules (or greenhouse gases) that there are in the atmosphere, the greater the greenhouse effect, and the greater, all other things being equal, the mean surface air temperature of the planet. There are many greenhouse gases – for example, methane, nitrous oxide, and

---

[3] Hansen et al. (2010). The average temperature in the United States from 1981 to 2010 was 0.5°F greater than it was from 1971 to 2000 (NOAA 2011).

perfluorocarbons – and they absorb and re-emit longwave radiation at different rates. But by far the most common greenhouse gas is carbon dioxide. Although its global warming potential is much lower than that of other greenhouse gases, its abundance makes it the greatest cumulative contributor to the greenhouse effect.[4] The concentration of greenhouse gases in the atmosphere, and carbon dioxide in particular, have increased dramatically since the start of the industrial revolution. The primary source of the carbon dioxide increase is the combustion of hydrocarbons or fossil fuels, principally oil, natural gas, and coal. There may be other contributing causes to the increasing global mean surface air temperature of the planet. Nevertheless, greenhouse gases emitted as a by-product of industrial human activity, and the climatic feedbacks that this causes, are the primary drivers.[5]

We are now at a point where we must confront *foregone global climate change*. Foregone global climate change is the amount of climatic change that is already "locked in" by virtue of existing levels of greenhouse gases in the atmosphere plus the most optimistic scenarios for future emissions. The reason that so much climate change is foregone is that greenhouse gases, and particularly carbon dioxide, remain in the atmosphere for a considerable amount of time, and the effects of elevated greenhouse gas levels on climatic and ecological systems can be persistent.[6] "About 50% of an [carbon dioxide] increase will be removed from the atmosphere within 30 years, and a further 30% will be removed within a few centuries. The remaining 20% may stay in the atmosphere for many thousands of years."[7] This means that the climate change that is occurring now is largely the result of the cumulative emissions since the Industrial Revolution. And the fact that emission levels have been steadily increasing at a dramatic rate means that even if future carbon dioxide emissions levels flatten out there will be more carbon dioxide in the atmosphere in 50 or 100 years than there is now, since carbon dioxide would still be being released into the atmosphere at a higher rate than it is removed.

It is not possible to predict precisely how high atmospheric greenhouse gas levels will reach. Therefore, it is not possible to know how much global mean surface temperatures will rise; what the broader climatic impacts of

[4] United States Energy Information Administration (2010).
[5] IPCC (2007a); United States Energy Information Administration (2010).
[6] Gillett et al. (2011).   [7] IPCC (2007b: 501).

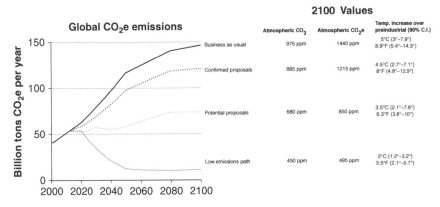

Figure 3.1   Projected greenhouse gas levels and temperature increases on possible future emissions scenarios. © Climate Interactive

the greenhouse gas and temperature increases will be; and how those climatic changes will impact local areas and, thus, people, places, and species. The reason for this is the enormous uncertainties involved. One source of uncertainty is a lack of data on such things as emissions levels and the current state of ecological and climatic systems. Another source is an incomplete understanding of the workings of the relevant systems – for example, regarding feedback processes and potential tipping points. But the largest source of uncertainty is the contingencies involved. How high car-bon dioxide (and carbon dioxide equivalent) levels will reach in the future depends upon the amount of emissions that occur. This, in turn, is contin-gent upon policies and practices that have yet to be determined, as well as on the feasibility of technologies that do not currently exist or are not yet widely implemented. Because of these contingencies, discussion of future climatic change must be done in terms of scenarios.

Figure 3.1 illustrates possible scenarios for future greenhouse gas emis-sions, and so future global mean surface air temperatures.[8] The Business as usual (BAU) scenario represents the current emissions trajectory. On BAU there would be an expected 3.0–7.9°C warming (5.4–14.3°F). That there is such a range even within one scenario represents the level of uncertainty involved. The mid-point of that range (which is what the line for each scenario represents) is 5.0°C (8.9°F).

---

[8] Climate Interactive (2011).

The Confirmed proposals trajectory represents probable future emissions given policies and targets to which national governments have committed, including those made under the United Nation's Framework Convention on Climate Change (UNFCCC). They have not all been implemented. The Potential proposals trajectory represents future emissions given the adoption of policies and targets that are currently being discussed, but that national governments have not yet committed to in any official respect. The Low emissions path represents what many climate scientists argue is necessary to prevent "catastrophic" or "runaway" global climate change – that is, limiting temperature increases to 2°C above preindustrial levels.[9] It is the most reasonably optimistic scenario, since it involves immediate and decisive action to pursue a pathway that has significantly lower emissions than do even current potential proposals, as well as developing the structural and technological capacities necessary to accomplish it.

Yet, even on the Low emissions scenario, global concentrations of carbon dioxide in the atmosphere would reach 450 ppm by 2100 (preindustrial levels were approximately 280 ppm and current levels are approximately 390 ppm). This would result in an increase in global mean surface air temperatures of 1.2–3.2°C (2.1–5.7°F) over preindustrial temperatures. This level of warming, though considerably less than on the BAU scenario, is still highly significant climatically.

As discussed above, there are substantial uncertainties and contingencies involved in the development of these scenarios. Given the subject matter, they cannot be avoided, though the models do take them into account (which is why each scenario has an outcome range, for example). Nevertheless, several general conclusions that are not dependent on the precise details of the models or scenarios are warranted:

Magnitude: Even according to the most optimistic scenarios, there will be large amounts of climatic and ecological change in comparison with the recent historical past.

Rate: Climatic and ecological changes will occur more rapidly than they have in the recent historical past.

Uncertainty: There is a tremendous amount of uncertainty, unpredictability, and contingency regarding future greenhouse gas

---

[9] Hansen (2007); Hansen and Sato (2007); Hansen et al. (2008); Spratt and Sutton (2008).

emissions and, therefore, the magnitude and impacts of future climatic and ecological change.

Variance: The magnitude, and so impacts, of future climatic and ecological change vary widely on different emissions trajectories.

In what follows, I discuss the implications of these features of global climate change for nonhuman species, as well as for place-based and restoration-oriented approaches to species preservation.

3.3   The challenge of adaptation

As long as there has been climate, there has been climate change, and with it ecological change. And as long as there have been systems of living organisms, adaptation to ecological change has occurred. However, the magnitude and rate of climatic and ecological change are not constant. Therefore, neither is the *challenge of adaptation*. The increased magnitude, rate, uncertainty, and variance associated with global climate change makes biological and cultural adaptation to ecological change more difficult, for both us and other species.[10] At the core of the concerns about global climate change is that species, ecological systems, and human societies will not be able to meet the adaptation demands, and that failure to do so will have high social, economic, ecological, and biodiversity costs. It is because people, populations of nonhuman species, and ecological and social systems cannot adapt (or adapt quickly enough) that there will be increased rates of species extinction, instability of ecological systems, agricultural and

---

[10] The challenge of adaptation associated with the high rate and uncertainty of ecological change is exacerbated by several factors. These include the types of ecological changes that are likely to occur, such as increased incidence of extreme weather events and large climatic variability, as well as the possibility of there being climatic "tipping points" that could result in abrupt changes in climatic and ecological trajectories. In addition, the range of possible climatic and ecological futures – for example, with respect to surface air temperatures, sea levels, species' ranges, weather events, precipitation, and air velocities – within a given time frame is expansive due to the rate of change and indeterminacy involved. Adaptation activities that are appropriate to increases in surface air temperatures of 2°C above preindustrial levels are not the same as those appropriate to increases of 4°C above preindustrial levels (let alone 6°C or 8°C) (New 2011). Adaptation is also made more difficult by other anthropogenic stressors on ecosystems, such as pollution, habitat loss, and the spread of pests and pathogens.

natural resource insecurities, exposure to severe weather events, incidence of disease, and ecological refugees (and associated climate injustice). With respect to impacts on people, the Intergovernmental Panel on Climate Change (IPCC) reports:

> Projected climate change-related exposures are likely to affect the health status of millions of people, particularly those with low adaptive capacity, through: increases in malnutrition and consequent disorders, with implications for child growth and development; increased deaths, disease and injury due to heat waves, floods, storms, fires and droughts; the increased burden of diarrheal disease; the increased frequency of cardio-respiratory diseases due to higher concentrations of ground-level ozone related to climate change; and, the altered spatial distribution of some infectious disease vectors.[11]

With respect to nonhuman species, studies have found that 35 percent of bird species and 52 percent of amphibians have traits that put them at increased risk of extinction due to global climate change;[12] that 20 percent of lizard species are likely to be extinct by 2080 due to global climate change (and that 4 percent of local populations already are);[13] and that 15–37 percent of species will be committed to extinction by 2050 on mid-level warming scenarios.[14] Nonhuman species populations that cannot quickly change their geographical ranges, such as those that disperse seed only locally or migrate slowly, are less likely to meet the challenge of adaptation than are those that are more mobile. For them, suitable habitat might contract, shift, or otherwise disappear more quickly than they are able to adjust.[15] Mountain and small island populations are also highly vulnerable, given the geographical limits (e.g., mountain tops and coasts) on their capacity to migrate as their environments change. So, too, are populations of species, such as corals, that are dependent upon very particular environmental conditions or on other species.[16] Species whose members are more ecologically flexible with respect to diet and habitat, such as starlings

[11] IPCC (2007a: 12).   [12] Foden et al. (2008).   [13] Sinervo et al. (2010).

[14] Thomas et al. (2004). Intraspecific reductions in genetic diversity will also be highly elevated (Bálint et al. 2011).

[15] It is estimated that species ranges are shifting altitude at a median rate of 11.0 meters per decade and in latitude at a median rate of 16.9 kilometers per decade in response to global climate change (Chen et al. 2011). See also, Burrows et al. (2011).

[16] Urban et al. (2012).

(*Sturnus vulgaris*) and house mice (*Mus musculus*), are less vulnerable. Moreover, populations of species that have fewer offspring and longer developmental periods (e.g., large mammals and hardwoods) are less likely to be able to biologically adapt to changing ecological conditions than are populations of species that reproduce rapidly and abundantly (e.g., weedy plants). Overall, the IPCC concludes:

> There is medium confidence that approximately 20–30% of species assessed so far are likely to be at increased risk of extinction if increases in global average warming exceed 1.5–2.5°C (relative to 1980–1999) [i.e., the Low scenario]. As global average temperature increase exceeds about 3.5°C [i.e., the Confirmed proposals scenario], model projections suggest significant extinctions (40–70% of species assessed) around the globe.[17]

Given that the background historical rate of extinctions is one species per million per year, this constitutes a dramatic increase in extinction rates, and "there are very strong indications that the current rate of species extinctions far exceeds anything in the fossil record."[18]

3.4 The dilemma

Global climate change is an anthropogenic ecological crisis, and species extinctions are at the core of it. Conservation biology is the crisis field of biology and ecology, and it has a basic commitment to preserving biodiversity. Therefore, conservation biology seems more relevant than ever. However, in practice, global climate change undermines conservation biology's core species preservation strategies.

Already, independent of global climate change, over three-quarters of the Earth's terrestrial surface has been significantly impacted by human activity – for example, by development, invasive species, resource extraction, and agriculture.[19] Many medium and highly impacted ecological systems are now "novel systems."[20] A novel system is one in which anthropogenic activities have resulted in a system in which the biotic features, such as species distributions, and abiotic characteristics, such as

---

[17] IPCC (2007a: 54).   [18] Magurran and Dornelas (2010: 3504).
[19] CIESIN (2005). Forty-one percent of marine systems have medium to high human impacts (Halpern et al. 2008). See also, Ellis and Ramankutty (2008).
[20] Hobbs et al. (2006).

soil composition, significantly depart from those of the pre-impacted system. The more novel an ecosystem, the greater and more numerous are the restoration thresholds or changes that must be accomplished in order to reestablish historical ecological conditions or trajectories. Therefore, the more novel the system, the more difficult is restoration.[21] It can be challenging enough to restore a large predator to a system even where its primary prey is already abundant. But it is much harder to do so, and potentially not viable at all, if it requires altering soil nutrients, reestablishing water flows, and eliminating invasive species so that the flora on which the prey depends can be reestablished, for example. Moreover, the greater the novelty of a system, the less naturalness (understood as independence from human impacts), natural historical continuity, and native species there are in the system to be preserved. Thus, in many places restoration and preservation already are decreasingly viable. Or, in order to be viable, they must be diminished. Restorations must have less historical fidelity and preservation will involve fewer native species and less historical independence.

Global climate change promises to further undermine place-based preservation and ecological restoration, since it will generate even greater novelty on an even greater scale. Moreover, it will do so by altering background climatic and ecological conditions, rather than locally originating, and so locally addressable, stressors.

3.4.1   The end of *in situ* preservation?

In situ preservation is preserving a species or population where it is, in its native habitat. It is in contrast to *ex situ* preservation, which is preserving a species outside its habitat, as in a zoo or a seed bank. As discussed above, *in situ* preservation has traditionally been favored by conservation biologists and environmentalists for reasons to do with their normative postulates. According to those postulates, ecological integrity and evolution are good, a species' value is in part related to its ecological and evolutionary situatedness, and independence from human design and control is value adding. It follows from these commitments that a species' value is fully realized only as long as its independent ecological and evolutionary situatedness is maintained. Preservation of eastern gorillas (*Gorilla beringei*), California condors (*Gymnogyps californianus*), and hyacinth macaws (*Anodorhynchus hyacinthinus*)

---

[21] Hobbs et al. (2009).

in zoos or environments where they are not endemic does not have the same value as having them in their habitat, where they live their form of life in the context of their co-evolved and ecological relationships.

The difficulty for *in situ* species preservation, given global climate change, is that both its effectiveness and its justification depend upon the ecological systems in which species are located remaining sufficiently intact. No ecological system is static. Therefore, an ecologically informed account of "intact" must accommodate historically standard rates and types of change.[22] However, global climate change represents non-normal spatial and temporal change, even on optimistic future emissions scenarios.[23] As a result, current habitats and species assemblages – that is, ecosystems – are coming apart at unusually high rates. Moreover, they are doing so in ways and for reasons that cannot be addressed or controlled by conservation biologists. It is the product of global climatic processes and not stressors local to the system, such as overuse, deforestation, direct pollution, or species harvesting, which might be reduced or eliminated by management plans. Indeed, given foregone global climate change, it is not in the power of anyone to constrain ecosystem change to normal historical rates. Because ecosystems – the assemblages of species, abiotic features, and processes that comprise ecological spaces – are coming apart, species increasingly cannot be preserved by protecting the places where they currently are or historically have been.

Perhaps the most prominent example of this is the effect that increased surface air temperatures are having on polar bear populations. Sea ice is a crucial component of polar bear habitat. The bears depend upon it as a platform for hunting seals and other marine mammals, which are their primary food source.[24] As the climate has warmed, the sea ice has begun breaking up earlier in the year.[25] Bears consequently have less time to build

---

[22] For this reason, Callicott has reformulated Leopold's land ethics as follows: "A thing is right when it tends to disturb the biotic community only at normal spatial and temporal scales. It is wrong when it tends otherwise" (2001: 216).

[23] Palmer (2011a) discusses some difficulties with determining "normal rates" of climatic and ecological change. From a geological perspective, comparative large and abrupt ecological changes are not abnormal (i.e., they regularly occur given a long enough time scale). As discussed above, the current rate and magnitude of change are abnormal in comparison with the recent historical past.

[24] Derocher et al. (2004); Stirling et al. (2004); Stirling and Parkinson (2006).

[25] National Snow and Ice Data Center (2011).

up the fat reserves that they need during the period of food scarcity until the sea ice reforms. They must also swim longer distances between ice platforms, further depleting their energy reserves. The result has been significant decreases in the average body weight of the bears in some populations. This has, in turn, led to higher mortality rates, lower percentages of bears having litters, and smaller litter sizes. Therefore, bear numbers are declining in those populations.[26] Because climatic change and not just local factors, such as hunting or extraction activities, are driving the decreases in population sizes, local management plans alone are inadequate for protecting them. Designating and protecting critical habitat areas will not itself preserve the bears' form of life in their current location, since it will not limit increases in surface air temperature.[27]

---

[26] Schliebe et al. (2006); Stirling and Derocher (2007); Regehr et al. (2010); Rode et al. (2010); Molnar et al. (2011).

[27] This is the reason that the polar bear's status on the US Endangered Species list has led to so much political and legal controversy in the United States. Currently, polar bears are listed as "threatened," rather than "endangered." Both designations protect individual members of the listed species from being taken (or harvested) and require that its critical habitat be protected. To protect the bears, the Alaska Fish and Wildlife Service has designated 187,000 square miles as critical hunting and denning habitat (Alaska FWS 2011). However, because the bears' habitat is threatened by climate change, meeting the provisions of the ESA also seems to require (or, at least, empower) the administering agencies – the Fish and Wildlife Service and the National Marine Fisheries Service – to limit future greenhouse gas emissions throughout the United States in order to try to mitigate increases in Arctic surface air temperatures. This, however, would constitute an enormous expansion of the regulatory power of the agencies in a way not intended by the ESA. Therefore, the Department of the Interior (in which the administering agencies are located) has done two things in order to avoid the regulatory implication. First, they have adopted a special rule for the bears – which they are authorized to do by the ESA for threatened species – that limits the administering agencies from acting outside the designated critical habitat area in order to protect the species. Second, at the time of the listing, they announced a broader legal finding that greenhouse gas emissions are not actionable under the ESA in order to protect listed species and their habitat when they are impacted by climate change. (One of the claimed bases for this is that it is not possible to causally link any particular emissions activities with any particular "taking," which assumes a very stringent causal requirement for regulatory action.) Both the special rule and the broader legal finding are highly contested, and they are both currently under litigation. The crucial point of this case for present purposes is that the controversy arises only because *in situ* preservation by local management alone is not viable, and the reason for this is that global climatic processes rather than local stressors are driving the habitat losses.

The polar bear is a particularly charismatic and high-profile case, but it is not an atypical one. Many species populations are dependent upon specific environmental conditions that will no longer obtain in their current and recent historical locations as a result of global climate change. For such populations, place-based preservation strategies are undermined. It is not possible to preserve coral reefs and the species that depend upon them by designating their locations marine sanctuaries when increases in ocean temperatures due to climate change and ocean acidification due to elevated atmospheric levels of carbon dioxide are the causes of coral declines.[28] It is not possible to preserve American pika (*Ochotona princeps*) populations in the western United States or golden toad (*Bufo periglenes*) populations in Costa Rica by protecting the mountain tops where they live, when climatically altered temperature and precipitation patterns and not local land uses are the threats to them.[29] It is not possible to preserve Canada lynx (*Lynx canadensis*) and wolverine (*Gulo gulo*) populations in greater Yellowstone through local management plans when it is increases in air temperature that are reducing their crucial snowpack habitat.[30] Place-based preservation strategies depend upon the stability of background climatic and ecological conditions. Global climate change disrupts that stability. To the extent that it does so in a particular location, place-based preservation strategies for the at-risk species that are there are less viable. They cannot preserve the species' form of life in their evolved ecological context.

Moreover, because ecological systems are transitory assemblages of overlapping species ranges, it is not the case that ecosystems (or species communities) will migrate as a whole in response to global climate change.[31] This is particularly so in places, such as North America, in which the composition of modern species communities is relatively

---

[28] NOAA Coral Reef Protection Program (2011).

[29] Pounds and Crump (1994); Pounds et al. (2006); FWS (2010a); Erb et al. (2011). The golden toad has already gone extinct.

[30] Aubry et al. (2007); United States Global Change Research Program (2009); Brodie and Post (2010); FWS (2010b).

[31] Root and Schneider (2006); Barnosky (2009). The evolved dependencies and interactions between species populations often have an effect of holding some species assemblages together under changing conditions. However, the paleoecological record shows that ecological change of the rate and magnitude projected to be associated with anthropogenic climate change (even on the more optimistic emissions scenarios) largely overwhelms these "adhesive" features.

geologically recent, such that species are not highly co-evolved.[32] The current ecosystems of New England are not, as a result of global climate change, going to be found largely intact in mid-eastern Canada in 2100. Rather, the 2012 Massachusetts ecosystems are going to disassemble – some species will disappear, others will become more prevalent, new ones will arrive – and the ecological features of the place will be changed. This will also be the case for ecosystems in mid-eastern Canada. Even if mid-eastern Canada comes to have approximately the same surface air temperature in 2100 as Massachusetts does in 2012, it will nevertheless be a new system, with different precipitation patterns, different species population densities and distributions, different topographies, and different ecological relationships more generally from those found in Massachusetts in 2012.

Thus, to the extent that global climate change occurs, place-based protections will be a less effective approach to preserving species *in situ* and maintaining ecological integrity more generally.

3.4.2   The end of native species prioritization?

Because *in situ* preservation aims to preserve species where they are – that is, in their historic and co-evolved ecological context – it has been tightly associated with native species promotion and alien or nonnative species removal. The justification for prioritizing native species over nonnative species (hereafter *native species prioritization*) in ecosystem management rests primarily on two considerations. The first, is that native species are more conducive to maintaining ecological integrity and biodiversity than are nonnative species. The second, is the normative postulate that the value of species is tied to their ecological and evolutionary situatedness. Both of these justifications for native species prioritization are undermined by global climate change, since they both depend upon the relative stability of background ecological and climatic conditions.

The reason that alien species are thought to pose a greater risk to ecological integrity and biodiversity than native species is that the latter have co-evolved with predators, prey, competitors, and other ecosystem "controls." Because of this, they are unlikely to rapidly become far more numerous and widespread than they are currently and, thereby, disrupt ecological

---

[32] Hunter et al. (1988).

processes, undermine ecosystem services, and displace other species (e.g., through direct competition, predation, or environmental modification). In contrast, nonnative species, which do not have co-evolved ecological controls in the recipient site, are more likely to become ecologically and economically problematic or *invasive*. The total estimated cost of invasive species – for example, European rabbit (*Oryctolagus cuniculus*) and Japanese knotweed (*Fallopia japonica*) – to the United Kingdom economy is £1.7 billion annually;[33] and in the United States, economic losses and expenditures attributed to invasive species – for example, zebra mussels (*Dreissena polymorpha*), Eurasian milfoil (*Myriophyllum spicatum*), kudzu (*Pueraria lobata*), purple loosestrife (*Lythrum salicaria*), brown rats (*Rattus norvegicus*), Asian carp (*Ctenopharyngodon idella*), and gypsy moths (*Lymantria dispar*) – exceed US$120 billion annually.[34] Moreover, because invasive species out compete and predate upon native species, they can be a driver of native species populations becoming imperiled, particularly in island and freshwater lake ecosystems.[35]

Although invasive species are (by definition) highly problematic, most nonnative species are not invasive. They do not result in significant economic losses, do not disrupt ecosystem services, and do not imperil native species populations.[36] For example, it is estimated that there are over 50,000 nonnative species in the United States, of which only 4,300 are at all ecologically problematic.[37] Nonnative species often increase species richness, as well as phylogenic and genetic diversity in an area. They also frequently provide social and economic benefits. This is clearly the case with respect to many nonnative agricultural and ornamental species, which, in addition to the economic activity they generate, provide food, recreation, and beauty. Nonnative species also sometimes have ecological benefits. They provide habitat and food for other species, are employed in environmental remediation, and can contribute to ecosystem services.[38] For example, in the United States, nonnative tamarisk (*Tamarix* spp.) is

---

[33] Williams et al. (2010).   [34] Pimentel et al. (2005).

[35] Wilcove et al. (1998); Sax and Gaines (2008); Davis (2009). Even in lake and island ecosystems, climate change will often play a larger role in biotic change than will nonnative species (Sharma et al. 2011).

[36] Sax and Gaines (2008); Davis (2009).   [37] FWS (2009).

[38] Hershner and Havens (2008); Davis et al. (2011); Schlaepfer et al. (2011); Thompson and Davis (2011).

the preferred nesting habitat for the endangered southwestern willow flycatcher (*Empidonax traillii extimus*), and introduced honeysuckle (*Lonicera* spp.) provides an abundant food source for native bird species, which results not only in greater numbers of those species, but also in a higher dispersal rate of other fruit-bearing plant species in the area.[39] Therefore, nonnative-ness should not be conflated with invasiveness, even though nonnative species have historically been more likely to become ecologically problem-atic than native species.

As discussed above, alien species have been more highly associated with invasiveness than have native species, because the former have tended to have fewer ecological controls. Native species have more controls because they co-evolved in a common ecological context with the other native species in the system – that is, it is a product of longitudinally developed ecological relationships among species and their environment. These rela-tionships, and thereby the controls, can be disrupted in either of two ways. A species can be removed from its evolved ecological context and intro-duced into a new system, as is the case with nonnative species, or the ecological system in which a species is located can be altered.[40] Removal of predator species from an ecosystem is a case of the latter. For example, the elimination of grey wolves and eastern cougars (*Puma concolor couguar*) in many areas of the United States has contributed to an explosion in the white-tailed deer (*Odocoileus virginianus*) population, from approximately 500,000 in the early 1900s to tens of millions today. In addition to causing billions of dollars in economic losses – primarily through car accidents and agricultural damage – the overabundance of deer is detrimental to individ-uals of many other species, including the plant species that they eat, the bird species that nest in those plant species, and the animal species with which they have common diets.[41] White-tailed deer have become an eco-logically problematic species in these places, not because they were moved to a new system, but because the systems that they are in have changed.

---

[39] Sogge et al. (2008); Gleditsch and Carlo (2010).

[40] "The invasion (as opposed to range expansion) of a native species into new habitats is similar in many respects to the introduction of an exotic species. However, instead of the introduced species being physically transported in space, the environment itself is shifted from hostile to benign for a species that already is geographically in place. The net result is the same; the in-place plant community is subjected to influences that are foreign to the co-evolved dynamics of the system" (Logan and Powell 2001: 170).

[41] Curtis and Sullivan (2001); Rawinski (2008).

In a rapidly shifting ecological context, where there are high levels of biotic and abiotic change – for example, population extinctions, introduced species (including pests and pathogens), new precipitation patterns, nitrogen eutrophication, altered soil chemistries, and increased surface air temperatures – the ecological relationships that are the basis of the ecological controls on native species will increasingly be disrupted. As a result, the factors that make native species less likely to be ecologically problematic than nonnative species will be diminished. This phenomenon is already occurring. Due to increases in the surface air temperature of its habitat, the mountain pine beetle (*Dendronctonus ponderosae*), which is native to North America, is expanding its range and producing larger and more severe outbreaks, thereby causing significantly elevated levels of tree mortality. A recent outbreak in British Columbia, for example, was of an order of magnitude greater in terms of area and mortality rates than any previously measured outbreak in the region.[42] Moreover, the beetles are increasingly threatening high alpine pine species, such as the whitebark pine (*Pinus albicaulis*), which had formerly been "protected" from severe outbreaks by colder high alpine temperatures. Whitebark pine are a charismatic keystone species for many alpine ecosystems, including Yellowstone National Park in the United States. Clarke's nutcracker (*Nucifraga columbiana*), red squirrel (*Tamiasciurus hudsonicus*), and grizzly bears (*Ursus arctos horribilis*) each depend upon whitebark pine seeds as a food source, and high alpine pines in general are crucial to snow capture and therefore to seasonal water flows.[43] A substantial reduction in whitebark and other high elevation pine populations would have large and diverse cascading effects throughout the system.[44] Already, the interaction effects of increased exposure to mountain pine beetles and a nonnative disease, white pine blister rust, have resulted in substantial declines in whitebark pine populations.[45] In its ESA evaluation of the whitebark pine, the United States Fish and Wildlife

---

[42] Taylor et al. (2006); Kurz et al. (2008).

[43] The Yellowstone grizzly's status on the United States endangered species list was recently restored due to its dependence upon whitebark pine as a food source (*Greater Yellowstone Coalition* v. *Wyoming* 2011, USCA 9th Cir., DC. No. 9:07-cv-00134-DWM).

[44] Logan and Powell (2001); Macfarlane et al. (2010).

[45] Logan et al. (2010). A 2009 survey of whitebark stands in greater Yellowstone found that 46 percent of the stands had suffered significant mortality, 36 percent had medium mortality, 13 percent low mortality, and only 5 percent no mortality (Macfarlane et al. 2010).

Service reports that "models predict that suitable habitat for whitebarks will decline precipitously, by about 70% by the 2030s and 97% within the next 100 years."[46] As with white-tailed deer, mountain pine beetles have become ecologically problematic due to a change in the system that undermines a control on their population. In the beetle case, the control is temperature, and the primary cause of the change is climatic.[47]

The mountain pine beetle case demonstrates that climate-change-driven ecological change can result in native species becoming ecologically disruptive, in much the same way as are invasive aliens, and for much the same reason – that is, the absence of ecological controls. The greater the magnitude and rate of climatic change, the more frequently this phenomenon is likely to arise. Therefore, to the extent that global climate change occurs, the ecological justification for native species prioritization will diminish. Native/nonnative will be an increasingly poor proxy for ecologically safe/ecologically risky.

Some biologists have argued that the native/nonnative distinction is already no longer practically useful, and that adherence to it fosters presumptions about ecological risk that lead to poor management decisions, such as using scarce resources in unlikely to succeed attempts to try to control or eliminate nonnative species that are not really ecologically problematic.[48] Advocates of this view propose that instead of evaluating species on the basis of their place of origin, ecosystem managers should focus on the actual impacts that they are having on the system, as well as on whether they have traits that make them likely to diffuse rapidly through disturbed or highly dynamic ecological systems. Moreover, they emphasize that the organism and group traits that foster rapid diffusion of a species

---

[46] FWS (2011: 42638). The evaluation concludes that: "Based on these threats [i.e., mountain pine beetles, blister rust, and climate-change-driven increases in competition with less cold-tolerant tree species], the whitebark pine is in danger of extinction, or likely to become so in the foreseeable future" (FWS 2011: 42638).

[47] Logan and Powell (2001); Logan (2007). Species introduction and altered ecological context can work in combination to produce invasiveness. For example, gypsy moths, which are invasive in the eastern United States, have yet to become established in the western United States, despite regular unintentional introduction of specimens. However, models suggest that global climate change will significantly increase the ecological suitability of some areas for gypsy moths, thereby dramatically increasing the likelihood of establishment with landscape scale impacts (Logan et al. 2007).

[48] Carroll (2011); Davis et al. (2011); Thompson and Davis (2011); Vince (2011).

population under those conditions, and therefore are indicators of a population's likelihood of becoming ecologically problematic, are the same for native and nonnative species.[49] Therefore, they conclude, knowing whether a species is native or nonnative does not provide much, if any, pertinent information about its likely future ecological impacts.

It is an empirical matter whether ecosystems in general, or some subset of them, are now sufficiently disturbed and dynamic that the native/nonnative species distinction lacks practical value in ecosystem management decisions. Some conservation biologists argue, contrary to the view described above, that it remains informative for many systems, particularly less impacted ones, while others argue that more research is needed to settle the question.[50] What is contested is not whether nativeness as such makes a species population less ecologically risky in comparison with alienness. No one believes that it does. Nor is anyone proposing not to address the problems caused by invasive species where feasible, or not to prevent the introduction of alien species with a high risk of becoming invasive. At issue is whether the native/nonnative distinction is informative regarding ecological risk and, thereby, useful for evaluating possible ecosystem management practices and policies.

There are, in general, two ways that the distinction might be informative about ecological risk: (1) if nativeness and nonnativeness are substantially differentially correlated with traits that favor rapid expansion in disturbed and dynamic systems; or (2) if nativeness and nonnativeness are substantially differentially correlated with the presence of ecological controls within the system. As discussed above, there is a growing body of evidence that the traits characteristic of invasive species are also associated with ecologically problematic native species. For plant species, the traits include

[49] "Invasive alien plants usually have the same general suite of traits exhibited by most successful plants in the world today, irrespective of their alien or native status. This conclusion is consistent with studies that showed that invasive aliens exhibited the same set of traits as did expanding, successful natives, that aliens and natives exhibit similar successional dynamics and that natives of disturbed, fertile habitats are indistinguishable from aliens of similar habitats ... The simplest interpretation of these findings is that, in the modern, human-dominated landscape, there is an increasingly sharp distinction between plant 'winners' and 'losers,' and that this distinction often owes rather little to native or alien status" (Thompson and Davis 2011: 156).

[50] Alyokhin (2011); Hulme et al. (2011); Lerdau and Wickham (2011); Lvei et al. (2011); Simberloff (2011); Simberloff et al. (In press); van Kleunen et al. (2011).

fast growth rates, short life cycles, copious seed production, and rapid germination.[51] Given this, the usefulness of the native/nonnative distinction turns on whether (2) will continue to hold generally. There are no studies that demonstrate decisively that the nativeness/nonnativeness distinction no longer indicates anything useful about the presence of co-evolved ecological controls and, thereby, ecological risk. However, looking forward in light of probable climate change scenarios, the situation is much different. The rate and magnitude of biotic and abiotic ecological change over the next century (and beyond) are projected to be so elevated in comparison with the recent past, even on the low emissions trajectory, that it is reasonable to believe that at some point in the near ecological future the distinction will cease to have practical value, even if it currently retains some. Climate-induced population extinctions and changes in temperature and weather patterns, in combination with intensive land use, eutrophication, and other types of anthropogenic ecological impacts are likely to disrupt the co-evolved ecological relationships that provide ecological controls on native species in such a widespread way that the native/nonnative distinction will cease to be informative about ecological risk. Therefore, to the extent that global climate change occurs, the ecological integrity justification for native species prioritization is undermined.

As mentioned earlier, there is a second justification for native species prioritization. Given the normative postulates of conservation biology and environmentalism, as well as those of many environmental ethics, having individuals of a species live out or express their form of life in their endemic habitat has more value than does preserving members of the species in an alien or *ex situ* context. It is polar bears in the Arctic, not polar bears in Central Park Zoo, that are able to fully pursue the polar bear form of life, which is what people find magnificent and valuable. Nonnative species that are introduced by human activities are extracted from their evolved, ecological relationships, and therefore have less value on the normative postulates than do native species. Thus, even when nonnative species are not ecologically problematic, they are less valuable or desirable than are native species.

As with the ecological integrity justification for native species prioritization, this natural or natural historical value justification depends upon a

---

[51] FWS (2009); Lerdau and Wickham (2011); Thompson and Davis (2011); van Kleunen (2011).

species' co-evolved ecological relationships remaining sufficiently intact. In this case, the relationships themselves have final value or else are the basis for species possessing final value. Therefore, the high rate and magnitude of ecological reconfiguration associated with global climate change undermines this justification for native species prioritization as well. To the extent that global climate change occurs, the relationships that are the basis for natural (and natural historical) value will be disrupted, and it is not within the power of ecosystem managers to prevent the changes, since they are the product of global processes.

As will be discussed in the next section, natural value needs to be understood in a way that allows for gradation. Some ecological disruption will not result in a sudden loss of all natural value. Therefore, native species still possess more natural value than do nonnative species, and they will continue to do so in the near future. However, the value differential will diminish as the rate and magnitude of anthropogenic ecological change accelerates. Thus, to the extent that global climate change and associated ecosystem reconfigurations occur, the natural value justification for native species prioritization is undermined. There may be some basis for it now (assuming the normative postulates), but it will become vanishingly small in the not-too-distant future given the projected scale of ecological change on probable climate change scenarios.

There may still be some justification for native species prioritization. However, if there is, it is fleeting. The evolved ecological relationships on which it depends are being rapidly eroded by global climate change and other anthropogenic impacts. Therefore, when ecosystem management plans and policies take a long-range ecological perspective, as they often should do, native species prioritization is unwarranted.

3.4.3   The end of restoration?

As with *in situ* preservation and native species prioritization, global climate change undermines ecological restoration as an effective, well-justified ecosystem management strategy for preserving biodiversity. Ecological restoration is a variety of ecologically assisted recovery – actively intervening in a space in order to improve it from an ecological perspective. An activity that degrades an area or leaves it no better off ecologically than it was prior to the intervention (or does not aim to make it better off) is not an assisted recovery. A particular assisted recovery is a restoration – as opposed to a revitalization, regeneration, or reclamation, for example – to the extent that *historicity* is incorporated into the project. Historicity typically involves returning something to the way, state, or place that it was previously. However, it also can be understood in terms of carrying forward an ongoing narrative or process that reaches back into the past. In the case of ecological restoration, these are often intertwined. Ecological restoration aims to improve the ecology of a place in the future by maintaining continuity with the past. This is accomplished by incorporating or amplifying elements, such as native species or abiotic features, which previously obtained in a particular place or region, or by establishing something of the ecology that would have obtained absent anthropogenic degradation – that is, by reestablishing a historical trajectory for the space or the species in it. Thus, as the terms are used here, ecological restoration is a type of assisted recovery that is distinguished by historicity;[52] an assisted recovery is a restoration to the extent that it is informed (in product, process, or vision) by the past; and historical fidelity is a commitment to historicity in assisted recovery.[53]

One of the primary justifications for emphasizing historicity in assisted recovery is that it helps to promote ecological integrity by setting goals and incorporating elements that are well suited to the site of the recovery, since they have obtained and thrived there in the past. Moreover, by grounding the goals of assisted recovery in the past ecological realities of a place, rather than in our desires or visions for it, a commitment to historicity functions as a check on prioritizing human wants for the space over what is more ecologically suitable or feasible.[54]

However, under conditions of global climate change, the ecological future is less likely to resemble the ecological past. The ecological impacts of global climate change will be geographically differential. They will be greater in some places than in others. But, in general, there will be substantial increases in the rate of ecosystem transitions. Therefore, historical ecosystems and ecological trajectories (and the reference conditions derived from them) will, in general, be increasingly poor proxies for

---

[52] This conception of ecological restoration is largely that developed by Higgs (2003). Its core elements are ecological integrity, historicity, and design.

[53] Sandler (2012a).   [54] Higgs (2003); Throop (2012).

ecological integrity. That the native/nonnative species distinction will be an increasingly poor stand-in for ecologically beneficial/ecologically detrimental is an instance of this.

Under conditions of rapid and uncertain ecological change, good assisted recoveries from the perspective of ecological integrity will, in general, involve less historicity. They will less strongly resemble the composition and trajectories of systems prior to their degradation. Moreover, too much historical fidelity would be a form of ecological insensitivity to ongoing ecological change. Rather than providing a check against implementing an ecologically unsuitable human vision for a place, too strong a commitment to historicity would involve imposing ourselves against ongoing ecological processes. For example, in the Long Island Sound, American lobster (*Homarus americanus*) populations are declining, while blue crab (*Callinectes sapidus*) populations are increasing, due in part to increases in water temperature. Actively intervening to restore the sound as fertile lobster habitat and, thereby, restoring prior ecological trajectories and cultural practices is not feasible. Even on optimistic global climate change scenarios, the sound is going to increasingly suit blue crabs rather than lobsters, since it is at the lobster's southernmost coastal range. This needs to be part of the ecosystem management plan for the Sound, and it needs to inform expectations for the place more generally.[55] The same holds for any management project for which climatic change has significantly altered ecological conditions and trajectories from pre-disturbance states. Whether it is the effect of altered temperatures on woodland restoration in North America,[56] carbon dioxide concentrations on savannah restoration in Africa,[57] sea levels on coastal dunes in Central America, or flow volumes on watersheds in Asia, what is ecologically feasible and responsible depends upon what the ecological conditions will be now and in the future. To the extent that global climate change occurs, the trajectory of the ecological future will deviate from the trajectory of the ecological past. History will not be such a good guide to ecological integrity.

In defense of historicity in assisted recovery, William Throop has argued that even as the effects of anthropogenic climate change increase, those with "the virtues of humility, sensitivity and self-restraint ... will tend to

---

[55] Long Island Sound Study (2011).
[56] Greater Yellowstone Coordinating Committee (2011); Throop (2012).
[57] Harris et al. (2006).

adopt conservative restoration goals ... that exhibit a high degree of historical fidelity."[58] For example, he suggests that, given climate change, restor-
ationists should use genetic stock from the southern portion of a species'
range, rather than look to a different species altogether. However, getting
genetic stock from a different place than the site of the restoration is to
incorporate less historicity. It is a diminished role for the history of the
place. Moreover, if the magnitude of ecological change is sufficiently large,
then even the more southerly stock (in the northern hemisphere) of a
species may not be well suited to the current and future ecological conditions of the restoration site. If this occurs systematically, then historicity
must diminish as a goal in assisted recovery, since ecological sensitivity will
be increasingly in tension with it. It is for this reason that the claim
defended here is conditional: to the extent that the ecological future less
resembles the ecological past (due to global climate change and other
anthropogenic causes), the ecological justification for historical fidelity is
diminished. However, as discussed above, given the current ecological and
climatic trajectories, as well as the trajectories on optimistic future emissions scenarios, the ecological future of most places will be quite different
from their recent ecological past. Thus, the implication of global climate
change for incorporating historicity into ecosystem management is that
prioritizing historical systems, elements of those systems, and past historical trajectories in assisted recovery will be less conducive to realizing the
ecological integrity goals of assisted recovery. Therefore, restoration is
undermined as an effective, and therefore well justified, approach to species preservation.

Another common justification for historical fidelity in assisted recovery
(and, thus, restoration) is based on natural value – that is, the value of the
continuity of ecological processes and the products of those processes by
virtue of their being free from human intervention and design. If ecological
continuity and human independence is value adding, then restoration
would seem to be preferable to other forms of assisted recovery, all other
things being equal. The historicity that is involved with restoration would
provide additional value to the recovery.

Some have argued that appeals to natural value cannot justify restoration
because it is part of the concept of the value that it cannot be recaptured

----

[58] Throop (2012: 56–57).

once lost. The need for restoration entails that the natural history, the basis of the value, has already been disrupted. Moreover, execution of the restoration involves further human intervention and design. Therefore, even a restoration high on historicity cannot increase or create natural value.[59] In response, advocates for restoration and historical fidelity might argue that natural value is not an all-or-nothing matter. Natural value can be possessed by systems and species populations to a greater or lesser degree based on the extent to which they are free of human intervention and design. In this way, an assisted recovery high on historicity would have more natural value, because it bears less of a mark of human intervention and design, than one that does not. Historical fidelity might then be justified, at least in part, because of its conduciveness to promoting natural value, including the natural value of species, in assisted recovery.

However, even granting this not-all-or-nothing conception of natural value, the relevant features of global climate change reduce the extent to which natural value justifies historical fidelity. This is because even as it would be in principle possible to reestablish or increase natural value through restoration, it is in practice going to be more difficult to do. As discussed earlier, given global climate change, assisted recoveries that aim for ecological integrity will involve less historicity. As a result, they will have less natural value. More intervention, not less, will be required to accomplish high levels of historicity. More intervention, not less, will be required to maintain the ecological and evolutionary situatedness of species. Therefore, even granting subjective natural value and/or objective natural historical value, as well as a conception of naturalness that admits of degrees, this justification for restoration over other forms of assisted recovery is undermined to the extent that global climate change occurs.

Alternatively, suppose that a previously degraded ecological place can develop natural value over time if it is free of human intervention, design, and control. On this conception of natural value, an ecological space can come to possess natural value proportional to the extent to which and duration for which it is free from human interference. This conception of natural value also fails to support historical fidelity. The reason is that on it natural value emerges by allowing places to develop independently.

---

[59] Katz (2000); Elliot (1982).

However, to the extent that global climate change occurs and the ecological future is accelerating away from the ecological past, realizing historicity will require greater intervention and control. Letting ecological systems regenerate or recover on their own will be less likely to result in systems that are highly analogous to the pre-impact systems and trajectories of the place.

Thus, the distinctive features of global climate change undermine the primary justifications for prioritizing historicity in assisted recovery – that is, it promotes ecological integrity and increases natural value. Because these are the core justifications for restoration, to the extent that global climate change undermines them, the case in favor of ecological restoration is significantly weakened. (Or, alternatively, a weaker historicity is justified.) However, they are not the only justifications that have been offered for historical fidelity. Another justification for restoration has been suggested by Eric Higgs, who argues that incorporating historicity into ecosystem management helps to fulfill our nostalgic needs.[60] However, given global climate change, such nostalgic needs – or desires for the ecological past – are increasingly in tension with the goal of ecological integrity. They would become nostalgic impositions on ecological integrity within the context of assisted recovery. As a result, they are unsatisfiable, or satisfiable only in a less robust or sustainable form. Moreover, they are in tension with ecological sensitivity and humility, which are among the important moral education goals of assisted recovery.[61] For these reasons, satisfaction of ecological nostalgia is another casualty of global climate change. Even this less prominent justification for historicity in assisted recovery is undermined by the distinctive features of global climate change.[62]

---

[60] Higgs (2003).   [61] Basl (2010a); Light (2000).

[62] Higgs (2003) also suggests that historical fidelity is conducive to developing connection to place, which is good in itself and conducive to promoting ecological integrity. However, there are other factors besides historicity that are conducive to developing connection to place. Many people's connection to a place has more to do with their history with the place and the opportunities (e.g., recreation, relaxation, education, study, and art) that it enables, than it does with the general history (or historicity) of a place. Moreover, connection to place can be effectively fostered through engaging in assisted recovery, even when the recovery does not include much historicity (Basl 2010a). Thus, this consideration does not provide justification for historical fidelity in assisted recovery, even independent of global climate change.

To the extent that global climate change occurs, appropriate ecological goals for a place will less strongly resemble its prior ecological trajectory. Context-specific assessments of the role of historicity in assisted recovery are, of course, needed, and historicity may play an appropriately larger role in some recoveries than in others.[63] Relevant considerations include the magnitude of global climate change's impact on the area (not all places will be equally affected); the purpose of the restoration (e.g., research, recreation, habitat, or ecosystem services); the desires and values of those involved; available resources; the time gap between the degradation and the recovery; the timeline for the recovery; and the novelty of the place's biotic and abiotic features. However, in general, historicity will be less conducive to promoting environmental values. Therefore, ecological restoration should have a diminished role in ecosystem management, including the preservation of species and biodiversity, under conditions of global climate change.[64]

3.5 Conclusion

Global climate change is an anthropogenic calamity from the perspective of species and ecosystem preservation. It also poses a dilemma for those committed to species conservation. One the one hand, global climate change will dramatically increase the number of species that are at risk of extinction. On the other hand, global climate change undermines the effectiveness of and justifications for the predominant approaches to species conservation: place-based preservation and restoration. Many conservation

[63] Harris et al. (2006).

[64] This is not to conclude that historical continuity of ecological processes or the products of those processes are any less or differently valuable given global climate change. The core argument is that, given global climate change, reestablishing natural value and ecological integrity through historically-oriented restoration will be increasingly difficult to achieve, so appeals to natural value and ecological integrity will do less to justify historical fidelity (or historicity) in assisted recovery. The basis of natural value is people's evaluative attitudes regarding processes, places, and products (e.g., species) that are independent of human control, impacts, and designs. Therefore, if more people value these (or value them more greatly), given their scarcity or fleetingness as a consequence of global climate change, then the significance of natural value would be increased in the age of global climate change. Alternatively, if people value naturalness less given the ecological realities associated with global climate change, then the significance of natural value would diminish.

biologists and environmentalists recognize this difficulty.[65] In response, some have begun to advocate for a new approach to preserving species under conditions of global climate change: assisted colonization. In Chapter 4, I conduct a value analysis and assessment of this emerging species conservation strategy.

[65] Donlan et al. (2005); Harris et al. (2006); Hoegh-Guldberg et al. (2008); Hobbs et al. (2009); UNEP (2009); Cole and Yung (2010); Hellmann and Pfrende (2011).

4   Assisted colonization

In response to the conservation biology dilemma, many conservation biologists, ecosystem managers, and environmentalists have begun to advocate for a new species preservation strategy, assisted colonization (or managed relocation). *Assisted colonization* is intentionally moving individuals of a species to a location where there is no existent population of the species, sometimes beyond their historic range, and the establishment of a viable independent population in that location, for the purpose of preventing the species from going extinct. The motivation for assisted colonization is that, unless some such practice is adopted, conservation biology will be reduced to "managing extinctions," rather than preserving species.[1]

> Moving species outside their historic ranges may mitigate loss of biodiversity in the face of global climate change ... We must contemplate the possibility that some regions of the Earth will experience high levels of warming (>4°C) within the next 100 years, as well as altered precipitation and ocean acidity. Under these circumstances, the future for many species and ecosystems is so bleak that assisted colonization might be their best chance.[2]

Assisted colonization is rapidly gaining proponents and, in some cases, practitioners. In the United Kingdom, two butterfly species have been successfully translocated northward to sites that climate-species models suggest will be more conducive to their long-term survival than their prior range.[3] In Canada, scientists have relocated dozens of tree species to locations beyond their recent historical range; in the United States, an environmental

---

[1] Donlan et al. (2005: 913).

[2] Hoegh-Guldberg et al. (2008: 346). See also, Donlan et al. (2005); Hobbs et al. (2006); United States Climate Change Science Program (2008); Richardson et al. (2009); Camacho et al. (2010); Minteer and Collins (2010); Vitt et al. (2010); Thomas (2011).

[3] Willis et al. (2008).

group called the Torreya Guardians has translocated specimens of *Torreya taxifolia*, a threatened conifer, from its present range in Florida to a more northerly location in North Carolina.[4] Several other species – such as the Quino checkerspot butterfly (*Euphydryas editha quino*) in California, the Iberian lynx (*Lynx pardinus*) in Spain, and the whitebark pine in British Columbia – have been proposed as candidates for assisted colonization,[5] and several models for guiding decision making on when intentional translocation is an appropriate conservation strategy have been developed.[6]

The momentum building behind assisted colonization is evidence of the acuteness of the conservation biology dilemma. As discussed in Chapter 3, conservation biologists and environmentalists have for decades had a strong commitment to native species over nonnative species, due to both the risk of invasiveness and their value orientation – that is, favoring natural over anthropogenic designs and processes, as well as maintaining ecological and evolutionary relationships. Yet assisted colonization is intentionally establishing viable populations of nonnative species. One set of commitments – prioritizing nature's independence and maintaining ecological and evolutionary situatedness – is in tension with another – preservation of biodiversity by forestalling anthropogenic extinctions. Advocates of assisted colonization are prioritizing the latter.[7]

---

[4] Marris (2008, 2009).   [5] Marris (2008); Morelle (2010); McLane and Aitken (In press).
[6] Hoegh-Guldberg et al. (2008); Richardson et al. (2009); McDonald-Madden et al. (2011).
[7] One possible reason for prioritizing species preservation over nature's independence might be that global climate change has ended nature's independence. As Bill McKibben (2000) has famously argued, once we affect the climate, we affect everything; no place is left untouched by human industrial activities. However, even if this descriptive point is true, it does not follow that the independence of nature has been ended. We may have altered the climate, but we do not control climatic processes. Moreover, there are many more features, forces, and processes that constitute nature's independence, including many that contribute to determining the climate, than the levels of greenhouse gases in the atmosphere. Furthermore, there remain many places with ecological features that are only slightly impacted by human activity (Caro et al. 2011). There may be no (or very few) places on land or in the oceans that are purely natural. But there is, nevertheless, still naturalness, independence from humans. Moreover, as argued in previous chapters, naturalness and natural value admit of degrees. Yellowstone, despite the impact of humans, is more natural than a manicured backyard, which is more natural than a shopping mall parking lot. Therefore, global climate change does not make preserving naturalness impossible. If we refrain from attempts to manipulate and control climatic and ecological systems, the process and product will be more natural than if we attempt to design and engineer them. Thus, the "end of nature" does not justify prioritizing

In this chapter, I conduct a value analysis and assessment of assisted colonization to determine if it is a well-justified species conservation strategy under conditions of rapid and uncertain ecological change. I argue that, with very rare exceptions, it is not. In the vast majority of cases, assisted colonization is not likely to preserve the value of species. Moreover, successful assisted colonizations, ones that are responsibly conducted and in which the target species becomes established without being ecologically disruptive, are likely to be highly uncommon. In addition, the opportunity costs associated with them will typically be substantial.

4.1 Environmental value analysis

Policies and practices aim to bring about goals that are taken to justify the costs, including the opportunity costs, associated with them. Therefore, it is possible to conduct a value analysis of any policy or practice by determining:

(1) what is good or valuable about the goal that the policy or practice aims to accomplish;
(2) to what extent the policy or practice is likely to accomplish or realize those goods or values;
(3) the possible or likely disvalues associated with the practice or policy;
(4) whether there are other approaches to realizing the goods or values that are likely to be more effective or efficient (or have fewer associated disvalues);
(5) whether the resources that would go toward the policy or practice could be used more effectively or efficiently in pursuit of other goods or values.

In the case of assisted colonization, the goal is to prevent species from going extinct, and this is thought to be justified because it preserves the value of individual species and/or biodiversity – that is, this is the answer that proponents of assisted colonization give to (1) above.[8] Therefore, a value analysis of assisted colonization must determine, for each of the types of value that species might have:

species preservation over promoting nature's independence, since nature's independence has not ended.

[8] Barlow and Martin (2004/2005); McLachlan et al. (2007); Hoegh-Guldberg et al. (2008).

(a) whether it is plausible that species possess the type of value – this is to assess the answer to (1);

(b) if species do possess the type of value, whether intentional translocation of populations of an endangered or threatened species is an effective way to preserve the value – this is to answer (2); and

(c) if translocation is an effective way of preserving the value, whether (and to what extent) this justifies committing resources to doing so, given the costs, risks, potential disvalues, and alternatives available – this is to answer (3)–(5).

The value of species was addressed in Chapter 2, where I argued that biodiversity and individual species have instrumental value, both present and option, but that not all species have it equally. I also argued that biodiversity and some species have subjective final value, both preference and integral, but, again, that not all species have it equally. With respect to objective final value, I argued that species do not have inherent worth, since they do not have a good of their own distinct from that of the individual organisms that comprise them, and that they should not be regarded as having natural historical value, since, although it is possible that there is such value, there is no adequate justification or argument for believing that it exists.

In what follows, the extent to which assisted colonization could be effective in preserving the instrumental and subjective value of species is discussed. Natural historical value is also considered, since a positive argument for its nonexistence was not presented (whereas a positive argument against the inherent worth of species was provided). The costs, risks, and potential disvalues of assisted colonization are then addressed and an overall assessment of assisted colonization as a species conservation strategy under conditions of rapid ecological change is provided.

4.2   Instrumental value and species translocation

As discussed in Chapter 2, ecosystem integrity is often valuable, and it can be so in multiple ways. It can have instrumental value, both present and option, subjective value, and/or inherent worth. Therefore, biodiversity or particular species are instrumentally valuable to the extent that they contribute to ecosystem integrity. Each species also has some instrumental value to us and other species, even if a very small amount. Does assisted colonization promote or protect the instrumental value of species or biodiversity?

The primary motivation for assisted colonization is to preserve the target species, not to address some problematic feature of the ecology of the recipient system.[9] Proposed guidelines emphasize that for any assisted colonization to be justified there must be sufficient evidence that it is unlikely that it will not be ecologically detrimental to the recipient system.[10] However, that an assisted colonization is not likely to be ecologically detrimental is not a reason in favor of doing it. It is the absence of a reason not to do it. Therefore, justifying an assisted colonization on the basis of ecological value requires more than demonstrating that the ecological risks of that particular translocation are relatively low, and that enabling low risk assisted colonizations does not encourage more risky ones.[11] It is also necessary to justify why even relatively low risks should be taken.[12]

Again, the primary concern regarding assisted colonizations is that they will be ecologically disruptive to the recipient systems.[13] In no case will the risk be zero, since it is always possible that the introduced species will become problematic, or that others who are either more hasty or less able to identify and assess ecological risks will be encouraged to engage in the practice. At best, there will be low ecological risks associated with a candidate assisted colonization, with respect to both likelihood and severity of disruption.[14] Moreover, even when a translocation has relatively low ecological risks, there is likely little ecological value to be gained from it. The fact that nonnative species are sometimes found to be beneficial does not imply that it can often be predicted with confidence when this will be the case, as would be necessary for ecological value to justify assisted colonization. Furthermore, the greater the ecological value a translocated species is intended to have in the recipient system, the greater the risks involved are likely to be, because its intended ecological impact will be greater. Thus, the ecological value of a species, which is relational to the system of which it is a part, is not a promising justification for assisted colonization.

---

[9] Barlow and Martin (2004/2005); McLachlan et al. (2007); Hoegh-Guldberg et al. (2008).
[10] McLachlan et al. (2007); Hoegh-Guldberg et al. (2008); Richardson et al. (2009).
[11] Schwartz (2004/2005).   [12] Hoegh-Guldberg et al. (2008); Lawler and Olden (2011).
[13] McLachlan et al. (2007); Hoegh-Guldberg et al. (2008); Mueller and Hellmann (2008).
[14] Schwartz (2004/2005); Davidson and Simkanin (2008); Mueller and Hellmann (2008).

When a species introduction is intended to be restorative or remediative to the recipient system, such as the reintroduction of wolves to Yellowstone, the relative ecological risks and benefits will often be quite different. However, such cases are not strictly assisted colonizations, as the paradigmatic cases of, and candidates for, assisted colonization indicate. These include relocating the Quino checkerspot butterfly to higher elevations,[15] the marble white skipper (*Melanargia galathea*) and small skipper (*Thymelicus sylvestris*) north in the British Isles,[16] the Florida torreya to North Carolina,[17] and the narrow-faced kangaroo rat (*Dipodomys venustus*) north of San Francisco.[18] In each case, the aim is to prevent the species from going extinct, not to improve the ecological conditions of the recipient system.[19] The ecological value of the species is not the basis for, and does not justify, the assisted colonization.

None of this assumes or implies that species-level biodiversity is not highly valuable. As discussed in Chapter 2, species-level biodiversity can have considerable ecological, instrumental, and option value. However, it does not follow from this that every species is also highly or equally valuable in these respects. Moreover, an assisted colonization, at best, does not diminish, but also does not significantly increase, the biodiversity of the recipient system, since only one or a few species are translocated. Therefore, assisted colonization is not justified by its potential contribution to the ecological value of biodiversity in the system.

Exceptions are possible. There may be cases in which assisted colonization of a species is likely to be significantly ecologically beneficial to the recipient system, the associated ecological risks are relatively low, and these can be predicted with confidence in advance of the translocation. However, the foregoing considerations suggest that such cases will be rare.

The same is true of the instrumental value of the species themselves – that is, their direct usefulness to human beings or other species,

---

[15] Zimmer (2007).   [16] Willis et al. (2008).

[17] Barlow and Martin (2004/2005); Schwartz (2004/2005); Fox (2007).

[18] Berdik (2008).

[19] This is why, in the definition of assisted colonization, reference is made to the goal of the translocation. It is distinctive of assisted colonization that the goal is to preserve the species. Translocation of species is nothing new, it has always been commonplace in agriculture and horticulture, and more recently in bioremediation and restoration, for example. It is the goal, the reasons for, and the conditions of the translocation that distinguish assisted colonization.

independent of their contribution to biodiversity and ecological integrity. The paradigmatic assisted colonizations, such as the Florida torreya and Quino checkerspot butterfly, are not justified by, and their advocates do not espouse, the instrumental value of the species. Moreover, the species have very little option value, or potential for future instrumental value, because the probability that they will be instrumentally significant in the future is extremely low. That these candidates for assisted colonization do not possess significant ecological or instrumental (including option) value is not happenstance. As discussed earlier, most species are low in such values. Only a small portion of species are keystone or dominant species, economically significant, medicinally useful, or scientifically crucial, for example. Moreover, candidate species for assisted colonization are especially likely to be low on instrumental value. They are rare and narrowly distributed, otherwise their preservation would not require translocation, so their present contribution to ecological integrity, ecosystems services, and other instrumental values is typically small.[20] Furthermore, with the exception of commercially significant species (which, again, are a tiny minority of species), they are often at risk of extinction because their instrumental value is not close to the economic value of the development and extraction activities that are so often threats to them. In addition, if a species does have substantial instrumental value, establishing an independent population through assisted colonization often will not be an effective means of promoting it, in comparison with *ex situ* cultivation, for example.

As with ecological integrity, exceptions are possible. There may be cases in which the target species is especially high in instrumental or option value, and assisted colonization is a comparatively effective way to protect and promote it. For example, a species might have high ecotourism value even once translocated, or it might become an important food source for charismatic fauna. However, the foregoing considerations suggest that such cases will be rare.

4.3   Subjective value and species translocation

An entity has subjective final value if people have preferences for it or value it for what it is or that it is, not merely for what it can do for them or others.

---

[20] Ehrenfeld (1988).

Many people value species in this way. Some people have (noninstrumental) preferences for the existence of some species, such that those species have preference value. Others value biodiversity or specific species in ways that flow from their worldviews or deeper value commitments, such that they have integral value. To what extent does this justify engaging in assisted colonization to prevent species from going extinct?

As discussed earlier, the existence value of species, because it derives from personal preferences, is not a particularly robust type of value. People's preferences regarding species vary over time, are more easily manipulated than integral valuing, and can be based on a lack of (or bad) information, for example. Moreover, different people have different preferences regarding particular species and biodiversity generally. This limits the extent to which preference value justifies assisted colonization. That some people have a preference for the existence of a particular life form is some justification for preserving it, but it does not have the sort of normative force that is sometimes associated with assisted colonization.[21] Therefore, even when some people have a preference for the existence of some species, this is not in itself a compelling justification for taking on the costs and risks associated with an assisted colonization.

The integral value of species provides a more promising basis for justifying assisted colonization than does preference value, since it is more stable and robust. Although, as discussed earlier, even on the legislative and reason-based (i.e., informed and coherent) conception of the integral value of species and biodiversity, it is still not fully secure, since it is highly contested and both the valuing and the legislative expression of it can and do change over time. Nevertheless, if a species possesses integral value, there is reason, stronger than that associated with preference value, to try to preserve the value. It does not, however, follow from this that assisted colonization is an effective approach to doing so.

In fact, the value currently attributed to species by the ESA, which on Callicott's view is the legislative expression of the integral value of species in the United States,[22] does not justify assisted colonization. Protection of species, as it is understood and operationalized within the ESA, involves not merely keeping them in existence, but doing so in their habitat and in a

21 Barlow and Martin (2004/2005); Southgate et al. (2008).
22 Callicott (2006); Callicott and Grove-Fanning (2009).

sustainable way. This is one of the features of the ESA that makes it a powerful piece of conservation legislation. Provisions of the Act are not met for a listed species if the species is kept in existence only *ex situ*, and not all individuals of a species are valued in the same way under the ESA. For example, hatchery raised and released salmon, despite being the same life form as wild spawned salmon, are not counted in ESA listing determinations. Therefore, it is doubtful that the ESA, which treats species as integrally valuable *in situ*, would treat a species as valuable (or as equally so) if it were moved sufficiently beyond its current or even historic range. An ecologically informed operationalization of the ESA should recognize that a species' habitat is in constant flux and that historic ranges often extend well beyond current ranges, particularly for endangered species. However, it does not follow from this that the ESA must recognize conservation in any suitable habitat[23] or any historic range[24] as *in situ* conservation. Thus, whether a candidate assisted colonization would, if successful, preserve the integral value of the target species depends upon the details of how *in situ* conservation is operationalized, as well as upon the details of the assisted colonization – for example, whether translocation is within or beyond the species' historic range.

If people value a species (or biodiversity) integrally – for example, for its beauty, complexity, diversity, spiritual significance, naturalness, wildness, wondrousness, or rarity[25] – then that is a reason to try to preserve it. However, it does not follow from this that assisted colonization is a well-justified approach to doing so. In many cases – such as with the ESA and natural value – what is valued is not merely the continuation of the species, but continuation of the species *in situ*. At least some varieties of assisted colonization, such as those that involve translocation outside the

---

[23] Chapron and Samelius (2008).   [24] Barlow and Martin (2004/2005).

[25] Rarity is sometimes a value-adding property. For example, some things (including individuals of some species) are more economically valuable because they are rare, and some things (including individuals of some species) are integrally valued because they are rare. But rarity itself does not make something valuable. In fact, all things are rare under some description or category. The apple tree at my son's school is the only edible-fruit-bearing tree at the school – that is, it is very rare under that description. However, if there is a type that is valued, and the individuals of that type are reduced, then the remaining individuals may have increased instrumental or subjective final value by virtue of their scarcity. Rarity is not relevant to inherent worth, since inherent worth is interest-based, and rarity does not itself create or alter interests.

species' historic range, do not accomplish this. In addition, if an assisted colonization poses a risk to some other threatened or endangered species, or may be otherwise ecologically disruptive, the integral values that support species conservation would likely favor refraining from attempting the translocation.

4.4   Natural historical value and species translocation

According to proponents of the natural historical value of species, species possess objective value as a result of their ecological and evolutionary situatedness. The value is thought to follow from each species being a distinctive historical form of life that is the product, process, and instrument of complex generative evolutionary processes stretching back through "deep time." I argued in Chapter 2 that the case in favor of natural historical value is not strong enough to warrant attributing it to species and ecosystems. However, I also argued that such value is conceptually coherent and possible. Therefore, the earlier arguments against accepting natural historical value notwithstanding, it is worthwhile considering whether such value, if it exists, would justify engaging in assisted colonization.

Even if it is granted that species possess natural historical value, it does not plainly justify assisted colonization. Species possess natural historical value by virtue of their roles and relationships within ecological and evolutionary systems and processes. As a result, "It is not preservation of *species* that we wish, but the preservation of *species in the system*. It is not merely *what* they are, but *where* they are that humans must value correctly . . . The species can only be preserved *in situ*; the species *ought* to be preserved *in situ*."[26] It is not clear whether preserving a species through assisted colonization is sufficiently *in situ* so as to preserve also its natural historical value. If an assisted colonization is successful, the evolutionary trajectory and potential of the species is not extinguished, although it is altered. The species continues to be ecologically situated in a way that it would not be in a zoo or botanical garden. However, the species may not be preserved in its current, recent, or even historic habitat. As discussed earlier, what constitutes *in situ* conservation must be informed by a dynamic conception of habitat, but this does not imply that preservation in any suitable habitat should be

---

[26] Rolston (2001: 411, original emphasis).

considered *in situ*. Consider, for example, bristlecone pines (*Pinus longaeva*), which can live for thousands of years under extreme conditions at elevations of two miles above sea level. Even if a viable population could be established elsewhere, under more hospitable ecological conditions, it would not retain what is most distinctive about their form of life: that is, they live for so long, with bare metabolism, under those circumstances.

For these reasons, even if species possess objective natural historical value, assisted colonization might not be an effective approach to preserving it. As with natural value, whether it would depends upon how *in situ* conservation is understood and on the details of the assisted colonization.

4.5   Against assisted colonization

In the previous sections, I argued that there is little value to be preserved through assisted colonization, except in rare cases where the translocated species would be ecologically or instrumentally valuable in the recipient site (and this can be reliably predicted in advance), or the species has final value by virtue of characteristics that are independent of ecological or evolutionary situatedness. This warrants the conclusion that very few assisted colonizations are justified, let alone obligatory. It is not, however, to argue that they ought not be done. In this section, I argue for the stronger conclusion that, except in rare cases, assisted colonization of species at risk of extinction largely due to global climate change should not be translocated for preservation purposes. Here is the core argument:

(1) Except in rare cases, there is little or no value to be preserved through assisted colonization, even when it is successful.

(2) Successful assisted colonizations – that is, those in which the target population is sustainably established and is not ecologically problematic in the recipient site – are likely to be rare.

(3) Responsible assisted colonizations – that is, those in which adequate pre-translocation research on the target species and recipient site is conducted, legal barriers are addressed, and public support around the recipient site is sought and secured – are likely to be difficult to accomplish, expensive, and have high opportunity costs.

(4) Successful assisted colonizations will be detrimental to some individuals in the recipient system, and are likely to be so for some of the translocated individuals as well.

(5) Therefore, assisted colonization is an unjustified response to species extinctions associated with global climate change, except in very rare cases.

Premise (1) of the argument – that there is little or no value to be preserved through assisted colonization, except in rare cases – is the conclusion of the value analysis conducted in the prior sections. If the analysis is accurate, the premise is true.

Premise (2) of the argument – that successful assisted colonizations are likely to be rare – follows from the features of global climate change. In order to accomplish a successful assisted colonization it is necessary to know where to relocate the target population in order for it to thrive. This requires identifying where suitable habitats are – for example, where there is appropriate precipitation, temperature, soil chemistry, or other species – not just now, but extended into the future. However, among the distinctive features of global climate change are the uncertainty and contingency of the ecological future. Because the ecological future depends so heavily on public policy decisions not yet taken and technological innovations still to be created and disseminated, as well as on incompletely understood effects of greenhouse gas levels on climatic systems and ecological processes, it is not possible to predict the climatic and ecological future of a particular place with any confidence. There are simply too many poorly understood and indeterminate (not just unknown, but unknowable) factors. Moreover, due to the abnormally high rates of climatic and ecological change and the elevated levels of uncertainty and indeterminacy, the range of possible ecological futures in any particular place is broader than in the recent ecological past. For example, the range of possible mean surface air temperature increases over preindustrial levels by 2100, just within the Confirmed proposals scenario discussed in Chapter 3, is 4.8–12.9°F (2.7–7.1°C) (a difference of 8.1°F [4.4°C]), and the range from the bottom end of the Low emissions scenario to the upper end of the BAU scenario is 2.1–14.3°F (1.2–7.9°C) (a difference of 12.2°F [6.7°C]). The difficulty in identifying an appropriate recipient site is particularly acute for populations of species that are less ecologically flexible, which are precisely those that would be most in need of assisted colonization, since they will typically have less adaptive capacity. Thus, one reason successful assisted colonizations are likely to be rare under conditions of global climate change is that it is not possible to predict with any confidence where suitable habitat for a species population will be 50 or 100 years from now. This difficulty is severely compounded by the many other anthropogenic drivers of rapid and macro-scale ecological change, such as nitrogen eutrophication, unintentional species introductions, and shifting land use patterns.

Moreover, because the rate of climatic and ecological change associated with global climate change is elevated, and there is no reason to believe that it will abate,[27] even if a recipient site is appropriate now, it might become unsuitable for the species population in 50, 100, or 200 years. This difficulty, like the previous one, is particularly salient for species that would be the primary candidates for assisted colonization, those whose populations have less adaptive capacity. As a result, under conditions of global climate change, even if an assisted colonization is initially successful, it is likely to be unsustainable. The same features – global climate change and habitat fragmentation and degradation – that are driving the need for translocation now will continue to obtain and, in the near future, will place many trans-located species populations in much the same position as they are pres-ently. Thus, the distinctive features of global climate change suggest not only that it will be difficult to successfully translocate in the short run, but that even temporarily successful translocations are unlikely to be the basis for long-term population stability.

An additional consideration relevant to premise (2) – that successful assisted colonizations are likely to be rare – is that for an assisted coloniza-tion to be successful, a viable population of translocated individuals must be established without it becoming a problematic invasive. As has already been discussed, the vast majority of translocated (or nonnative) species are not invasive. However, the ones that are can be highly ecologically and econom-ically detrimental. Some have argued that there remains an inadequate understanding of invasive species and associated ecological processes for predicting which species are likely to become invasive in particular ecolog-ical contexts, a problem that is exacerbated by the uncertainties and inde-terminacies associated with global climate change.[28] To the extent that this is correct, it will make successful assisted colonizations still more difficult to foretell and execute.

---

[27] Gillett et al. (2011).
[28] Ricciardi and Simberloff (2009). For an alternative assessment of the state of knowledge regarding invasion and assisted colonization, see Mueller and Hellmann (2008).

Premise (3) – that responsible translocations are likely to be difficult to accomplish, expensive to execute, and have high opportunity costs – is based on an inclusive conception of what constitutes a responsible translocation. In some cases, it may be possible for a small group of individuals, acting on their own, to translocate a species relatively easily. This appears to have been the case with the Florida torreya translocation, for example. However, such translocations are not responsible, for several reasons. They may be risky with respect to invasiveness in the recipient system; they may be inconsiderate of the valuations of others regarding the recipient system; they may be detrimental to individuals in the recipient system and/or translocated individuals; and they may be illegal. A responsible assisted colonization must attend to the relevant ecological, legal, social, and cultural considerations associated with a candidate species and recipient site. One framework for such inclusive and multidimensional evaluation suggests assessing any candidate assisted colonization on both social and ecological grounds with respect to focal impact, collateral impact, feasibility, and acceptability, and it includes multiple considerations (and subconsiderations) within each of the categories.[29] Executing a responsible assisted colonization involves studying the potential effects on the recipient system – for example, on other species and on ecosystem services. It involves assessing alternative conservation strategies with respect to feasibility and cost; identifying and consulting all stakeholders, with due process and diligence; and addressing all relevant legal considerations, such as reviews, permits, and liability.[30] This will typically require resource intensive longitudinal study, on the part of both ecologists and social scientists, as well as extensive social, cultural, and legal engagement – and even then the translocation may not be supported.[31]

If a candidate relocation is determined to be technically feasible, low in ecological risk, socially and culturally acceptable, legal, and preferable to alternative conservation strategies, it must still be executed. Depending upon the species, there could be considerable time and resource costs associated with capture, transport, and postintroduction monitoring and management. Thus, overall evaluation, execution, and management costs, in terms of time, effort, and resources, will often be significant. They will differ by case – for example, the costs associated with a large mammal

---

[29] Richardson et al. (2009).   [30] Shirey and Lamberti (2009).   [31] Vilá and Hulme (2011).

relocation are likely to be much higher than those for an easily propagated plant species. Nevertheless, in all cases there will be nontrivial costs, and in many cases quite substantial ones.[32] Due to the scarcity of conservation funding, particularly given the scale of ecosystem management challenges under conditions of global climate change and rapid population growth (among other ecological stressors), these opportunity costs must be considered. Resources that are flowing to assisted colonization might otherwise be supporting alternative, less risky, and more likely to succeed conservation practices – for example, corridor creation, place protections, and *ex situ* approaches to species preservation.[33] Moreover, an assisted colonization, even if successful, preserves only one or two target species. It is a quintessential fine-filter approach to species preservation.[34] Therefore, justifying resource allocations for an assisted colonization, as opposed to a more coarse-filter approach to species preservation, such as reserve and corridor creation intended to "capture" whole systems and communities, requires that the target species possesses high value that can be preserved through translocation.

Premise (4) – that even successful assisted colonizations will be detrimental to some individuals in the recipient system, as well as to some of the translocated individuals – concerns the welfare of organisms impacted by an assisted colonization. I argued in Chapter 2 that individual organisms have a good of their own that we ought to care about – that is, they have inherent worth. A successful assisted colonization results in the establishment of a population in the recipient system, the individuals of which consume resources – for example, sunlight, water, and shelter – that individual organisms of other species would have used. To the extent that individuals of the translocated population out compete other individuals in the recipient system, they are detrimental to them. When a translocated species is predatory on individuals in the recipient system, the harm is more direct. As discussed previously, that all living things have inherent worth does not imply that we ought to consider them all equally or respond to their worth in the same way. Therefore, the weight of this consideration against a candidate assisted colonization depends upon both the ecological facts about the relocation – for example, the expected impacts on

---

[32] Hunter (2007).   [33] Hunter (2007); Webber et al. (2011).
[34] Hunter et al. (1988); Hunter (1990, 1991).

individuals in the recipient system – as well as on the facts about the individuals affected – for example, whether they are sentient.

Translocation can also be detrimental to the individuals that are relocated. The process of capture, transport, release, and monitoring can be stressful, and injury is possible. This is particularly so for sentient animals that have psychological awareness (though not an understanding) of what is happening to them. In addition, the relocated individuals are taken from a familiar environment and placed in an unfamiliar environment, which may make meeting their basic needs more challenging, particularly if they were bred in captivity. Moreover, if predatory species are held in captivity for some time prior to their translocation – for example, to increase their population or return members to good health – they will need to be fed individuals of other species.[35] Again, the significance of this consideration depends upon the psychological complexity of the individual organisms involved and the facts about the case – for example, expected mortality rates and whether the translocation involves such things as capture, restraint, anesthesia, prolonged captivity, marking, and tracking.[36] But at least in some cases, particularly those that involve large predators, it is reasonable to believe that a successful assisted colonization will be detrimental to more organisms of similar capacities than it is beneficial. The reintroduction of wolves in Yellowstone, which caused a dramatic reduction in the coyote population through both direct predation and indirect effects, would seem to be an instance of this.[37]

The foregoing considerations, taken together, suggest that assisted colonizations, except in quite rare cases, are ill-advised. Only with respect to a small number of species is there value to be preserved through a successful assisted colonization. But successful, responsible assisted colonizations are themselves likely to be quite rare, given the distinctive features of global climate change, the characteristics of species that are likely to be most in need of relocation, and the possibility that there will be significant

---

[35] Bekoff (2010). This is particularly relevant for animals bred in captivity, which would not have existed, and so would not have eaten, absent the breeding program. Predators that are brought into captivity from the wild would have killed prey if they were not being relocated. However, in the case of wild caught animals, the fact that they would have done the killing themselves in the wild, whereas humans do the killing during the captivity period, may make an ethical difference.

[36] MacDonald et al. (2010).   [37] Berger and Gese (2007).

stakeholders who will be resistant to them. Moreover, even in the rare cases of responsible, value preserving, and likely to be successful relocation, there are likely to be significant disvalues, including opportunity costs and negative impacts on the welfare of individual organisms.

This does not imply that all assisted colonizations are unjustified. It may be that there are candidate species: (a) that are high in subjective and/or instrumental value, in ways that are not dependent upon their ecological and evolutionary situatedness; (b) that are likely to be ecologically success-ful in the recipient systems, though not invasive, now and into the future, even given high rates of ecological uncertainty and change; (c) whose relocations will not be overly costly, with respect to resources and welfare; and (d) whose relocations are widely supported. However, these are sub-stantial criteria that, taken in combination, imply not only that such cases will be exceedingly rare, but that the burden of establishing that a case is an exception is quite high. It involves not only a comprehensive ecological justification, but also a social (so social science) and value (so ethical) one.

4.6 Pleistocene re-wilding

The most ambitious species translocation project that has been proposed is the Pleistocene re-wilding of North America:

> The idea is to actively promote the restoration of large wild vertebrates into North America in preference to the "pests and weeds" (rats and dandelions) that will otherwise come to dominate the landscape. This "Pleistocene re-wilding" would be achieved through a series of carefully managed ecosystem manipulations using closely related species as proxies for extinct large vertebrates, and would change the underlying premise of conservation biology from managing extinction to actively restoring natural processes.[38]

Advocates of North American Pleistocene re-wilding propose translocation of wild (or de-domestication of nonwild) tortoises, camels, cheetahs, horses, elephants, and lions from Asia and Africa, among other places, to expansive parks in the Great Plains and western United States. They believe that the species are appropriate ecological proxies for the large vertebrates that went extinct in North America 13,000 years ago, in part due to over-hunting by humans. They argue that re-wilding would provide an intercontinental

---

[38] Donlan et al. (2005: 913). See also, Donlan et al. (2006).

refuge for the threatened translocated species, rejuvenate the ecological and evolutionary potential of North American ecological systems (which have been depleted by species eliminations, habitat fragmentation, and intensive land use), and provide economic benefits (for example, jobs and ecotourism) to depressed areas of the midwestern United States.

Re-wilding, so conceived, involves multiple coordinated species trans-locations for conservation purposes. In this respect, it is a massive assisted colonization program. Moreover, because the selection of species is histor-ically "inspired" and the goal is to improve the region from an ecological and evolutionary perspective, it is also an ambitious ecological restoration project.[39] However, re-wilding goes beyond assisted colonization and eco-logical restoration in that the purpose is not merely to preserve the target species and reestablish lost ecological trajectories, but also to reimagine and redesign entire ecological systems on a landscape scale. Proponents of re-wilding argue that it constitutes an optimistic, active, and creative agenda for conservation biology, in contrast to what they describe as "the negative slope of our current conservation philosophy,"[40] in which the primary activities are monitoring, managing, and mitigating extinctions. In what follows, I evaluate Pleistocene re-wilding as an ecological restoration and as an assisted colonization, before addressing its vision as a positive philoso-phy for conservation biology under conditions of widespread and rapid ecological change. First, however, it is necessary to differentiate Pleistocene re-wilding from other re-wilding activities.

Pleistocene re-wilding is distinguished from other types of re-wilding by virtue of its ambition and its temporal and spatial scales.[41] It seeks to reestablish an ecological trajectory inspired by the distant past (the Pleistocene). It seeks to do so over "vast areas" of the Great Plains. It includes numerous species introductions, often from distant locations, which are meant to be proxies for species that have not been in the recipient system for a very long time. It aims to have large, system-wide impacts. There are other, much more modest, re-wilding projects. For example, in the Netherlands, Konic ponies, Heck cattle, and Galloway cattle have been introduced as proxies for extinct herbivores in two comparatively small reserves, Millingerwaard and Oostvaardersplassen, and the reserves are much more lightly managed, with respect to both their flora and fauna,

---

[39] Donlan et al. (2006: 664).   [40] Donlan et al. (2006: 674).   [41] Callicott (2002).

than is typical in the region. Several similar efforts are being planned throughout Europe.[42] In addition, reintroductions of species into their former ranges have become quite common – for example, Przewalski's horses (*Equus ferus przewalskii*) in Mongolia, Bolson tortoises (*Gopherus flavo-marginatus*) in the southwestern United States, Eurasian beavers (*Castor fiber*) in Scotland, and grey wolves in Yellowstone. However, in all of these re-wilding and reintroduction cases, only one or a few species are involved. Moreover, the species have been absent from the area for a much shorter period of time, the spatial scales are much smaller, and the intended impacts are much less dramatic than would be the case with Pleistocene re-wilding.[43]

As discussed above, one of the justifications offered in support of Pleistocene re-wilding is that it would improve the target system from an ecological and evolutionary perspective. In this respect, it is being pro-moted as an ecological restoration with a deep and distant historical com-mitment. However, the biotic and abiotic features of North American ecosystems have changed substantially over the past 13,000 years, with respect to soil compositions, species distributions, and atmospheric carbon dioxide concentrations, for example.[44] Moreover, as a consequence of global climate change, the magnitude, rate, and unpredictability of ecolog-ical change will be greater in the future than it has been in the past. As discussed in Chapter 3, this implies that less historicity is appropriate in ecological assisted recoveries. The fact that Pleistocene re-wilding involves such a remote historical benchmark opens it to several objections that collectively suggest that, even if invigorating the evolutionary and

---

[42] Rewilding Europe (2011). There are a number of places that have become wilder over time, but that do not constitute re-wilding projects, since there has been no assisted recovery or management plan for them. The radioactive exclusion zone in Ukraine and Belarus around the Chernobyl nuclear power plant, which had a meltdown in 1986, is an instance of this. So, too, is the demilitarized zone between North Korea and South Korea. The wilding of these places is an unintended consequence of human activities, in one case technological and in the other case political.

[43] There is a species reintroduction project in the Siberian region of Yakutia that is sometimes referred to as "Pleistocene Park." Thus far, it covers only 160 square kilo-meters and involves only small herds of herbivores, including reintroduced musk oxen (*Ovibos moschatus*). However, if the pilot is successful it could expand over greater areas and incorporate large predators, such as the Siberian tiger (*Panthera tigris altaica*) (Zimov 2005).

[44] Smith (2005).

ecological potentials of North American ecosystems should be adopted as an ecosystem management goal, Pleistocene-inspired introductions and trajectories are an unjustified approach to doing so.

Due to the temporal distance, there is an information deficit regarding Pleistocene systems and the species that populated them in comparison with what we know about modern species communities and populations. For example, far more complete and reliable information is available regarding the behavior and ecological impacts of cougars and wolves in the United States than is available for the long-extinct American lion (*Panthera leo atrox*) and American cheetah (*Acinonyx trumani*).[45] As a result, it is much more difficult to anticipate the ecological impacts of Pleistocene-inspired reintroductions on the recipient system than it is for more local and modern species reintroductions, which are themselves often difficult to execute and predict (and will be increasingly so given global climate change).[46] In addition, since many of the proposed Pleistocene proxies would involve intercontinental relocation, the risk of introducing novel (to the recipient system) diseases and pathogens is elevated.[47] Thus, claims about the ecological benefits of Pleistocene reintroductions are more speculative and the risks amplified in comparison with possible reintroductions of species that are more local and more recently lost to the system.[48] Therefore, Pleistocene proxies are not the most appropriate choice for reinvigorating the ecological and evolutionary vitality of North American ecosystems. If re-wilding is the goal, reintroduction of more recent and more local species, such as Eastern cougars, grey wolves, bison (*Bison bison*), bobcat (*Lynx rufus*), badgers (*Taxidea taxus*), jack rabbits (*Lepus townsendii*), and prong-horn sheep (*Antilcapra americana*) is preferable from an

---

[45] This also makes identifying appropriate proxies more difficult. There may be ecologically significant phenotypic and behavioral differences between the extinct Pleistocene species and candidate modern proxy species that it is not possible to identify (Caro 2007).

[46] Rubenstein et al. (2006).

[47] This particular concern may be manageable. Proponents of Pleistocene re-wilding emphasize that many of the proxy species already exist in significant numbers in captivity and on ranches in North America (Donlan et al. 2005). However, animals from captivity often are not as successful in reintroductions as are wild caught animals. Therefore, some intercontinental translocations may be nevertheless necessary (Rubenstein et al. 2006).

[48] Rubenstein et al. (2006); Caro (2007).

ecological perspective to using Pleistocene proxies.[49] The reintroductions are more likely to be successful; they are less likely to impact negatively on other species populations in the recipient systems (including already stressed and threatened ones); and they can perform the ecological functions (e.g., predation and grazing).[50]

Moreover, more local and recent introductions actually involve more historicity than do most of the Pleistocene proxies, which are not the same species as those that went extinct from the area 13,000 years ago (with a few exceptions, such as Bolson tortoises). The Pleistocene proxies have different genetic and evolutionary histories than did the extinct species, and they are being introduced into a different ecological context. Therefore, the evolutionary potentials of the lost species are not reestablished by Pleistocene re-wilding; new potentials for the proxy species are being created. For all of these reasons, the historicity involved with Pleistocene re-wilding is far too remote for it to be a viable approach to assisted recovery. The Pleistocene component of Pleistocene re-wilding is unjustified.

In addition to reinvigorating the ecological and evolutionary potential of North American ecosystems, Pleistocene re-wilding has the goal of helping to preserve threatened species by establishing viable independent wild populations in a new location. In this respect, it constitutes an ambitious multispecies assisted colonization. The proxy species proposed by proponents of Pleistocene re-wilding are large, charismatic megafauna that are high in subjective final value. Whether they will have the same (or more) subjective final value in their translocated location is an empirical and open question. I do not know of any study that addresses whether people will value lions and elephants on a reserve in Kansas as much as they do on a reserve in South Africa. However, even granting that they would – that is, even if the species would retain their value across the translocation – the assisted colonizations involved with Pleistocene re-wilding are ill-advised.

---

[49] Dinerstein and Irvin (2005); Schlaepfer (2005); Rubenstein et al. (2006).

[50] These considerations do not apply uniformly to all proposed Pleistocene proxies, since they have differential ecological and evolutionary profiles in relation to the recipient site. For example, the translocation of Bolson tortoises, whose geographic range at one point extended to (or near to) the recipient site, and which are not ecosystem transformers, would be less risky than the translocation of African savannah elephants (*Loxodonta africana*).

For an assisted colonization to be justified there must be strong reasons to believe that it will be possible to establish the target population in the recipient site without its being ecologically problematic. As discussed above, Pleistocene re-wilding fails to satisfy this condition. The translocated species are likely to be difficult to establish in comparison with recent and local reintroductions. But more important is that there are substantial ecological risks involved, with a high likelihood of negative impacts on species and individuals in the recipient site. A careful and controlled incremental approach to the translocations may mitigate these concerns to some extent. However, given the scope of the information deficits involved, the features of the proxy species (e.g., that several of them are ecosystem transformers or large predators), the time frame that the pilot studies would require, and the scale of the intended impacts on the recipient systems, it is unlikely that such an approach could establish with adequate confidence that the risks involved are acceptable.[51]

A second condition for a justified assisted colonization is that it be conducted responsibly – that is, that legal barriers are addressed and that public support around the recipient site is sought and secured. Satisfying this condition would be enormously challenging for Pleistocene re-wilding. It would require securing the requisite land and gaining federal and state legal approvals on species transport, introduction, and commercial use (if there is to be ecotourism involved). Moreover, it would require gaining informed consent from impacted communities. Given that Pleistocene re-wilding involves the introduction of large predators and ecologically transformative species, which are likely to compete for scarce resources (e.g., water and prey) and have the potential to cause large amounts of agricultural damage, this is likely to be exceedingly difficult. Even familiar predators, such as wolves, mountain lions, and grizzly bears have found acceptance difficult in the Great Plains and western United States.[52] Many North American conservation organizations are also likely to oppose the relocations, given the potential for deleterious impacts on native plant and animal species.

Finally, for an assisted colonization to be acceptable it must be an effective and efficient approach to conservation of the species in comparison with other possible approaches. Pleistocene re-wilding fails to meet this

---

[51] Rubenstein et al. (2006).   [52] Caro (2007).

condition as well.[53] In this case, the alternative is to preserve the target species in or near their current or recent historical locations. Some of the proposed proxy species, such as the African elephant, are not currently threatened and have robust numbers in parts of their current range. For several other proxies, such as lions and cheetahs, there are robust and ongoing *in situ* conservation efforts, which include habitat protection, community engagement programs, and wildlife corridor creation, for example. For still other species, there are recent and local reintroduction projects – for example, the Przewalski horse in Mongolia. Longitudinal preservation of most of the proxy species is more likely to be accomplished by these and related conservation efforts, particularly in combination with complementary *ex situ* programs, than through intercontinental translocation, given the robust ecological and social challenges involved with Pleistocene re-wilding.[54] This is so even given global climate change, which exacerbates the difficulties involved with both *in situ* and translocation-oriented preservation efforts. Moreover, preservation of the proxy species through Pleistocene re-wilding would be enormously more expensive than ongoing species preservation efforts, even if those efforts were to be substantially amplified. Pleistocene re-wilding will require purchasing or leasing (or otherwise securing) large amounts of land, addressing the legal and cultural issues and challenges, conducting the relocations (including piloting and monitoring), and setting up compensation funds (for displaced economic activities and damage caused by translocated species), for example; and it will require doing so at comparatively high North American prices. Furthermore, the economic and scientific resources committed to Pleistocene re-wilding would likely draw resources away from *in situ* preservation efforts, both for the proxy species and for threatened North American species, and so have significant opportunity costs. It could also come into competition with other ongoing North American conservation projects, and negatively impact ecotourism-oriented conservation efforts in Asia and Africa.[55] Finally, *in situ* preservation of a species has more natural

---

[53] As with several of the ecological and historical considerations discussed above, this applies to most, but not all, of the proposed species. Again, the Bolson tortoise, because it is a recent and local species, is an exception.

[54] Chapron (2005).   [55] Rubenstein et al. (2006).

value than does preservation through translocation. Because Pleistocene re-wilding would be more expensive, more disruptive of other conservation efforts, more ecologically risky, less likely to succeed (particularly in a responsible way), and less *in situ* than alternative approaches to preserving the target species, it is unacceptable when considered as an assisted colonization effort, just as it was when considered as an ecological restoration.

The third element of the case for Pleistocene re-wilding is that it provides a positive, hopeful, and creative vision for conservation biology under conditions of rapid ecological change. Pleistocene re-wilding involves reimagining landscapes on large spatial and temporal scales and populated by charismatic megafauna. This is in contrast to what proponents describe as the dominant "doom and gloom" agenda of merely reducing the rate of biodiversity loss as we slowly move toward a landscape dominated by "pests and weeds (rats and dandelions)." However, as discussed above, landscape-scale re-wilding in parts of North America, including reestablishing large predators and herbivores, can be accomplished by using local and recently lost from the system species. Moreover, this is more justified, both ecologically and with respect to natural value, than Pleistocene-inspired introductions.

Furthermore, there is an aspect of the Pleistocene re-wilding vision that is ecologically insensitive. It is overly dismissive of the ecological and evolutionary values and potentials that currently exist in North American ecosystems, and it involves a lack of openness to the ecological and evolutionary future of species and places. The Pleistocene re-wilding agenda is not only creative, it is destructive; and evaluating it requires attending carefully to what could be lost. Rats and dandelions are not primarily pests and weeds. They are forms of life with ecological profiles and evolutionary potentials. An alternative positive vision for conservation biology under conditions of rapid and uncertain climatic change is one that involves appreciation of novel ecological systems and species assemblages, even if they are not the ones that we would choose. The associated ecosystem management agenda would be one that promotes the dynamic and creative process of spontaneous (i.e., not human-guided) ecological reconfiguration. In Chapter 5, I argue for a revision of standard ecosystem management goals that is much closer to this alternative positive vision than it is to the Pleistocene re-wilding ecosystem engineering vision.

4.7 Conclusion

A value analysis of assisted colonization reveals that, even if successful, it will only occasionally preserve the value of the target species, while it always runs some risk of decreasing value in the recipient system. Moreover, given global climate change and other ecological stressors, successful and responsible assisted colonizations are likely to be quite rare. Furthermore, there will very often be significant opportunity and welfare costs associated with evaluating, executing, and monitoring candidate assisted colonizations. Therefore, assisted colonization ought to have, at most, a very minor role in the portfolio of ecosystem management practices, even as they pertain to species conservation under conditions of rapid climate change. Advocates for a particular assisted colonization have the burden of demonstrating not only that the ecological and social risks and costs associated with it are sufficiently low, but also that the instrumental or integral value of the candidate species is such that it justifies taking on those risks – that is, that translocation of the species constitutes an exceptional case. Pleistocene re-wilding fails to meet this burden of justification. Both the ecological and species preservation goals associated with it are likely to be accomplished more readily, and with less cost and risk, by alternative conservation strategies.

Global climate change undermines both of the traditionally dominant strategies for species conservation: place-based preservation and ecological restoration. Moreover, the emerging alternative, assisted colonization, is only very rarely justified. How, then, should we respond to the enormously elevated rates of species extinctions associated with global climate change? I address this question in Chapter 5.

5 Shifting goals and changing strategies

I have argued that traditional species conservation approaches – that is, place-based preservation and ecological restoration – are undermined by global climate change, and that the emerging alternative – assisted colonization – is almost always unjustified. In this chapter, I develop a more positive account of how we ought to respond to the biodiversity losses expected to be associated with global climate change.

The first part of the chapter concerns adapting ecosystem management to conditions of rapid and uncertain ecological change. I argue that global climate change requires not only exploring new strategies to accomplish traditional ecosystem management goals, but also reconsidering the goals themselves and, in many cases, deemphasizing species preservation. I then discuss the implications of rapid and uncertain ecological change for the goals and strategies of ecosystem management in less impacted systems and highly impacted systems, respectively. The aim is to identify the values that are salient within each type of ecosystem, and indicate the sort of management goals and practices that they favor. The discussion is normative, not predictive. It is not meant to describe how ecosystem management and conservation biology will evolve in the future, but rather the values that ought to be considered in that evolution.

The second part of the chapter concerns the implications of the value of species for mitigation of global climate change, including geoengineering approaches to it – that is, intentional large-scale manipulation of ecological and climatic systems. I argue that appropriate responsiveness to the prospective biodiversity losses associated with global climate change involves aggressively reducing emissions, so that fewer species are at risk of extinction and the magnitude of the conservation biology dilemma is lessened, but not by means of geoengineering.

5.1   Reconsidering species preservation

Many proponents of assisted colonization are, despite their advocacy, less than enthusiastic about it. Several of the decision models would have it as a last (or near last) resort, and then only if the ecological risks and associated costs are sufficiently low.[1] The implicit view, sometimes explicitly stated, is that it would be preferable not to have to move species to save them.[2] There are, after all, costs and risks involved, and the value commitments characteristic of conservation biology and environmentalism favor place-based preservation and restoration if possible. Moreover, assisted colonization is a more interventionist species preservation technique than are place-based preservation and restoration. Design is a component of all ecosystem management; we must decide where to manage, what to aim for, and how to go about accomplishing it.[3] But assisted colonization is a particularly assertive form of management, in comparison with more restraintful place-based preservation and more deferential restoration, which makes use of prior ecological history to define recovery goals.

Nevertheless, as proponents of assisted colonization emphasize, the ecological reality is now one of rapid climatic change, and the implications for biodiversity are stark. For many species, the alternatives to assisted colonization are anthropogenic extinction or *ex situ* preservation. Therefore, assisted colonization is the lesser evil. It is what needs to be done if we are to preserve species in nature, rather than "manage extinctions." Thus, in the view of assisted colonization proponents, we must come to accept that global climate change will require a much more interventionist attitude and approach toward ecosystem management:

> The upshot is that we simply have no choice but to think beyond the traditional parks-and-preservation model if we wish to save species in an era of rapid climate change. This will require coming to grips with a significantly more activist and hands-on approach to species conservation than we have taken in the past. It will also mean redeploying our funds and research efforts as we shift them from traditional preservationist agendas toward more pragmatic and interventionist programs for conservation science and action on a rapidly changing planet.[4]

---

[1] Hoegh-Guldberg et al. (2008).   [2] Stone (2010).
[3] Vogel (2002); Higgs (2003); Sandler (2012a).   [4] Minteer and Collins (2010: 1802).

The core contention expressed in this passage is correct. The goal of species preservation cannot be accomplished effectively by traditional ecosystem management strategies under conditions of rapid, high magnitude, and uncertain ecological change. *If* we wish to save species, then adopting novel, more interventionist approaches to doing so is needed.[5]

However, there is another option. If a goal cannot be accomplished by the standard strategies, then one can either change the strategies or modify the goal. This applies to ecosystem management goals and practices under conditions of rapid climatic change:

> Over time, some ecosystems may undergo state changes such that managing for resilience will no longer be feasible. In these cases, adapting to climate change would require more than simply changing management practices – it could require changing management goals. In other words, when climate change has such strong impacts that original management goals are untenable, the prudent course may be to alter the goals. At such a point, it will be necessary to manage for and embrace change.[6]

Proponents of assisted colonization advocate developing a new strategy to accomplish a traditional goal. However, they implicitly accept that it can sometimes be more justified to let a species go extinct than to move it, otherwise there would not be a prominent ecological harm criterion in the decision models. That is, they recognize that more intervention is not always advisable, even when forestalling extinction. In Chapter 4, I argued that this is, in fact, almost always the case with assisted colonization. Given a right understanding of the value of species and a full appreciation of the challenges posed by global climate change, it is usually more justified to let

---

[5] An intervention can be aimed at either the ecosystem level or the organism level. Assisted colonization, re-wilding, and ecosystem engineering are examples of ecosystem-level intervention. Cloning or genetically modifying extinct, endangered, or threatened species are examples of organism-level intervention. This chapter, like the prior two chapters, concerns ecosystem-level management. The ethics of engineering transgenic organisms, whether for agricultural, biomedical, or conservation purposes, is discussed in Chapter 6. Ecosystem- and organism-level interventions can be intertwined within a conservation program – for example, if genetic engineering were used to help a threatened population adapt to novel ecological conditions, or if individuals of a formerly extinct species were cloned from preserved tissue and then re-wilded (Crist 2010).

[6] United States Climate Change Science Program (2008: ch. 9, 3). See also, Camacho et al. (2010).

a species population go extinct than to move it significantly beyond its present range to create an independent population. I also argued that it is not feasible to keep modern species communities intact where they are now or restore them to where they have been. Thus, under conditions of rapid and unpredictable ecological change, it is very often more justified to change the goals of ecosystem management away from species conservation than it is to take on more interventionist approaches to accomplishing it. To the extent that global climate change occurs, species preservation should be deemphasized as an ecosystem management goal.

As the case of species preservation demonstrates, determining appropriate responsiveness to the ecological changes driven by global climate change requires identifying when it is appropriate to adopt novel and more interventionist ecosystem management strategies to accomplish traditional goals, as opposed to reconsidering or revising the goals. A crucial component to doing this is identifying the types of value that are most salient in a space, which depends heavily upon the features of the place – whether it is largely intact, biodiverse, heavily manipulated, agricultural, novel, or hybrid, for example. Ultimately, whether more or less interventionist approaches to ecosystem management are justified depends upon the goals or values at stake, as well as what strategies are effective for protecting and promoting them. Each of these – values, goals, and strategies – needs to be reevaluated for different system types under conditions of rapid and uncertain ecological change.[7]

In the next two sections, I discuss the implications of the value of species and the distinctive features of global climate change for ecosystem management goals and strategies for two different types of landscapes:

---

[7] Reassessing values, goals, and strategies is a crucial complement to adaptive management in the context of global climate change. Adaptive management aims to identify the most effective and efficient strategies with which to accomplish management objectives – for example, preserving species, promoting ecosystem integrity, or maintaining ecosystem services. It involves evaluating possible strategies in a particular context by testing hypotheses and methods, gathering information where needed, implementing those strategies that appear most effective and efficient, and iterative assessment and refinement of the strategies in light of changing circumstances and new data. Value analysis is crucial to adaptive management, since it identifies the values operative in a space, evaluates what management objectives are most justified based upon those values, and determines whether any strategies would undermine the values that support or justify the objectives.

comparatively intact and lightly impacted systems, on the one hand; and highly novel, multiple use, and manipulated systems, on the other hand. These represent the poles of a continuum of human impacts on systems and species. In actuality, most systems fall in between them. However, by discussing the divergent types, the implications of different values for defining objectives and informing approaches to ecosystem management can be more clearly delineated.

5.2   Less impacted systems: in defense of parks and reserves

In the past, the most effective approach to preserving many valued landscapes, systems, and species, as well as many ecosystem services, was through parks and reserves – that is, designated and protected wilderness areas in which external stressors were reduced and human activity was limited. There was thus a large amount of practical convergence between the goals of species and ecosystem preservation, on the one hand, and the goals of protecting wilderness and respecting the individual organisms that constitute it, on the other hand.[8] However, under conditions of rapid ecological change, these sets of traditional ecosystem management goals will be increasingly in tension. Providing ecosystem services, maintaining valued environmental entities, and preserving species will often require intensive management, thereby resulting in a diminishment in wilderness and naturalness (understood as independence from human design, control, and

---

[8] It is often argued that while nature (or wilderness the place) exists independently in the world, the wilderness ideal of nature-without-humans is largely constructed and, in many respects, problematic (Cronon 1995). We are ourselves natural – biologically evolved organisms dependent upon and in constant exchange with our environments – so there is not a sharp metaphysical boundary between nature and us. Moreover, wilderness has, since the beginning of *Homo sapiens*, been inhabited by humans. The idea that nature-without-humans is ideal nature therefore seems to be a particular historically located phenomenon and, on many people's view, has problematic implications for environmental justice in conservation practice (Sandler and Pezzullo 2007; Dowie 2009). However, one can be supportive of reserve-oriented conservation without being committed to the wilderness ideal, much less to the metaphysical views and cultural biases that have in some cases been the underpinnings for it. There are values located in wilderness areas (independent of the wilderness ideal) that often make those places worth protecting, and the protections need not include exclusion of all human inhabitants and activities.

impacts).[9] As a result, those who wish to continue to prioritize species preservation as an ecosystem management goal often see climate change as the final "nail in the coffin" of the reserve-oriented approach to ecosystem management, since it "is mismatched to a world that is increasingly dynamic."[10] Human activity has already significantly reduced low impact areas, such that there are ever fewer places with high levels of natural historical continuity, independence from humans, and pristine native species communities; and now increasingly intensive human intervention is needed to maintain ecological relationships threatened by local stressors and rapid ecological change. Therefore, under conditions of global climate change, parks and reserves will be increasingly ineffective in accomplishing traditional management objectives that depend on maintaining those relationships, such as species and system preservation.

However, it does not follow from this that the park and reserve model of ecosystem management is not well justified under conditions of global climate change. To assess whether global climate change undermines the justification for parks and reserves, one must first identify the value of less impacted and comparatively lightly managed places under conditions of rapid ecological change, as well as the appropriate management objectives for them given that value.[11] Then one must determine whether reserve-oriented strategies are an effective method for accomplishing those goals. When this is done, it turns out that parks and reserves remain well justified as an ecosystem management approach under conditions of rapid ecological change for two reasons: (1) they are comparatively effective for building resilience and adaptive capacity among species and systems; and (2) they are an effective approach to accomplishing other worthwhile ecosystem management goals.

Although parks and reserves will be less effective for conserving particular species, species assemblages, and ecosystems under conditions of

---

[9] "What we need to do to save species and what we need to do to save the wilderness aspect of nature are diverging" (Barnosky 2009: 202). "Changing climate conditions may ... make it impossible to maintain the combination of goals we have come to expect of landscapes designated as reserves: historical continuity, protection of current features, and 'naturalness' in the sense that ecological processes occur with only limited human direction or assistance" (Camacho et al. 2010: 24).

[10] Camacho et al. (2010: 21). See also, Donlan et al. (2005) and Minteer and Collins (2010).

[11] Caro et al. (2011).

global climate change than they have been in the past, they are likely to maintain *comparatively high* ecological (including species conservation) value, when measured against nonprotected areas. Protected areas and corridors provide some adaptive space, and so more adaptive possibilities, for populations and systems. Moreover, more biodiverse places, often (though not always) the target of protection, are likely to have more species with sufficient behavioral and evolutionary potential to meet the adaptation challenge posed by global climate change. Therefore, protecting biologically diverse and rich habitats (including diverse physical environments[12]), establishing wildlife corridors and ecological gradients[13] (particularly "climate-connection corridors"[14]), promoting landscape permeability,[15] and fostering rejuvenation/regeneration (which can also contribute to carbon sequestration[16]) continue to be well justified under conditions of global climate change. Again, they will better protect and promote ecological value, including the conservation of species and species communities, than the alternatives – for example, the absence of place-based protections and assisted colonization. They are ways in which the adaptive potential of species and systems can be increased by stepping back and removing human impediments to adaptation, rather than through greater intervention, which, as argued earlier, undermines operative values in these spaces (e.g., natural and natural historical value) and is less likely to be successful under conditions of rapid ecological change.

In addition, familiar stressors of ecosystems and species populations – for example, pollution and extraction – decrease their resistance and resilience and, thereby, their adaptive capacity. Therefore, reducing or managing such stressors can increase the adaptive potential of species and ecosystems, again by removing anthropogenic impediments, rather than by more interventionist activities.[17] Thus, traditional "managing for

---

[12] Hunter et al. (1988).   [13] Smith et al. (2001); Brodie et al. (2010).

[14] Barnosky (2009: 206); Hannah (2011).   [15] NPS (2010); Wapner (2010).

[16] In this way, "we decelerate climate change while increasing the adaptive capacity of people and ecosystems alike" (Turner et al. 2009: 278). It is thus a win-win-win (mitigation, adaptation, biodiversity preservation). See also, Paterson et al. (2008).

[17] "Many best-management practices for conventional ecosystem stressors also reduce the tendency of these stressors to intensify climate change effects. Therefore, one approach to adaptation is to reduce the risk of adverse outcomes by increasing the resilience of systems and supporting the ability of natural systems and species to adapt to change" (NPS 2010: 14). "Many existing best-management practices for 'traditional'

resilience" and protection of biodiverse places and corridors increases the adaptive potential of populations and systems to global climate change. It can make global climate change less bad in terms of species and population losses, and decrease the magnitude of the conservation biology dilemma.

The second reason that global climate change is not the final "nail in the coffin" of the park and reserve model is that, under conditions of rapid ecological change, the approach is often justified for nonpreservationist reasons – that is, because it is conducive to accomplishing appropriate nonspecies preservation ecosystem management goals, both traditional (e.g., wilderness protection) and emerging (e.g., ecosystem reconfiguration). For example, protecting less impacted areas is often an effective approach to maintaining ecosystem services and providing instrumental goods (e.g., clean water, storm surge protection, and carbon sequestration[18]), particularly when measured against nondesignated areas.

In addition, naturalness has significant integral value in some places and cultures – for example, North American environmentalism. Highly managed species populations and ecosystems have less natural value than do more lightly managed ones, and systems that are assembled by us have less value than those that do so spontaneously. The background of anthropogenic climate change is the same, whether we engineer new systems or they develop independently of our intentions. Thus, whatever the extent to which anthropogenic climate change compromises natural value, it does so for all systems equally. However, more intensive ecosystem management involves further reduction in natural value. Therefore, those who endorse natural value ought, other things being equal, to be supportive of less intervention, even under conditions of global climate change.

The same is true of natural historical value. Global climate change is now part of the natural history of this planet. The more space that species populations and communities are given to adapt and reconfigure independent of our vision or influence, the more ecologically and evolutionarily situated they will be from a natural history perspective. The value is, perhaps, diminished from what it might have been absent global climate change. But it would seem to be still further diluted by more intensive management.

stressors of concern have the added benefit of reducing climate change exacerbations of those stressors" (United States Climate Science Program 2008: ch. 1, 1).

[18] Turner et al. (2010).

The inherent worth of wild organisms also supports reserve-oriented management. Inherent worth concerns the value of organisms in and of themselves. Each organism possesses the value equally, regardless of whether it is harmless or dangerous, a member of a species that is common or rare, or is treasured or disdained by people. Appropriate responsiveness to the inherent worth of organisms varies according to facts about the organism – for example, compassion is appropriate to hyacinth macaws and meadow voles (*Microtus pennsylvanicus*), but not to bristlecone pine and giant kelp (*Macrocystis pyrifera*), since only the former are sentient. So, too, does appropriate treatment of them – for example, releasing rescued American alligators (*Alligator mississippiensis*) into the Everglades is compassionate, whereas releasing rescued bottlenose dolphins (*Tursiops truncates*) there would be cruel. Nevertheless, that organisms have equal inherent worth favors not privileging some individuals over others, all other things being equal – for example, given their possessing similar psychological complexity and so comparable interests. This, in turn, favors less intervention into ecological systems, since all interventions benefit some individual organisms and harm others.[19] This was seen, for example, with assisted colonization, where for any translocation some individuals in the recipient system will be benefited (e.g., by having new prey), while others will be harmed (e.g., by having a new predator).

Under conditions of global climate change, parks and reserves will be less effective for preserving endangered or vulnerable species and communities. Nevertheless, populations still have a better chance of adapting in protected areas than in systems that are unprotected and more stressed. Moreover, lightly managed spaces will continue to have value as places where ecological and evolutionary processes play out independently (or comparatively so) of human intention, design, and manipulation. Therefore, natural value, natural historical value, and the inherent worth of wild organisms continue to be supportive of reserve-oriented management. Thus, the view that global climate change represents the end of traditional place-based park and reserve approaches to ecosystem management is mistaken. They remain very well justified under conditions of global climate change, as do many associated management strategies, such as remediation, rejuvenation, and corridor creation.[20] However, appropriate goals for such places

---

[19] Taylor (1986).   [20] Andam et al. (2008); Gaston et al. (2008); Rands et al. (2010).

must shift away from preservation of particular species and assemblages (i.e., traditional preservationism and compositionalism[21]) to promoting adaptive capacity, maintaining ecosystem services, and allowing for ecosystem reconfigurations.[22] This, in turn, requires changing expectations as to what these approaches can (and cannot) accomplish. It also requires shifting management practices appropriately – for example, deemphasizing historicity in assisted recovery, reducing native species prioritization, and refraining from intensive efforts to prop up dwindling populations or communities when they are associated with climate-change-driven ecosystem transitions.[23]

Again, the goal of park and corridor management under conditions of rapid ecological change should not be to maintain particular species assemblages interacting with particular abiotic features: the number of species at risk of extinction, and rate of ecological change generally, is too high; the causes cannot be controlled by ecosystem managers; modern species assemblages often are recent and not highly co-evolved; and the historical record shows that climatic changes of this size and rate, even on the most optimistic future emissions scenarios, result in the coming apart of ecological systems. Ironically, under conditions of rapid ecological change, place-based protection, rather than being valuable for maintaining a space largely as it is or preserving the components that are there, is valuable for the processes of change that occur – that is, human-independent adaptation and reconfiguration.

In addition to revising management goals, expectations, and practices for protected places, global climate change requires adapting our attitudes

---

[21] Callicott et al. (1999).

[22] "Retaining the somewhat static view of ecosystems as particular assemblages in particular places will become increasingly unrealistic and is likely to shackle conservation and restoration efforts to ever more unreasonable expectations and objectives" (Hobbs et al. 2009: 604).

[23] Refraining from invasive techniques to protect dwindling populations includes not killing large numbers of a nonnative species (particularly sentient ones) to protect endemic or endangered species – for example, culling ruddy ducks in the United Kingdom to protect white-headed ducks. If the changes in species distributions are partly in response to shifting climatic and ecological conditions, such that maintaining the prior species or excluding the recent one is decreasingly tenable, then, in addition to the animal welfare (or inherent worth-oriented) concerns that are standardly raised against such practices, the ecosystem management goals that the killing aims to realize are less justified.

toward those places and to ecological change more broadly. *Openness* toward
the ecological future, *accommodation* of human-independent processes in
determining that future, and *appreciation* of new ecosystem arrangements
(even if they are partly anthropogenic) are crucial to place-based management, as well as to good ecological engagement more generally, under
conditions of rapid ecological change.[24] These attitudes involve cultivating
sensitivity and appropriate responsiveness to the value of biotic systems
and living things that are the successors or beneficiaries of rapid ecological
change – that is, for the species that thrive and species assemblages that
emerge – even if they are not the ones we would have preferred or prioritized.[25] The human-independent ecological and evolutionary processes that
produced what is valued now will continue, and over time will generate
new species populations, communities, and systems. These attitudes may
also involve developing new ways of conceiving of, relating to, and valuing
nature, naturalness, and wildness, as well as new conceptions of ecological
integrity and sustainability (both ecological and ecosocial) that are suited to
rapid rates of change, high levels of contingency and unpredictability, and
human-influenced climatic and ecological background conditions.[26] The

[24] Openness of just this sort is exemplified by managers of the Millingerwaard re-wilding
project in the Netherlands. They are refraining from interventionist management of
the flora. One reason for this is that the space has passed several significant restoration
thresholds. For instance, the soil composition has been altered by industrial activities
in and around the space, and the species distributions of the seeds deposited by the
flooding of the Rhine (which bounds one side of Millingerwaard) have changed due to
canals connecting it to other waterways upstream. The other reason is that they
recognize that they cannot effectively predict which species will be suited to the
place in the future, given global climate change. Therefore, instead of actively managing the flora, they are accommodating and appreciating what develops. In contrast, the
Galloway cattle that have been introduced there as one of the proxies for extinct
herbivores in the area will soon be inappropriate for the site. The long-haired cattle
are having difficulty coping with the increases in temperature associated with global
climate change. Thus, this project demonstrates both the necessity of openness in
ecological management and the difficulties with species translocations under conditions of global climate change.

[25] As discussed in Chapter 4, some of the advocacy for Pleistocene re-wilding suggests an
absence of this sort of appreciation: "The idea is to actively promote the restoration of
large wild vertebrates into North America in preference to the 'pests and weeds' (rats
and dandelions) that will otherwise come to dominate the landscape."

[26] McKibben (2010); Thompson (2010); Wapner (2010); Thompson and Bendik-Keymer
(2012).

salience of related attitudes, such as *flexibility*, *tolerance*, and *restraint*, are also amplified in place-based management and ecological engagement, given the uncertainties involved with the ecological future and the rate at which ecological change will occur.[27] So, too, is the salience of *patience*, since ecological transitions, the reconfiguration of systems, and the evolution of populations may not occur or abate on the time scale that we might prefer.

For the vast majority of species and species communities, the most justified response to their inability to meet the challenge of adaptation is not to engage in highly interventionist activities to preserve them in nature, but to let them go. (However, as discussed above, less interventionist approaches to increasing their adaptive capacity so that they might better meet the challenge of adaptation are justified.) For this reason, the significance of *reconciliation* is increased under conditions of global climate change. Reconciliation, in environmental contexts, is the disposition to accept and respond appropriately to ecological changes that, though unwanted or undesirable, are not preventable or ought not to be actively resisted. Reconciliation has always been relevant to ecological practice. Even independent of global climate change, ecosystems are always dynamic, and individuals, species, and abiotic features are always coming into and going out of existence. Good ecological engagement – for example, love and wonder toward nature – and practice – for example, ecosystem management – require accepting and not resisting too strongly such changes and losses. The increased rate and magnitude of ecological change and loss associated with global climate change makes reconciliation still more necessary.

Reconciliation is not indifference. Species are rapidly going extinct, ecological relationships are being disrupted, and human activities are the cause. We are responsible for an enormous loss of value in the world. *Recognition* of the magnitude of the loss and *remorsefulness* for our contributions to it are appropriate. The fact that we are now at the point where we often should not actively aim to prevent the losses or attempt to restore or replace what is lost, and instead need to reconcile ourselves to them, is tragic.

But we can respond better or worse to this tragedy of our making. Significant environmental values remain, even under conditions of rapid,

---

[27] Several of these environmental virtues are discussed in Sandler (2007). See also, van Wensveen (1999) and Sandler and Cafaro (2005).

human-caused, ecological change. Good ecological engagement involves cultivating attitudes that facilitate recognition of those values, adopting ecosystem management goals that are justified by them, and developing ecosystem management practices and policies that protect and promote them. With respect to less impacted systems, species preservation should be deemphasized as an ecosystem management goal, while human-independent adaptation and ecosystem reconfiguration should be elevated. As a result, restraintful park- and reserve-oriented management remains well justified, whereas highly interventionist species conservation strategies, such as assisted colonization and re-wilding, are not. Moreover, attitudes associated with restraint, such as openness, patience, reconciliation, appreciation, and accommodation are crucial ecological virtues.

5.3   Manipulated and engineered landscapes

Most of the terrestrial surface of the Earth has been impacted to some extent by human activities, such as resource extraction, development, agriculture, and pollution.[28] In many places – for example, urban, industrial, and intensively cultivated areas – the resultant systems are highly novel and manipulated. They have biotic and abiotic characteristics, such as surface permeability, species distributions, soil composition, and precipitation patterns, which diverge substantially from the pre-impact system. These systems are often not realistic candidates for being managed to preserve or establish natural or natural historical value, for reasons to do not only with global climate change, but also with use demands (e.g., agriculture and habitation), ecosystem thresholds (both biotic and abiotic), and cost (time, effort, and expense).[29] In addition, individual species in such places often have diminished natural, natural historical, and ecological value, even if they are native to the location, since their ecological and evolutionary context is so altered. Moreover, due to the stresses and use demands on such spaces, they are often places where the independent adaptive capacity of species communities is low, as is the resilience and ecological integrity of the systems themselves. Therefore, light management of these systems is not justified on either compositionalist (i.e., preserving parts and

---

[28]   What follows applies, *mutatis mutandis*, to aquatic ecosystems, over a third of which are moderately to highly impacted by human activities.

[29]   Hobbs et al. (2006, 2009).

relationships) or functionalist (i.e., promoting ecological integrity and ecosystem services) grounds, and they do not possess the type of value (i.e., natural and natural historical) that favors restraintful management.

Instead, the primary values operative in highly manipulated systems are instrumental and subjective (though not natural value). Because of this, appropriate management goals for a highly manipulated and ecologically novel space are determined largely by how people value it, both instrumentally and subjectively.[30] There is, thus, a crucial social science component to developing management goals and plans for such places. In addition to ecological assessments, it is necessary to determine how people value and use the place, as well as identify their preferences for it. This is accomplished by engaging community members and interested citizens in planning processes (e.g., through comment periods, public forums, and outreach to stakeholders), determining patterns of use (e.g., through observation), and conducting surveys regarding people's attitudes about the place and hopes for it. These activities ought not to involve only passive data collection. Effort needs to be made to ensure that people's preferences for, and valuations of, the place are as informed as possible by relevant ecological possibilities and constraint, as well as costs and trade-offs. The importance of robust community engagement processes to effective adaptive management and conservation biology practice is frequently emphasized.[31] Global climate change will further amplify the need for community engagement and inclusiveness in environmental decision making, since its impacts will generate greater ecological novelty and require the reassessment of existing management goals and strategies both in general and for particular places.[32]

A possible outcome of a robust community engagement process is that preservation of certain species (or individuals) is highly valued. In these instances, intensive species conservation efforts may be appropriate, for precisely the sorts of reasons discussed in Chapter 3 – that is, the particular

---

[30] For such systems, more so than for lightly impacted systems, "Decisions about how much conservation and restoration investment is appropriate will depend on shifting cultural values about historical fidelity and ecological integrity, sentimentality about ecosystems of the past, local species diversity, priorities for livelihoods and sustainability (i.e., historically faithful restorations versus ecosystem services-oriented projects), and designs for resilience" (Hobbs et al. 2009: 604).

[31] Shindler and Cheek (1999); Berkes (2004); Norton (2005); Stringer et al. (2006).

[32] Sutherland et al. (2010); Turner et al. (2010).

species or set of ecological relationships are high in subjective value. Because (nonnatural) subjective and instrumental values are predominant in highly impacted spaces, and ecological integrity and natural value have less significance, several of the considerations that pull against establishment of independent wild populations through assisted colonization do not apply in intensively manipulated spaces. The type of values operative typically are not opposed to or undermined by more intensive management. Therefore, when intensive management is effective and efficient in accomplishing the goals that the subjective and instrumental value of a place justifies, including when those goals include species preservation, it is often appropriate. Assisted colonization into intensively manipulated systems, though not what proponents typically advocate, has a different value profile than it does into a system that is higher in ecological integrity and natural value (though ecological risk and inherent worth constraints still apply). Thus, approaches to species preservation in highly impacted systems, such as reconciliation ecology or backyard preservation, can be justified even for nonnative species, as long as the target species are highly valued, not just by researchers, but by those who use and are invested in the recipient spaces.[33] *Ex situ* preservation approaches, such as seed banking and managed refuge creation, can also be well justified for instrumental (including option) and subjective value reasons – for example, in case of future agricultural need or to preserve culturally significant species.[34]

It is possible that the operative cultural or instrumental values of a place incline toward aesthetic values or ecosystem services, rather than species conservation. Again, due to the salience of subjective and instrumental values in highly impacted and manipulated systems, and because intensive management is often consistent with them, such management on the basis of them is frequently appropriate.[35] For example, public urban green spaces should be managed so as to realize the goals of citizens and to satisfy their reasonable preferences, which may be aesthetic, recreational, ecological, or communal. Management needs to be conducted in ways that are ecologically sensitive and respectful of the inherent worth of living things.

---

[33] Rosenzweig (2003); Lerman and Warren (2011).

[34] *Ex situ* preservation typically is not justified on the basis of the ecological, natural, or natural historical value of species, since such values depend upon species populations maintaining their ecological and evolutionary situatedness.

[35] McClanahan et al. (2008).

However, management goals are properly determined by the informed and reasonable subjective values of those who make use of the space, and ongoing active management will often be required to accomplish them. Active intervention and intensive manipulation will often also be necessary for promoting human health and well-being in many highly impacted systems: pollution needs to be remediated; places of high cultural significance need to be protected (when feasible); ecosystem services need to be maintained; and, increasingly, ecological threats (such as sea level rise) and disasters (such as hurricanes) need to be addressed.[36]

Given the prominence of subjective values within highly impacted systems, it is worth revisiting the ways in which such values can be critically assessed. Integral valuing, like preferences, can be based on incomplete information or misinformation, and can be incongruent with a person's other beliefs or with facts about the world. This is the case, for instance, when replication of a past system is highly valued for a space where biotic and abiotic features have crossed significant ecological thresholds, such that a restoration high on historicity is not feasible. Valuing of and preferences for spaces need to be informed by ecological understanding, awareness of alternatives, and cost considerations, for example. With respect to global climate change, this means appreciating the ways in which rapid and uncertain ecological change must inform management goals, practices, and designs. Thus, even in highly impacted systems, where the operative values are not in principle contrary to intensive manipulation or engineering, the difficulties in predicting and controlling ecological features of the system under conditions of global climate change favor less control-oriented and precision-dependent management goals and strategies. Management goals and plans that are flexible and accommodating of ecological uncertainty are more likely to be successful than those that are not.

In addition, as mentioned above, inherent worth is an operative value in highly impacted spaces. Individual organisms, even if they live in novel or manipulated systems, have a good of their own that we have reason to care about, independent of the attitudes or preferences of valuers. As discussed in the previous section, all other things being equal, inherent worth favors less interventionist approaches to ecosystem management. However, for the reasons elucidated at the start of this section, such restraint is often not

---

[36] Jackson and Hobbs (2009).

a viable or well-justified option for manipulated and intensively used systems – that is, all other things are not equal. Nevertheless, inherent worth can inform ecological goals and practices, since not all interventions or management strategies are equally caring of living things and compassionate toward sentient animals. If a candidate use or management plan for a place requires culling large numbers of animals – for example, Canada geese, American crows (*Corvus brachyrhynchos*), or ruddy ducks (*Oxyura jamaicensis*) – or destroying large numbers of living things – for example, dredging a biologically rich river – the inherent worth of the individuals that would be harmed counts against the plan or practice, and alternatives for realizing the management goals (and the goals themselves) ought to be considered. Inherent worth, though objective, is not an absolute value. Therefore, it does not justify refraining from all interventionist practices that harm living things. However, as far as a practice or plan involves causing harm to living things, particularly unnecessarily or for trivial ends, it does constitute a reason against it. Management strategies that are compassionate and respectful of living things are preferable to those that are not. Thus, while subjective values are highly salient in these systems and might be compatible with (or even require) highly interventionist management approaches, there are bases – inherent worth, opportunity costs, and ecological viability – for critically evaluating them.

The discussion in this and the prior section has been general, and as with assisted colonization, there will be exceptions. The point has been to elucidate the salience of different environmental values – including the value of species – in different sorts of ecological systems, and to indicate generally the types of management that they favor under conditions of global climate change. With respect to comparatively lightly impacted ecological systems, the operative values typically favor restraintful park- and reserve-oriented management approaches, even under conditions of global climate change. With respect to high use and manipulated systems, the operative values are not contrary to more intensive intervention and design. Appropriate goals for such a place are heavily dependent upon the particular instrumental values associated with it and people's evaluative attitudes and preferences for it. In some cases these will favor preservation of particular species or ecosystem features, even by interventionist means (including translocation), and in other cases they will not.

5.4   The value of species and climate change mitigation

I have been emphasizing the extent to which global climate change is foregone, even on the most optimistic future emissions scenarios. However, there is quite a lot of potential climatic and ecological change that is not "locked in." The remainder of this chapter concerns the implications of the value of species for determining appropriate mitigation levels and strategies.

It is common in the discourse regarding global climate change to distinguish between prevention, mitigation, adaptation, and compensation. *Prevention* is taking steps that would result in global climate change not occurring. Prevention is no longer feasible. The closest option to prevention still "on the table" in the climate change discourse are some of the more intensive or "hard" forms of geoengineering – for example, scrubbing the atmosphere of carbon dioxide or reducing the amount of solar radiation that enters the atmosphere. I discuss geoengineering in the next section. *Mitigation* is "anthropogenic intervention to reduce the anthropogenic forcing of the climate system; it includes strategies to reduce greenhouse gas sources and emissions and enhancing greenhouse gas sinks."[37] *Adaptation*, which has been the focus in this and previous chapters, involves adjusting "natural and human systems" to climate change and its effects in a way that "moderates harm or exploits beneficial opportunities."[38] Finally, *compensation* involves recompensing those that are harmed by global climate change.[39] If adaptation is successful, then compensation is not needed. Compensation is appropriate only if adaptation efforts fail or are inadequate, such that wrongs or harms occur.

A central policy issue with regard to global climate change concerns whether, and to what extent, mitigation or adaptation should be prioritized.[40] There will be economic and social costs associated with responding to global climate change, whether it is done now with mitigation or later with adaptation. The policy question is to how to distribute efforts and costs. Should we aggressively mitigate now so that adaptation costs are lower later, or should we do less mitigation now and face higher adaptation costs later? One influential approach to addressing this question is welfare

---

[37] IPCC (2007a: 878).   [38] IPCC (2007a: 869).   [39] Caney (2010).
[40] Lomborg (2001, 2007); Jamieson (2005); Stern (2006); Nordhaus (2007a, 2007b); Posner and Sunstein (2007); Caney (2008, 2010); Gardiner (2010).

economics, which aims to identify the distribution of mitigation and adaptation that is socially and economically optimal – that is, that would bring about the best balance of social and economic benefits over costs. Nicholas Stern, for example, has argued in favor of aggressive mitigation on the grounds that it will cost much less socially and economically to mitigate now than it will to adapt later.[41] William Nordhaus, however, has argued that the socially and economically optimal approach would be to begin with some mitigation now (but not nearly as much as Stern advocates) and then increase the intensity of mitigation over time.[42] Bjørn Lomborg, in contrast to both Stern and Nordhaus, has argued that the opportunity costs of addressing global climate change are sufficiently high that the socially and economically optimal approach would be to use those resources to help the world's worst off in other ways – for example, through providing the desperately poor with medicine, education, and resources for economic development.[43]

One of the primary reasons that welfare economic studies of global climate change produce divergent results with regard to mitigation and adaptation is that they use different normative assumptions. For example, in order to make all social and economic costs calculable, welfare (e.g., pleasure, suffering, subjective well-being, and death) needs to be quantified in monetary metrics. There are no obvious or standard rates for converting, for example, malnutrition or being a refugee into a monetary metric, so there is often divergence with respect to value assignments and conversion rates. However, the normative assumption that primarily drives welfare economics calculations apart concerns the relative weight placed on the present versus future generations.

It is common in economics to increasingly "discount" the future – that is, not to count a dollar today the same as a dollar tomorrow, but rather to count a dollar today as worth more than a dollar in the future, and still more than a dollar in the further future. One reason for this is the expectation that a dollar today will be worth more than a dollar in the future in terms of purchasing power or goods acquisition. Purchasing power is used in economics as a proxy for the capacity to satisfy preferences. This, in turn, is taken as a measure of (or, in some cases, as being constitutive of) welfare or

---

[41] Stern (2006).   [42] Nordhaus (2007a, 2007b).

[43] Lomborg (2001). Posner and Sunstein (2007) defend a similar view. In his more recent work, Lomborg (2007) has distanced himself from his earlier view.

well-being, which is the ultimate concern of welfare economics. Thus, different economists will use a different discount rate if they have different views about future economic growth or contraction. A second reason for divergence in the discount rates used by welfare economists is that they adopt different pure time preference rates, in which the welfare of future generations is discounted simply because they are in the future. The greater the pure time preference, the less the interests or welfare of future generations is considered (or counted) in comparison with the welfare of present generations. Stern employs a near zero pure time preference. In his climate change cost calculations the welfare of individuals in future generations is counted as virtually the same as the welfare of individuals in the present generation. Nordhaus uses a larger pure time preference. In his climate change cost calculations the significance of the welfare of individuals in future generations diminishes over time in comparison with that of individuals in the present generation. Therefore, future adaptation costs carry much more weight in Stern's calculus than they do in Nordhaus'. This makes taking on greater mitigation costs now much more justified on Stern's calculus than on Nordhaus'. The more that harms to individuals in future generations matter, the more it makes sense to take on costs now to avoid them later.[44] The harms associated with global climate change are back-loaded; they will be greater in the future than they are now.[45] The reasons for this are that some greenhouse gases, including carbon dioxide, can persist in the atmosphere for many decades, centuries, or millennia, and that the impacts of greenhouse gas increases on climatic and ecological processes can take a considerable time to manifest. Therefore, calculations on whether to prioritize mitigation or adaptation to global climate change, and at what time points to do so, are particularly susceptible to variations in the discount rate.

The extent to which the welfare of future generations should be discounted against the welfare of present generations (if at all) is a normative question that cannot be addressed by economics or any descriptive science or social science alone. It has to do with how future generations ought to be

---

[44] It is not necessary to adopt a near zero discount rate in order to justify immediate aggressive mitigation on welfare economics grounds. Other normative considerations, such as strong aversion to catastrophe, can also result in conclusions that favor aggressive mitigation (Dumas et al. 2010).

[45] Gardiner (2006); Gillett et al. (2011).

valued. This is a vexing question, since future generations do not currently exist and are contingent on the actions and policies of present generations – that is, which future people there are depends on what present people do, including what they do with respect to global climate change. Different climate change policies and technologies will result in different people meeting under different circumstances and, ultimately, having different children. As a result, individuals in future generations cannot be made worse off by us than they would otherwise be – that is, harmed in the standard sense – since, for any future person, the alternative is not being better off, but not being at all (i.e., nonexistence).[46] Nevertheless, future people can come into conditions that are more or less conducive to their flourishing. Moreover, it is possible to compare the welfare of possible future generations.

Concerns about welfare economics approaches to the mitigation/adaptation question have been raised on the ground that they have so far not adequately attended to the philosophical and ethical issues associated with the value and moral standing of future generations.[47] However, a welfare economics calculus that includes a thorough and critical examination of the pure discount rate still does not constitute a comprehensive evaluation of the considerations relevant to the mitigation/adaptation question. For example, even if prioritization of adaptation over mitigation is justified on welfare economics grounds – that is, it would bring about the best balance of benefits and costs in the aggregate or overall – it might nevertheless be unjust. Wealthy people are disproportionately responsible for greenhouse gas emissions (per capita), since they consume more goods and energy than do those who are poor.[48] They are also better resourced economically, technologically, and socially to adapt to the impacts of global climate change. Climate justice proponents believe that such considerations – for example, regarding historical responsibility, present adaptive capability, and distribution of benefits and burdens more generally – need to inform discussion of not only who should be responsible for mitigation

---

[46] Parfit (1982, 1983, 1984).   [47] Caney (2008); Gardiner (2010).

[48] In 2005, the wealthiest 20 percent of the world were responsible for 76.6 percent of global consumption and the wealthiest 10 percent were responsible for 59 percent of global consumption, whereas the poorest 20 percent were responsible for 1.5 percent of global consumption and the poorest 10 percent for 0.5 percent of global consumption (World Bank 2008).

and adaptation, but also whether to prioritize mitigation over adaptation.[49] For instance, mitigation reduces the magnitude of global climate change, and so has widely distributed benefits, whereas adaptation is more localized and targeted, based on who has access to resources. For this reason, environmental justice considerations seem to favor mitigation over adaptation.

Other ethical considerations may also favor more intensive mitigation. For example, Simon Caney has argued that anthropogenic global climate change violates human rights and that this consideration favors mitigation over adaptation and compensation:

> A human rights approach ... requires us to reconceive the way in which one thinks about the costs involved in mitigation and adaptation. Some have argued that it would be extremely expensive to prevent dangerous climate change and hence that humanity should not do this. If, however, it is true that climate change violates human rights then this kind of reasoning is inappropriate ... If a person is violating human rights then he or she should desist even if it is costly ... The implications for mitigation and adaptation are clear. That mitigation and adaptation would be *costly* similarly does not in itself entail that they should not be adopted. If emitting greenhouse gases issues in rights violations it should stop, and the fact that it is expensive does not tell against that claim. A human rights approach thus requires us to reframe the issues surrounding the costs of mitigation and adaptation.[50]

On Caney's view, human rights are "moral thresholds" and this means that violations of them are not justified by appeal to other goods (including compensation). Since, on his view, climate change will result in human rights violations, reducing the magnitude of climate change and its impacts is required so that those violations are minimized. This holds even if

---

[49] Hoerner (2006); Baer et al. (2008); Shepard and Corbin-Mark (2009).

[50] Caney (2010: 171). "A second illustration of the point in hand concerns the question of whether it is appropriate to devote resources to mitigation now for the benefit of future people. It is sometimes argued that because, and to the extent that, future generations are wealthier than current generations it would be wrong to mitigate. This, however, is not a compelling argument if it turns out that future generations are wealthier than current generations but that some in the future are deprived of the basic necessities of human life. By virtue of its aggregative nature, a cost–benefit approach is concerned only with the total amount of utility, and therefore the total wealth of current and future generations, and it is indifferent to the plight of the very severely disadvantaged if their disutility is outweighed by the utility of others. A human rights approach, however, is not vulnerable to this charge because it establishes moral thresholds below which persons should not fall" (Caney 2010: 170).

aggressive mitigation has high costs and does not maximize overall social welfare. Human rights violations are wrongs that cannot be undone, and they are not tradable or substitutable for other goods and values.

It is possible that something similar holds for the value of species.[51] If species have a type of value that cannot be substituted or compensated for, and this value is lost through climate change due to species extinctions, then this would seem to favor aggressive mitigation over adaptation, even if it does not maximize overall social utility. Do species possess this sort of value?

The instrumental value of species, *qua* instrumental value, fits neatly into the cost–benefit or welfare economics model of evaluation. If something is instrumentally valuable as a means to an end, it is possible to compare it with other potential means to the same end. Moreover, if it is lost, but some other equally adequate means becomes available, then there is no net value loss. It is also fungible or substitutable, and loss of it is compensable. Therefore, the instrumental value of species does not challenge the welfare economics approach to questions about mitigation, adaptation, and compensation. It is not the sort of value that would require "us to reframe the issues surrounding the costs of mitigation and adaptation," and it does not (by virtue of the sort of value it is) favor mitigation, adaptation, or compensation.

What of the final value of species? Does it favor mitigation, adaptation, or compensation? On natural and natural historical accounts of the final value of species their value is tied to their ecological and evolutionary situatedness. Because of this, it is not the sort of value that could be fully replaced once lost or replicated elsewhere. However, it does not follow from this that species have absolute value in the sense that their value must be preserved at all costs or that destroying it is in principle unjustifiable. Even advocates of assisted colonization recognize that it is more justified to let a species go extinct than to try to save it when the ecological risks and costs are too high. Nor does it follow that the final value of species is incomparable or not tradable, since it is possible to value something as an end (even integrally), but not value it as much as some other end. Thus, it is not the case that the final value of species requires all out mitigation, without regard to costs.

Nevertheless, final value is not subject to pricing in the ways that are applied as standard in welfare economics. Even if a price can be put on

---

[51] Palmer (2011a).

something that has final value – that is, there is some finite value people are willing to pay for it or that they would take to sell it – the price does not fully capture how or why it is valued. So it is not the case that the final value of species that are lost through climate change can be substituted for or justified by other values later, such as benefits to others or costs avoided. Therefore, to the extent that species have final value, their value implies that a strictly welfare economics approach to questions about mitigation, adaptation, and compensation is incomplete.

Moreover, given the relational properties that are crucial to the final value of species and biodiversity, interventionist adaptation efforts to preserve their value (e.g., assisted colonization) are often not an effective method of doing so. Nor is compensation a viable option. Because species do not possess a good of their own or interests, compensation *to them* is not possible, even when they exist, and, if they go extinct as a result of global climate change, they do not even exist. Their extinction is a loss of value in the world, but it is not a wrong or harm to the species. Compensation to others, such as those who value an extinct species, would be misplaced. It is because people value species as ends – that is, noninstrumentally – that species have substantial final value. The loss of the final value of a species (or biodiversity) is therefore not a harm to those who value them. It might well have harmful effects on them – for example, by depressing them or depriving them of potentially pleasurable experiences. But the loss of the final value is not itself a harm to the valuer, such that the valuer could be compensated in ways that would make up for the value loss.

The final value of species cannot be fully assimilated into a welfare economics approach to mitigation–adaptation–compensation decisions. Moreover, because the final value of species is based on their ecological and evolutionary properties, it cannot be replicated elsewhere. Its loss is also not compensable. Therefore, the final value of species favors mitigation over adaptation and compensation. The strength of this justification for prioritizing mitigation is dependent upon the scope and magnitude of the final value of species and biodiversity. As discussed earlier, the valuing of them is integral and widespread among environmentalists and conservation biologists, among others.

In addition to favoring mitigation over adaptation and compensation, the value of species is relevant to evaluating forms of mitigation and adaptation.[52] There are approaches to mitigation that, although effective in reducing greenhouse gases in the atmosphere, are potentially detrimental to integrally valued species or biodiversity. For example, iron ocean fertilization to promote phytoplankton growth that would sequester carbon dioxide when it descends to the depths of the ocean would be ecologically disruptive, even if it were successful in pulling significant amounts of carbon out of the atmosphere.[53] Alternative energy technologies can also be ecologically problematic, even when they produce electricity with little emission of greenhouse gases. Hydroelectric dams, for example, are frequently an impediment to the migration and spawning of fish species, including endangered ones. Similarly, some methods of adaptation, such as expansion and intensification of agriculture, though perhaps beneficial for people (at least in the short run), might be detrimental to biodiversity. If a particular method or approach to mitigation, adaptation, or compensation is detrimental to valued species or systems, then that is a reason against pursuing it. In contrast, approaches to mitigation and adaptation that are also conducive to species preservation are preferable, all other things being equal. For example, the UNFCCC Reducing Emissions from Deforestation and Degradation (REDD and REDD+) program aims to reduce emissions by protecting forested areas in developing nations. Because such areas are high in biodiversity, protecting them is justified both on mitigation grounds and by the final value of species.

Thus, the final value of species favors mitigation over adaptation and compensation, and should be considered when evaluating potential mitigation and adaptation strategies.

5.5   The value of species and geoengineering

The final value of species favors mitigation over adaptation. The most interventionist approach to mitigation currently "on the table" is geoengineering.[54] *Geoengineering* refers to attempts to manipulate climatic or ecological processes on a large enough scale to significantly reduce the magnitude

---

[52] Palmer (2011a); Sandler (In press).

[53] Blain et al. (2007). The potential of ocean fertilization to sequester carbon, in fact, appears to be rather limited (Zeebe and Archer 2005; Strong et al. 2009).

[54] Keith (2001); Wigley (2006); Schrag (2007); Chu (2009); Royal Society (2009a); Blackstock and Long (2010).

of global climate change.[55] Several approaches to geoengineering have been suggested, including solar radiation management, atmospheric scrubbing, and carbon sequestration. Solar radiation management aims to decrease the amount of solar radiation that enters the atmosphere. Methods of solar radiation management that have been proposed, and in some cases are under development, include stratospheric sulfur injections, space-based mirrors, and brightening marine clouds with seawater mist.[56] Atmospheric scrubbing involves removing carbon dioxide (or other greenhouse gases) already in the atmosphere. Methods of atmospheric scrubbing under study include introducing catalysts into the atmosphere to increase the rate at which greenhouse gases break down, and capturing greenhouse gases by filtering ambient air. Ocean fertilization is a carbon sequestration approach to geoengineering. It involves seeding the ocean with iron (or other fertilizers) to increase phytoplankton growth and thereby carbon absorption, which is then sequestered when the phytoplankton die and descend to the ocean floor. Another carbon sequestration method currently under development is carbon capture and storage. Carbon capture and storage involves capturing carbon dioxide at its source point – for example, fossil fuel power plants – and sequestering it in geological formations and aquifers.

If geoengineering were successfully implemented, it would reduce the magnitude of global climate change and, thereby, forestall some species extinctions. Moreover, the value of species favors mitigation over adaptation, and geoengineering is aggressive, technologically-oriented mitigation. Given this, does the value of species support development and deployment of geoengineering technologies?

Part of the case against assisted colonization is that it is difficult to conduct successful and responsible species translocations without excessive opportunity costs. One of the primary reasons for this is the contingency and uncertainty characteristic of global climate change, which amplify the challenge of intervening effectively and predictably in complex

---

[55] As I use the term in what follows, geoengineering refers to projects intended to have a significant impact on ecological and climatic processes, with respect to both scope and magnitude. Smaller "geoengineering" projects, such as planting a few trees or painting some roofs white, are not sufficient to significantly impact climatic and ecological processes. However, a coordinated effort to plant billions of acres of trees or to paint all roads and roofs in the United States white would constitute geoengineering (Preston 2012).

[56] Fecht (2011a, 2011b).

ecological systems, particularly longitudinally. This difficulty is not specific to assisted colonization. It is an implication of the distinctive features of global climate change and the complexity of the systems involved. Unintended, unexpected, and uncontrolled by-products of environmental interventions have always occurred. Therefore, humility regarding our capacity to predict and control ecological systems has always been appropriate. But the distinctive features of global climate change raise the salience of humility, and warrant greater restraint with respect to how strongly we impose our designs and desires on ecological spaces and systems that are not already highly manipulated and engineered.

The difficulty with large-scale, technological, interventionist approaches to manipulating climatic and ecological systems to mitigate global climate change is that they depend for their success on our capacity to predict and control the impacts of the intervention, as well as on the ability to effectively address all of climate change's significant climatic and ecological dimensions.[57] The first of these – that is, identifying and controlling the impacts of large technological interventions in ecological systems – has not been done well in the past, even on local or regional scales and even absent the challenge of rapid climatic change. For example, intensive, technologically-oriented industrial agriculture, which has transformed terrestrial ecosystems as much or more than any other activity, has resulted in diminished topsoil, reduced fresh water availability, aquatic dead zones, biodiversity losses, and large amounts of greenhouse gas emissions. Industrial agriculture has for the most part been successful in accomplishing its goal of increasing yields. But it has done so with expensive inputs and enormous externalized costs, both ecological and social.

Geoengineering involves intervening in atmospheric, climatic, and ecological systems at a global scale using technologies that cannot be tested on comparable scales within like systems, in the context of highly contingent and uncertain variables.[58] Given this, and in light of the outcomes of prior large-scale interventions, it is reasonable to believe that unanticipated and unwanted detrimental side-effects are likely to be common, severe, and difficult to address. For example, solar radiation management might alter precipitation patterns, which could have transformative impacts on local

---

[57] An additional issue, not discussed here, is how to establish adequate oversight and governance of geoengineering (Royal Society 2009a).

[58] Robock et al. (2010).

ecosystems; and by reducing radiation reaching the Earth's surface, it might substantially reduce biological productivity and, thereby, food production.

Moreover, most geoengineering proposals do not even purport to address all of the significant climatic and ecological dimensions of increased atmospheric greenhouse gas concentrations. For example, even if solar radiation management successfully reduced the global mean surface air temperature by reflecting radiation out of the atmosphere, it would not address the serious problems associated with carbon dioxide accumulation and ocean acidification.[59]

Technology must play a prominent role in mitigation of, and adaptation to, global climate change. However, the ethical profiles of climate-related technologies vary dramatically. Some technologies address the cause of the problem – for example, hybrid vehicles, solar panels, green roofs, and insulation help to reduce greenhouse gas emissions. Other technologies help us adapt to the ecological realities that we confront – for example, flood hazard mapping, storm warning systems, and drought-tolerant crops. Geoengineering, in contrast, involves further manipulation of climatic and ecological systems. In a context marked by amplified climatic and ecological uncertainty, technologies that are more control-oriented and more precision-dependent are likely to be less successful than those that are not, and technologies that are more interventionist into complex and inadequately understood systems are likely to be less successful and have greater unanticipated effects than those that are not. This is a straightforward function of complexity and uncertainty in dynamic and integrated systems. It is no different for geoengineering than it is for assisted colonization. The greater the complexity, unpredictability, possibilities, and uncertainties, the more circumspect we should be regarding our capacity to intervene effectively and responsibly, particularly at a global scale.

Therefore, while it is true that, *if successful*, some forms of geoengineering could forestall significant species extinctions and ecological changes, and thereby preserve the value of species, there are strong reasons, amplified by the distinctive features of global climate change, for believing that successful geoengineering – that is, geoengineering that accomplishes

---

[59] Wigley (2006); Hegerl and Solomon (2009); Robock et al. (2009). For a more extensive discussion of the relationship between the value of species and solar radiation management, see Sandler (2012b).

its goal without significant problematic side-effects – is highly unlikely. Moreover, many forms of geoengineering, such as ocean fertilization and solar radiation management, would, even if successful, significantly alter the ecological context of species through massive human intervention. Therefore, they are not an effective approach to preserving the natural, natural historical, or ecological value of species. Because geoengineering is highly unlikely to be successful in preserving significant numbers of species and, even when it is successful, the value of species that are preserved is likely to be undermined, geoengineering is not a well-justified approach to species preservation.[60] The value of species strongly favors mitigation over adaptation, but not by means of hard geoengineering. It pulls toward aggressive, soft mitigation, such as reducing fossil fuel combustion and increasing forest and soil sequestration, which are scalable, terminable, reversible, noninterventionist, and do not involve manipulating systemic processes.

5.6 Conclusion

Under conditions of rapid climatic and ecological change, the goal of species preservation and the strategy of reserve-oriented management come apart. The issue then becomes whether to shift management goals away from species preservation or to change management strategies to something other than parks and reserves. I have argued that which of these is more justified for a particular place depends upon the types of values that are most salient in it. Adopting novel, interventionist species conservation strategies can sometimes be appropriate, particularly in already highly impacted and manipulated systems. However, in less impacted systems, the more justified response is to revise management goals away from species preservation and retain park- and reserve-oriented management approaches. These approaches can increase the adaptive capacity of systems and populations by removing local stressors and adaptation barriers. They also provide space for human-independent ecological transition and reconfiguration. These processes and their products have been valuable in

---

[60] These considerations do not apply equally to all approaches and methods of geoengineering. For example, they apply more strongly to atmospheric sulfur injection than they do to carbon capture and storage.

the past, and they will be so again in the future. The anthropogenic species losses associated with global climate change are tragic, and should be lamented. Yet in many cases it is more justified to let species go than to take "heroic" measures, such as hard geoengineering and assisted colonization, to try to save them. Instead, aggressive "soft" mitigation to reduce species extinctions, and reconciliation to those losses that cannot (or should not) be resisted are required.

6   The (in)significance of species boundaries

The first part of this book concerned the value of species, particularly as it relates to species preservation and ecosystem management under conditions of global climate change. The second part, which begins with this chapter, concerns the ethical or normative significance of species boundaries, particularly with respect to species modification and species creation. Discussion of the value of species will not be left behind, however. One way to formulate the issue regarding the ethical significance of species boundaries is to ask whether species boundaries have value and, if they do, what sort of value it is, what the grounds for it are, and what the practical significance is of their having it.

This chapter concerns the ethical significance of nonhuman species boundaries. It addresses whether these are normatively significant in a way that provides an intrinsic (i.e., not outcome-oriented) justification against creation of transgenic organisms. *Homo sapiens* species boundaries are the focus in Chapter 7.

6.1   Interspecific hybrids and chimeras

The operative conception of species is that they are groups of biologically related individuals that are distinguished by their form of life. Members of different species have different ways of going about the world. There is, of course, variation within species. However, it is possible to distinguish the form of life of gorillas from that of chimpanzees and, still easier, from that of giant kelp and whitebark pine. They are different life forms, in that they have different genetic and phenotypic traits; and they go about the world in different ways, with respect to food, habitat, social interactions, and reproduction. Individual organisms are conspecific (i.e., members of the same species) if they are members of a biological group that share a sufficiently distinct form of life.

The basis for an individual's form of life is largely genetic. Individual organisms have the sort of features that they have, and attempt to go about the world as they do, primarily because of their genotype: that is, what genes they possess, how they are organized, and their patterns of expression. Environmental factors influence what genes do, and are crucial to explaining an individual's phenotypic traits. For example, environment plays a substantial role in determining the height, intelligence, and culinary preferences of individual human beings. But it is a person's genotype that determines whether he or she goes about the world as a human being, as opposed to a llama (*Lama glama*), cuttlefish (*Sepia latimanus*), or bristlecone pine. Therefore, concerns about mixing or violating species – that is, not respecting the normative significance of species boundaries – standardly arise in the context of interspecific genetic mixing.

As the terms are used here, *transgenic organisms* include both *interspecific hybrids* and *interspecific chimeras*. Interspecific hybrids are organisms whose cells contain genetic material from more than one species. In a hybrid, the genetic material of multiple species is combined at the cellular level and this recombined genetic material occurs throughout the cells of the organism. Interspecific chimeras are organisms that contain cells derived from individuals of more than one species. Thus, rather than having cells that contain genetic material from more than one donor species, interspecific chimeras are comprised of cells of different species.[1]

---

[1] Interspecific hybrids and chimeras are considered together in what follows because they both involve genetic mixing (albeit in different ways and by different means), and the issue here is whether that is in itself (or intrinsically) problematic. This is not to claim that they have the same ethical profile overall. For example, there is a concern regarding chimeras that if two chimeras that are primarily of one species interbreed their offspring might be of a different (i.e., the donor) species – for example, two mice chimeras could mate and have a human embryo. This is not a concern that arises with respect to hybrid animals that contain only a single donor gene. Chimera research also often involves embryonic stem cells (including human embryonic stem cells), whereas hybridization typically does not. Moreover, the goal of chimera research (e.g., stem-cell-based therapeutics) will often differ from those of hybrid research (e.g., agricultural productivity). Thus, that hybrids and chimeras are considered together here does not imply that they should not be disambiguated when identifying their overall ethical profile, evaluating risks and benefits, and developing research regulations. In addition, the focus on interspecific transgenics should not be taken as implying that ethical issues do not arise

Interspecific hybridization is common in the wild. It is more frequent among plants than animals, for reasons to do with biological compatibility and reproductive strategies, and the resultant individuals are very often fertile and able to reproduce. Interspecific wild animal hybrids do occur, however, and have been documented in species combinations such as grizzly bear–polar bear, white-tailed deer–mule deer, white rhinoceros–black rhinoceros, ruddy duck–white-headed duck, Galapagos finch species, and *Heliconius* butterflies species.[2] There is also evidence of interspecific hominid crossing – for example, Neanderthal genes in the modern *Homo sapiens* genome.[3]

People have been intentionally crossing individual organisms, including individuals from different species, using breeding and grafting techniques since the beginning of agriculture. This is more frequently done in plants than animals, since it is more readily accomplished with them (due to reproduction rates, processes, and fecundity, as well as the costs and care demands involved) and the offspring are often viable and fertile – for example, apple trees, tomato plants, carnations, and tangelo trees. However, there are a large number of intentionally created interspecific hybrid animals as well, such as the zorse (zebra–horse), mule (donkey–horse), beefalo (domesticated cow–bison), and liger (lion–tiger).

Although immensely successful in producing organisms with desirable and useful traits, hybridization through traditional breeding techniques has significant limitations. There is a lack of control over which traits offspring receive from each parent; there are constraints on possible genetic combinations (e.g., due to sexual compatibility and viability); and it is possible to deviate only so much from the base life forms. Beginning with the development of recombinant DNA techniques in the 1970s, these constraints have been increasingly loosened. Recombinant DNA techniques enable the isolation of genes that code for particular desired traits in individuals of one species and insertion of those genes into the genome of another species. In this way, genetic material from individuals of almost any species can be inserted into the genome of individuals of another species, in order to

with respect to intraspecific transgenics (Russell and Sparrow 2008). Intragenics simply do not raise the species boundaries issues that are of concern here.

[2] Grant (1993); Salazar et al. (2010). The population and range changes associated with global climate change may lead to increased prevalence of hybridization, which could contribute to population extinctions (Kelly et al. 2010).

[3] Green et al. (2010).

create organisms that have genomic material from species that could never have reproduced or combined in the absence of intentional gene-level intervention – for example, chimpanzees with jellyfish genes, goats with golden orb spider genes, rice with maize genes, maize with bacteria genes, mice with human genes, and salmon with ocean pout genes. As indicated above, genetically engineered hybrids have been created primarily for agricultural, biomedical, and scientific purposes.[4] However, they are also used in recreational contexts. For example, GloFish® are zebra fish (*Danio rerio*) with an introduced florescent protein gene. In addition, some conservationists are interested in using genetic engineering, as well as cross-species cloning techniques, in species preservation contexts: for example, to help threatened populations adapt to novel ecosystems; to increase the genetic diversity or population size of endangered species; or to bring species (such as the woolly mammoth [*Mammuthus primigenius*], Pyrenean ibex [*Capra pyrenaica pyrenaica*], and New Zealand huai [*Heteralocha acutirostris*]) back from extinction.[5]

The knowledge base and technology needed for genomic sequencing, isolating genes, determining gene functions, knocking out genes, and

---

[4] It is estimated that, in the United States, revenues from genetically modified products – crops, biologics, and industrial biotechnology – exceeded US$300 billion and constituted more than 2 percent of GDP in 2010 (Carlson 2011). In the United States in 2011, 94 percent of the planted acreage of soybeans was genetically modified, as were over two-thirds of the planted acreage of corn and cotton (USDA 2011). It is estimated that globally in 2010, 81 percent of the planted acreage of soybeans, 64 percent of the acreage of cotton, and 29 percent of the acreage of corn were genetically modified (James 2010). An increasingly prominent argument for genetically modified crops is that, in order to feed a global population of over 7 billion people, it will be necessary to genetically engineer food crops that have traits, such as drought resistance, heat tolerance, pest resistance, and increased efficiency, that are well adapted to rapidly changing, unstable, and extreme agricultural conditions, which will often be associated with global climate change (Ortiz 2008; Royal Society 2009b).

[5] Lanza et al. (2000); Ryder et al. (2000); Ryder (2002); Holt et al. (2004); Crist (2010). Cross-species cloning involves inserting the genome of one species into an enucleated oocyte of another species. In conservation contexts, the DNA of an individual of an endangered, threatened, or extinct species is typically combined through nuclear transfer with the oocyte of an individual of a closely related nonendangered species. The chimera is then coaxed into developing and implanted into the surrogate. If the endangered or extinct species' genome has been modified or "supplemented" with genomic material from an individual of a different species, then the chimera is a genetic hybrid as well. For concerns about the use of cloning as a species conservation tool, see Yule (2002) and Ehrenfeld (2006).

assembling genomic material, while still quite imperfect, has progressed to the point where it is possible to intensively engineer genomes using elements from multiple biological and synthetic sources. As described in the Introduction, one research group has engineered a metabolic pathway in yeast that produces high concentrations of artemisinic acid – the precursor to artemisinin, an antimalarial drug – using genomic material from sweet wormwood and several bacteria species. Industrial production of artemisinin using the yeast is underway.[6] The trend in genomic design and construction is that the base organism is less and less a constraint on what can be created. The goal of some synthetic biology researchers is to develop a vast, ever expanding repository of biological (and nonbiological) parts and assembly instructions that can be used efficiently, precisely, and relatively easily to design and construct organisms with desired functionalities.[7] Synthetic biology accelerates the trend of loosening constraints on species engineering, and its emphasis on interchangeability constitutes a technical breaking down of species boundaries.

Research involving interspecific chimeras is often biomedical. Chimeras are used to study the behavior, development, migration, and fate of cells and tissues *in vivo* and *in vitro*. Human stem cells have been introduced into nonhuman organisms for these reasons. Understanding where stem cells migrate within a system, how and why they differentiate into different types of cells, and how they integrate with existing tissues is necessary in order to develop safe and effective stem-cell-based therapies. Chimeras can also be used as a source of materials for both research and therapeutic purposes, since nonhuman animal hosts can be used to grow human cells, tissues, and organs. Human cells have been introduced into fetal and embryonic mice, rats, sheep, fowl, and primates,[8] and research involving insertion of human DNA into enucleated nonhuman oocytes has been

---

[6] *E. coli* have been genetically engineered to break down cellulose in switchgrass (*Panicum virgatum*) and convert it into fuel (or fuel precursors) for diesel, jet fuel, and petrol (Bokinsky et al. 2011). Similarly, *Clostridium cellulolyticum* have been genetically engineered to convert cellulose into isobutanol (Higashide et al. 2011). Another strain of *E. coli* has been genetically engineered to detect the presence of a human pathogen, *Pseudomonas aeruginosa*, and then produce and deliver a toxin to kill it (Saeidi et al. 2011).

[7] iGem (2010); Registry of Standard Biological Parts (2010); Schwille (2011).

[8] Brustle et al. (1998); Ourednick et al. (2001); Goldstein et al. (2002); Almeida-Porada et al. (2005).

approved in the United Kingdom.[9] As stem cell research continues to progress and therapies begin to be developed it is likely that research on and cultivation of chimeras will become more widespread – for example, to demonstrate safety and effectiveness in nonhuman animal subjects prior to human trials and as a source of stem cells for therapeutic purposes.[10]

Not all chimeras involve human cells; and not all chimera research is biomedical. There is a history over many decades of the use of interspecific cell transplants in embryology and developmental biology more generally. Chimera plants, amphibians, birds, fish, and mammals have all been created, and in many cases have developed into adult organisms – for example, wood mouse–house mouse chimeras[11] and sheep–goat chimeras (or geep).[12] Some environmental applications for chimeras have even been suggested, such as using nonendangered species of fish as surrogates to produce endangered species for *ex situ* preservation or to replenish depleted wild stocks. For example, trout spermatogonia inserted into otherwise sterile male and female salmon can result in salmon that have only trout offspring.[13]

These practices – interspecific hybridization through traditional breeding, recombinant DNA techniques, and synthetic genomics, as well as interspecific chimerization through stem cell injection, tissue grafting, and oocyte enucleation and DNA insertion – have the potential to produce individuals that, to some degree, do not fit neatly into preexisting species categories. However, they do not violate or breach species boundaries in the sense that the species are themselves somehow mutilated, violated, or mixed. There are two reasons for this. First, the techniques and technologies typically do not change species categories at all, but rather modify or engineer organisms. For example, the breeding of ligers does not alter the form of life of either African lions (*Panthera leo*) or Bengal tigers (*Panthera tigris tigris*). Those species continue just as they were before. Instead, it creates individual organisms that are only to some extent lions and only to some extent tigers – that is, individuals that do not fit squarely within one

---

[9] Human Fertilisation and Embryology Authority (2007).

[10] It is worth noting that the preponderance of cells within the human body – 90–95 percent on many estimates – are microbial (Turnbaugh et al. 2007). There is, therefore, an attenuated sense in which all humans (and nonhuman animals) are always naturally occurring chimeras.

[11] Rossant and Frels (1980); University of Chicago Medical Center (2007).

[12] Meinecke-Tillmann and Meinecke (1984).   [13] Okutsu et al. (2007).

or the other of those species categories. Second, as discussed in Chapter 2, species do not have interests distinct from those of the individuals that comprise them. Therefore, species cannot be harmed or wronged, and so violated in that sense, by the technologies. Again, what the technologies do is create organisms that have features associated with more than one species – for example, goats that produce proteins in their milk that can be refined into silk or mice that grow human neural cells. Therefore, when something is described as "crossing species boundaries," "mixing species," or "violating species," what is occurring is not changes or alterations to species or species boundaries, but rather the creation of individual organisms that do not fit neatly or purely into prior species categories.

As discussed above, the mere existence of interspecific individuals is not out of the ordinary. They obtain on any conception of species, and in the absence of human intervention, due to the vagaries and dynamism of an evolved and evolving biological world. Nevertheless, many people find the *intentional* creation of such individuals to be ethically objectionable, and they often do so on grounds that are *intrinsic*, as opposed to *extrinsic* or *consequential*. That is, they believe that to intentionally create transgenic or interspecific individuals is objectionable or wrong, independent of the consequences or outcomes of doing so. (As discussed below, many people have significant consequentialist concerns as well.) The view that creating such individuals is intrinsically wrong is often expressed in language such as "unnatural" and "playing God."[14]

The remainder of this chapter addresses whether, and to what extent, species boundaries should be taken as having value or normative significance, such that they provide a reason not to intentionally create individual organisms with features of more than one species. The most prominent arguments both for and against the view that intentionally creating interspecific individuals is intrinsically problematic are presented and evaluated.

6.2 Arguments from nature

An argument frequently raised in support of the conclusion that creating interspecific individuals is not intrinsically problematic is the *argument from*

---

[14] OTA (1987); Rollins (1995); Program on International Policy Attitudes (2003); Human Fertilisation and Embryology Authority (2007).

nature.[15] According to this argument, since interspecific individuals are common in nature, there is nothing problematic about our intentionally creating them. The key normative premise in this line of reasoning is something like this: *if some type of event occurs or state of affairs obtains in the natural world, independent of human beings, then it is permissible (or not ethically problematic) for human beings to intentionally cause that type of event or state of affairs.* This premise is highly implausible, for reasons classically articulated by John Stuart Mill.[16] States of affairs and events that are abominable when intentionally done by humans are ubiquitous in the natural world: forced copulation, territorial killing, and selective reduction of newborns, to name but a few. What happens in nature is not, by virtue of its occurring there, permissible for us to do or cause.

Interestingly, there is another argument that appeals to what occurs in the natural world that is sometimes raised against creating interspecific individuals through gene-level intervention. This is the argument that it is *unnatural* to do these things because they could not have occurred in nature – for example, spiders could not breed with goats and chimpanzees could not breed with jellyfish.[17] The key normative premise of this *argument from*

---

[15] Robert and Baylis (2003).

[16] "In sober truth, nearly all the things which men are hanged or imprisoned for doing to one another are nature's every-day performances. Killing, the most criminal act recognised by human laws, Nature does once to every being that lives; and, in a large proportion of cases, after protracted tortures such as only the greatest monsters whom we read of ever purposely inflicted on their living fellow creatures. If, by an arbitrary reservation, we refuse to account anything murder but what abridges a certain term supposed to be allotted to human life, Nature also does this to all but a small percentage of lives, and does it in all the modes, violent or insidious, in which the worst human beings take the lives of one another. Nature impales men, breaks them as if on the wheel, casts them to be devoured by wild beasts, burns them to death, crushes them with stones like the first Christian martyr, starves them with hunger, freezes them with cold, poisons them by the quick or slow venom of her exhalations, and has hundreds of other hideous deaths in reserve ... Next to taking life (equal to it according to a high authority) is taking the means by which we live; and Nature does this too on the largest scale and with the most callous indifference. A single hurricane destroys the hopes of a season; a flight of locusts, or an inundation, desolates a district; a trifling chemical change in an edible root starves a million people. The waves of the sea, like banditti, seize and appropriate the wealth of the rich and the little all of the poor with the same accompaniments of stripping, wounding, and killing as their human antitypes. Everything, in short, which the worst men commit either against life or property is perpetrated on a larger scale by natural agents" (Mill 1904: 17–18).

[17] Verhoog (2003); Myskja (2006); Schouten et al. (2006a, 2006b).

unnaturalness is something like this: *if some type of event does not (or could not) occur or state of affairs does not (or could not) obtain in the natural world, independent of human beings, then it is not permissible (or is ethically problematic) for human beings to intentionally cause that type of event or state of affairs.* This premise, like the normative premise from the argument from nature, is highly implausible. It would rule out far too much (whereas the normative premise in the argument from nature allowed far too much). Almost all technologies, from toasters to computers, would be impermissible, as would be most human endeavors, from manufacturing clothes to staging sporting events. What does not occur in nature is not, by virtue of its not occurring there, impermissible for humans to do or cause.

In some cases, the claim that a technology or practice is "unnatural" is intended in the prescriptive sense of "wrong" or "forbidden." Here is an example of an argument that employs this type of claim: (1) genetically modified crops are unnatural; (2) anything unnatural is wrong; (3) therefore, genetically modified crops are wrong. However, such arguments either assume their conclusion or else equivocate on the meaning of "unnatural." If by "unnatural" is meant "wrong" or "forbidden," then the argument does not prove its conclusion, it just asserts it: that is, premise (1) is just the claim that genetically modified crops are intrinsically problematic. However, if "unnatural" does not mean "wrong," then for the argument to be sound there must be some meaning of the term "unnatural" that makes both premises (1) and (2) true. However, there is no such meaning. The fact that something is uncommon in nature, does not occur at all in nature, or is not the evolved function of something does not make it problematic. If it did, then marathons, science fiction, recreational sex, flannel, being left-handed, and ever-bearing strawberry plants would each be intrinsically objectionable.[18]

The upshot of the failures of these arguments is that nature simply is not normative for human beings. It is not a guide or template for what we ought

---

[18] Religious proponents of this argument might appeal to the will of God, such that "unnatural" is identified with divinely forbidden. But, of course, this would not constitute a naturalistic explanation for why species boundaries have normative significance. In fact, such an appeal eviscerates the normative significance of naturalness, rather than salvages it, since the normativity would then be grounded in the will of God. It should also be noted that hybridization has been accepted by almost all religious traditions, and some religious ethicists have argued that genetically modified crops are permissible (Feit 2002; Perry 2002).

and ought not to do.[19] There must be some independent basis or standard for determining which things in nature are appropriate for us to emulate and which things in nature are not. In this case, that means some independent account of why we should regard species boundaries as having normative significance.

6.3 Argument from incremental change

There is an argument often paired with the argument from nature, which might be called the *argument from incremental change*. This is the argument that technologically advanced genetic mixing techniques, such as recombinant DNA techniques and synthetic biology, are permissible because they differ only in degree, and not in kind, from prior techniques, such as hybridization, which in turn differ only in degree from selective breeding. Therefore, if selective breeding is not intrinsically objectionable – which is not at all in doubt – then technologies that create interspecific individuals, such as plant hybridization and synthetic biology, must not be intrinsically objectionable.[20]

This argument makes the problematic assumption that a difference in degree cannot be ethically significant. The fact that two things differ only in degree does not imply that there is no ethical distinction between them. Sending a child to his room alone for five minutes can be appropriate punishment, sending him there for two days is child abuse. The difference is only a matter of degree, length of time, but it makes an ethical difference. Good-humored joking differs only in degree from ridicule. Strict dieting differs only in degree from anorexia. Torture differs only in degree from interrogation. Identifying a property of some practice, even a crucial one, and showing that it differs only in degree from some ethically (or socially or environmentally) unproblematic practice does not establish that it is also unproblematic. The difference in degree may be ethically significant, or there may be other properties that are relevant to (intrinsic) ethical evaluation.

Moreover, the argument from incremental change is problematic even if it is assumed (contrary to what has just been argued) that differences in degree are not ethically significant, since in that case it would beg the question: why is it that creating interspecific individuals is only a difference

---

[19] Vogel (2002).   [20] NAS (1987).

in degree, not a difference in kind, from selective breeding? To claim that it is (in combination with the claim that differences in degree are not ethically significant) is merely to assert the conclusion.

It does not follow from this that the differences between these practices – for example, hybridization and recombinant DNA techniques or recombinant DNA techniques and synthetic biology – are ethically significant. It is only to claim that the fact that they are differences in degree (if it is a fact) is not determinative of whether there is an ethically significant difference between them or whether creating interspecific individuals by means of them is intrinsically problematic.

6.4   Arguments from the nonexistence of fixed species boundaries

Another type of argument against the normative significance of species boundaries is based on the claim that there are not any fixed boundaries to begin with.[21] On the *nominalist* view of species, there are only individual organisms, and people (e.g., biologists) simply group them in different ways and at different levels, including the species level, for different purposes.[22] Thus, species delineations are only constructed conventions. One motivation for this view comes from the fact that several different species concepts are used in biology – for example, phylogenetic, genetic, ecological, and morphological. Each of these captures biological differences between groups of organisms, such as lineage, ecosystem role, or genetic and phenotypic characteristics. In addition, each of them is more useful than others in some scientific context. As discussed in the Introduction, the phylogenic species concept is more useful than the ecological species concept in evolutionary biology, but often not in ecology, where ecological relationships, rather than evolutionary history, are the primary object of study and mode of explanation. Moreover, none of the concepts captures some feature of organisms that is more biologically fundamental than the others. All organisms have an evolutionary history, are ecologically situated, and have a phenotype and genotype, and these are causally (and so explanatorily) interrelated. Another motivation for the view that species categories are just constructed conventions is that every species concept used in biology is

---

[21] Robert and Baylis (2003).   [22] Ereshefsky (1998).

imperfect. There are always individuals that do not fit neatly into a single species category; and there is often ambiguity about whether a particular group of organisms constitutes a distinct species or subspecies. According to the *argument from species nominalism*, because species concepts (including the form of life concept) are just conventions, so too are species boundaries. Therefore, species boundaries do not have any normative significance.

An argument against the ethical relevance of species boundaries that is similar to the argument from species nominalism is the *argument from species fluidity*. This argument emphasizes that, even if species categories are real, they are shifting or dynamic.[23] The characteristics that define a species (on a particular species concept) depend upon the individual organisms that comprise it.[24] Because the traits of the individuals can change over time, the characteristics that define a species can do so as well. For example, the individuals that comprise a particular species of bird might, over time, migrate south for the winter less frequently, perhaps due to changes in climate and environment (e.g., food availability), or as a result of modifications to their physiology (e.g., feathers that increase cold tolerance). As a result, the characteristic life form of the species, and its ecological niche, are altered. According to the argument from fluidity, the dynamism of species suggests that transgenic individuals should not be understood as falling outside fixed species boundaries, but rather as redefining them. Therefore, they are not problematic by virtue of not conforming to established species boundaries.

Both the argument from nominalism and the argument from fluidity have problematic assumptions. The fact that a category is conventional does not imply either that it is arbitrary or that it cannot have normative significance. The form of life conception of species (like other conceptions of species) is not a convention in the sense of being without biological grounding. Chimpanzees really do have genetic and phenotypic traits and behaviors that are different from platypuses and silver maples. Which differences are the basis for species categorizations has a conventional component, but it does not follow from this that they are not based on real biological differences. Therefore, they are not arbitrary, and they are biologically informed.[25] Moreover, national boundaries and citizenship criteria are, in large part, conventional. However, it does not follow from this that there are

---

[23] Robert and Baylis (2003).   [24] Barker (2010).   [25] Crane and Sandler (2011).

not good reasons for preferring some criteria for citizenship over others, or that people do not have an ethically significant relationship with their fellow citizens, *qua* fellow citizen, that they do not have with noncitizens.[26] In addition, convention-based categories, such as citizenship or community affiliation, are often valued by people, and so have subjective final value. Similarly, that a category is fluid does not imply that it cannot have normative significance. Conceptions and legal operationalizations of citizenship are often shifting. So, too, are conceptions and compositions of families. The fact that there are a plurality of shifting conceptions of family (e.g., defined biologically or attitudinally), which are appropriately used in different contexts, does not imply that no conception of family has ethical or normative significance. Likewise, there may be multiple, shifting conceptions of species, yet some species concepts (and so boundaries) are ethically significant.[27]

Furthermore, the fact that species categories are imperfect – that is, there are individual organisms that do not fall cleanly into one and only one species category – does not imply that they are ethically insignificant. The category "moral agent" is ethically significant, since it is the class of entities that can be held morally responsible for their actions. As a result, there are forms of consideration and expectations that are appropriate for members of the category that are inappropriate toward nonmembers. This holds despite the fact that there are marginal cases, individuals that possess many of the capacities necessary for moral agency to at least some degree, but not all the capacities fully – for example, nonhuman primates, severely mentally handicapped humans, very young children, artificial intelligences, and psychopaths.

Thus, even if it is true that species categories are conventional, fluid, and imperfect, it does not follow that species boundaries lack ethical significance.[28]

6.5 Argument from repugnance

As discussed earlier, significant numbers of people have a negative emotional response to the idea of intentionally creating interspecific organisms.

---

[26] Nathanson (1993).   [27] Streiffer (2003).

[28] An additional difficulty with the argument from nominalism is that there may be a plurality of real species concepts: that is, species pluralism does not imply nominalism (Crane 2004).

Some bioethicists have argued that, at least in some cases, such "repugnance" responses to unfamiliar practices or technologies should be taken as "the emotional expression of deep wisdom."[29] The idea is not that repugnance to things is what makes them wrong (or ethically problematic), but that the repugnant response should be taken as evidence or indication of their wrongness.

A frequently identified difficulty with the *wisdom of repugnance* view is that many practices and technologies that elicited widespread repugnance in the past are now widely accepted – for example, interracial marriage and *in vitro* fertilization.[30] A possible response to this objection is to claim that the repugnance is appropriate (i.e., those practices really are objectionable), and we have simply become accustomed to some ethically problematic things. However, even if one takes this response to have some purchase with respect to novel technologies, it is an outrageous response with respect to many social practices formerly considered repugnant, such as interracial marriage. There are many good reasons, independent of our emotional responses, to believe that all people have equal worth, that skin color should not determine the bounds of community membership, and that freedom of association should be protected, for example.

That many technologies and social practices once seen as repugnant are now widely accepted demonstrates that repugnance responses can be significantly socially and culturally influenced. This may be more the case with some things (e.g., *in vitro* fertilization) than with others (e.g., incest). But it shows that repugnance responses cannot be taken as tapping into deep emotional wisdom, merely by virtue of the repugnance response, since the response might arise from cultural biases or lack of understanding or experience.

Moreover, if the practices or technologies that many people have repugnance responses toward really are ethically problematic, then one would expect that repugnance to them would grow as familiarity, understanding, and experience of them increases. But just the opposite has happened with respect to *in vitro* fertilization and interracial marriage, for example; and already there is evidence of diminishing repugnance with respect to genetically modified crops and same sex marriage.[31]

---

[29] Kass (1997: 557). See also, Kass (2001, 2002, 2003).
[30] Rollins (1995); Robert and Baylis (2003).   [31] Pew Research Center (2011).

In addition, repugnance responses, even when widespread, are not universally shared. It is true that some people have a repugnance response toward cloning, chimeras, and human enhancement, for example. But not all do. Some people do not have any significant emotional response one way or another, and others have quite strong positive responses. When there are conflicting emotional or attitudinal responses, how are we to adjudicate or determine which are veridical? One way to adjudicate is to prioritize responses that are based on familiarity and understanding. Since many things once widely regarded as repugnant are now not found to be repugnant, given increased knowledge and experience of them, this seems to favor taking a skeptical stance with regard to the "wisdom" of repugnance toward new technologies and unfamiliar practices. (Though, on this view, repugnance responses that are widespread and persistent should be given more credence – for example, those regarding bestiality and incest.)

Another, better, way to adjudicate is to determine if there is any basis for the wrongness that the repugnance is supposed to track. This does not involve looking for an explanation for the repugnant responses themselves, or why some people have them and others do not. It involves establishing if there is any justification for the response: that is, reasons either for or against the practices or technologies. In the case of intrinsic concerns regarding interspecific individuals, it requires determining whether there are considerations (independent of our repugnant responses) that constitute reasons for ascribing normative significance to species boundaries: that is, reasons to think that creating interspecific individuals is itself ethically problematic. Therefore, at most, repugnance should be taken as an invitation for further inquiry.

The foregoing establishes that repugnance responses to interspecific individuals do not constitute a reason for believing that there is anything objectively intrinsically problematic about them. However, the fact that many people have such responses suggests that they subjectively value species purity. The implications of this subjective valuing are discussed in section 6.9.

6.6   Arguments from the integrity of the organism

Another type of argument against intentionally creating interspecific individuals appeals to the integrity of the organisms that are engineered. One way to understand "organism integrity" is in terms of an organism's good, interests, or well-being, such that an organism's integrity is compromised if, and only if, it is harmed. Because this understanding of "organism integrity" is connected to outcomes – that is, how and whether an organism is benefited or harmed – it cannot establish that transgenic organisms are problematic by virtue of their being interspecific. Therefore, integrity-based intrinsic objections to transgenic individuals often appeal instead to the *integrity of their genome*.[32] Here, for example, is the Dutch Committee on Animal Biotechnology:

> Biotechnology interventions are not only a problem because of the potential negative effects on the health and welfare of the animals, but also because changing their genetic material interferes with their identity. By genetically modifying animals, their properties are deliberately and specifically changed for human benefit. These genetic modifications are described as a violation of the genotypical integrity of the animal.[33]

But why should the integrity of an individual's genome be taken as ethically significant, if not for reasons to do with its welfare? The passage above suggests that the genetic "identity" of the organisms is salient: that is, that creation of such organisms might compromise or interfere with their identity. However, creation of transgenic individuals cannot alter their identity unless they existed (i.e., had an identity) prior to the genetic modification. In most (but not all) cases, intervention to create transgenic individuals occurs prior to organism development – for example, during breeding, *in vitro*, or in embryonic stages. Therefore, there is no prior identity of the organism that is altered. Moreover, as discussed earlier, interspecific individuals do not alter the identity of species.

A similar difficulty applies to the claim that "the more the animal loses of its species-specific capacities and characteristics, the more serious the integrity violation."[34] Particular animals, if they do not exist as nontransgenics prior to becoming transgenic, do not lose any capacities or characteristics at all. A transgenic pig that does not root or a transgenic chicken that does not scratch is not a formerly rooting pig or scratching chicken. It is an

---

[32] Lammerts van Bueren et al. (2003); Verhoog et al. (2003); Lammerts van Bueren and Struik (2005).

[33] Translated in de Vries (2006: 470).

[34] Rutgers and Heeger (1999: 49). See also, Bovenkerk et al. (2002).

individual organism that lacks that behavioral tendency. For this reason, animal disenhancement – that is, genetically modifying (or selectively breeding) animals to have diminished capacities so as to reduce animal suffering in agricultural or other animal use contexts – is not intrinsically problematic by virtue of the alteration of "species-specific" capacities.[35]

Moreover, why is alteration of an individual's genome problematic in cases where a preexisting organism's capacities (or characteristics) are changed in ways that deviate from those that are "species-specific"? Such deviations are not necessarily bad from the perspective of the altered organism. In some cases, altering species-specific behavioral tendencies can be beneficial. For example, it might be good for pigs to lack the urge to root or for chickens to lack the urge to scratch in contexts where these urges could not be satisfied, thereby causing frustration or suffering (as is arguably the situation in standard industrial agriculture conditions). In other cases, deviations might involve expanded capacities that enable beneficial or worthwhile experiences that the individual would not otherwise be capable of having: that is, it would augment the range or types of goods available to the individual.[36] Treating an animal well does not always require refraining from genetically altering its species-specific capacities, behaviors, or, even, good.[37]

Once the concept of organism integrity is detached from that of organism welfare, it is difficult to see where it would get its normative significance. Appeals to genetic integrity are not helpful, since they beg the question. They assert that mixing genomic material from individuals of different species is in itself problematic, but the issue is why that should be and what could ground that norm. Moreover, pointing out that transgenic individuals will often have some, but not all, of the capacities associated with a species is merely to describe what they are. It is not to provide a

---

[35] For discussion of the ethics of animal disenhancement, beyond the species integrity issue addressed here, see Rollins (1998); Sandøe et al. (1999); Gravel Ortiz (2004); Sandøe and Christensen (2008); Thompson (2008); Palmer (2011a).

[36] Streiffer (2005).

[37] "Although it is clear that animals strive to realize their specific good, it is doubtful whether they strive to *preserve* that specific good, in the sense of trying to prevent their *telos* from being changed into another . . . This means that even though animals have an interest in realizing the specific *telos* they have, they do not have an interest in preserving that *telos*" (de Vries 2006: 477).

reason that creating such individuals is, by virtue of their being that way, problematic.

Another argument that has been offered in support of the view that creating transgenic individuals violates the integrity of organisms is the *argument from reductionism*. According to this argument, engineering transgenic individuals is intrinsically problematic because it treats organisms not as living things, but as chemical machines and components:

> [Genetic engineers] increasingly view life from the vantage point of chemical composition at the genetic level ... for they truly believe that they are only transferring chemicals coded in the genes and not anything unique to a specific animal. By this kind of reasoning all of life becomes desacralized. All of life becomes reduced to a chemical level and becomes available for manipulation.[38]

This argument assumes, without evidence, that those who engage in (or, presumably, support) creating transgenic individuals have a reductionist perspective regarding organisms: that is, they view organisms as nothing more than their chemical parts. However, this is not the case. It is possible to understand individual organisms as instantiating a form of life, and to appreciate them as such, while also supporting or practicing transgenic research.[39] The claim that engaging in such research fosters a desacralized attitude toward living things is also unsubstantiated and implausible.

When considering the integrity of transgenic organisms, it is necessary to take a comparative perspective. All agriculture (and agricultural research) involves the use of nonhuman organisms for human purposes. Most of it involves organisms that have been modified by humans, as well as intentionally creating organisms that will later be killed. Similarly, biomedical research on nonhuman animals standardly involves intentionally manipulating them in ways that are detrimental to them (e.g., inducing disease and introducing chemicals), as well as killing them during or after experimentation. Given this, it is difficult to find a basis for asserting that creating and using transgenic organisms in agriculture and biomedical (or other scientific) research offends their integrity in ways that do not apply as well to nontransgenic individuals.

---

[38] Rifkin (1985: 53).   [39] Rollins (1995).

6.7   Consequential concerns

Several objections to the creation of transgenic individuals have to do with their potential detrimental effects. If transgenic individuals, by virtue of being transgenic, pose significant (and unnecessary) hazards to human health, the environment, social justice, or other significant values, then that could be a ground for a norm or rule against them: that is, for ascribing ethical significance to species boundaries. In normative theory terms, this would constitute a rule consequentialist approach to establishing the normative significance of species boundaries. According to rule consequentialism, the correct rules or norms are those that the general adoption of which would bring about as good or better consequences than any other possible rules; and an action is right if it accords with those rules.[40] Therefore, if a prohibition (or presumption) against creating transgenic individuals brings about as good or better consequences than other possible rules regarding their creation, then, on a rule consequentialist approach, species boundaries are normatively significant.

Many environmental organizations have argued against genetically modified crops on the ground that they are a hazard to wild species and ecosystems.[41] Some genetically modified organisms do have considerable potential to be ecologically disruptive. For example, genetically modified creeping bentgrass, which is engineered to be herbicide resistant and have high fecundity, has been found to disperse easily and be difficult to contain, due to the lightness of its seed.[42] Genetically modified salmon, which have been engineered for rapid growth, could result in increases in waste effluents from aquaculture and pressure on wild fish stocks (which provide feed), particularly if they contribute to the expansion of the market for salmon.[43] However, other genetically modified organisms do not appear to pose significant ecological risks and might well be ecologically beneficial – for example, genetically modified pigs that produce waste with less sulfur, genetically modified cows that produce less methane, and

---

[40] Hooker (2000).   [41] Greenpeace (2002).
[42] Watrud et al. (2004); Reichman et al. (2006).
[43] Naylor et al. (2000); Smith et al. (2010). Concerns regarding the possibility of accidental escape and impacts on wild salmon populations have also been raised.

genetically modified crops that use less water.[44] Therefore, it is not common to all genetically modified organisms, let alone all transgenic individuals, that they are a significant ecological hazard.

The same is true with respect to transgenic organisms and human health. Some transgenic organisms – for example, virulent microorganisms – could be harmful to human health if people were accidentally or intentionally exposed to them. But not all transgenic organisms pose serious risks to human health. In fact, some genetically modified organisms appear to be beneficial to human health – for example, genetically modified bacteria that produce insulin for diabetes patients, genetically modified rice that contains beta-carotene (the precursor to vitamin A), genetically modified soybeans that are high in omega-3s, and genetically modified cassava that is virus resistant. That some transgenic organisms pose significant and unnecessary ecological or human health risks, while others do not, implies that a general prohibition (or, even, presumption) against them on human health and ecological grounds is not justified. Instead, differential assessment of them is needed.

There is too much diversity among engineered transgenic organisms for concerns regarding the possible outcomes of their creation and use to apply uniformly to all applications and research programs – for example, that they favor industrial agricultural practices and corporate control of the food supply, will increase or exacerbate underserved inequalities, will lead to reduced respect for the value of life, will cause suffering to the individuals modified, or will be used for bioterrorism. That interspecific organisms are transgenic is only one of their characteristics and, at most, only a small part of their overall consequential profile. Other relevant considerations include their intended use, who controls them, what oversight is in place, what the risks are, what benefits they confer, how the benefits and risks are distributed, whether they increase (or decrease) autonomy, how they change relationships and power distributions, and whether the organisms involved are harmed or benefited.

For these reasons, it is not plausible that a general rule or presumption against the creation of transgenic organisms will bring about the best consequences. When it comes to concern about justice, ecological risk, human health, and other consequential concerns, differential assessment

---

[44] Marris (2010).

of modified organisms, synthesized organisms, and chimeras is needed.[45] Therefore, consequential concerns do not establish the normative significance of species boundaries.

6.8 Virtue-oriented concerns

Virtue-oriented concerns regarding transgenic individuals claim that creating them is contrary to virtue or expresses vice. The view that creating genetically modified organisms expresses and promotes a problematic reductionist attitude toward living things and the view that it is disrespectful to the integrity of the organisms themselves are virtue-oriented concerns. However, as discussed earlier, there is no necessary or even very strong connection between creating interspecific individuals and the view that living things are only complex biochemical systems to be manipulated toward human ends. It is quite possible to support and engage in their creation and also wonder at the complexity, beauty, and otherness of non-human species and natural systems. Understanding the genetic and chemical complexity of organisms can even lead to greater appreciation of and wonder toward the evolved natural world. Therefore, even if the attitude that life is nothing more than complexly organized chemicals were detrimental to its possessor or tended to promote negative consequences, and was thereby a vice, it would not follow that creation of interspecific individuals expresses that vice or is contrary to virtue. Moreover, as also discussed earlier, there is no sense in which the integrity of transgenic organisms is violated by virtue of their being transgenic. Thus, supporting their creation is not disrespectful to them or otherwise contrary to virtue for organism integrity reasons.

A virtue-oriented concern regarding transgenic organisms that has not yet been discussed is that creating and deploying them to address ecological and human health challenges expresses and encourages hubris in two respects.[46] First, it involves an overestimation of our capacity to predict and control the effects of our technological interventions into complex biological and ecological systems. Second, it involves a problematic

---

[45] This is frequently recognized in policy and regulation, see, for example, DEFRA (2004); New Zealand Ministry for the Environment (2004); UNFAO (2004); Human Fertilisation and Embryology Authority (2007); the Vatican (2009).

[46] McKibben (2000); Plumwood (2002); Raffensberger (2002).

disposition to favor control-oriented technological fixes that treat the effects of problems, rather than addressing the causes of the problems by modifying behaviors, social practices, and institutions. These two worries are related. Technologically-oriented solutions to ecological, human health, and other social challenges find support in the confidence that they can be executed efficiently and effectively, with minimal undesirable side-effects.

The disposition to favor narrowly focused control-oriented technological "solutions" to complex ecological and human health challenges is problematic. It has contributed to the creation of ecological and social problems in the past. Such strategies are, because of their narrowness, highly susceptible to unanticipated and undesirable consequences. Moreover, their success often depends upon the ability to control the effects of the technology in complex biological systems (organism and ecological), as well as on the capacity to find new technological solutions for whatever undesirable side-effects the latest technological fix might have.[47] A tendency to favor more comprehensive approaches to solving ecological and human health challenges – that is, those that address underlying social, economic, political, and lifestyle factors as well – is more justified.[48]

Some transgenic organisms fall neatly into the control-oriented techno-fix paradigm. This is arguably the case with many first-generation genetically modified crops – for example, insect- and herbicide-resistant corn, soybeans, and cotton. They are part of the general chemical pesticide and herbicide strategy that is central to industrial agriculture, and as such they do not address the larger social, economic, ecological, and evolutionary contexts that give rise to the need for a "GM solution" for food security in the first place. An alternative would be to modify our lifestyles, including our diets, and our agricultural practices, so that they are more attuned to the limits and distribution of our agricultural and environmental resources, as well as to address the social, economic, and institutional factors that contribute to our agricultural challenges – for example, agricultural subsidies, political instability and insecurity, regulatory capacity and infrastructure, market and distribution systems, international trade practices and agreements, and population growth. However, the fact that some transgenic organisms are employed as a techno-fix does not constitute an argument against the creation and use of all transgenic organisms. In fact, there

---

[47] Scott (2005).   [48] Sandler (2007).

is no reason that genetically modified crops (or transgenics more generally) cannot be included as part of an integrated response to agricultural (or other environmental and human health) challenges that also addresses the underlying social, institutional, cultural, or economic causes. There is nothing about them that precludes their being part of, for example, crop diversity in agriculture or reforms in resource allocations and distribution systems. Nor is there anything about them that requires that they be developed and owned by large transnational corporations and inadequately regulated by national governments and international trade organizations.

The genetically engineered yeast that produces artemisinic acid, the precursor to artemisinin, illustrates this. It is intended to address a significant social issue, suffering and death from malaria, and benefit those who are worst off: that is, those that cannot afford or do not have access to more expensive or scarce treatments. In 2008, 247 million people contracted malaria, and nearly 1 million people died from the disease, the vast majority of them children.[49] Development of the engineered yeast was largely funded by the Bill and Melinda Gates Foundation, and its production and commercialization is being led by the nonprofit Institute for OneWorld Health, in collaboration with Sanofi-Aventis, a global pharmaceutical company. There are possible negative effects of the widespread availability of the drug, including the impacts on farmers who grow wormwood, the agricultural source from which the drug is derived. It will be necessary to provide adequate notice before distribution begins, so that farmers have ample time to cultivate alternative crops before the price of artemisinin drops. Moreover, there is the possibility of evolved malarial resistance to artemisinin. This concern is already being addressed by the World Health Organization through the promotion of combination therapies, though synthetic artemisinin could exacerbate the challenge by making the drug less expensive and more widely available.[50] Overall, synthetic artemisinin produced by transgenic microbes is a technology with the potential to significantly benefit a large number of the world's worst off: that is, it is compassionate and just. It is not without risks or costs. But its development and implementation is proceeding with social, ecological, and evolutionary sensitivity.

That transgenic individuals are involved in the development or production of some drug, food, or therapy does not itself imply that the project is

---

[49] WHO (2010).   [50] Dondorp et al. (2009); Lancet (2010).

hubristic and contrary to virtue. Differential assessment is needed. In some cases their creation and use is compassionate, just, and ecologically sensitive, in other cases it is not.

6.9   The value of (non-*Homo sapiens*) species boundaries

Each of the arguments discussed above aims to establish an objective basis for the ethical significance (or lack thereof) of species boundaries, and each was found wanting. Nevertheless, many people consider species boundaries to have ethical significance. They might do so because they find some of the arguments discussed above compelling or because it comports with or follows from significant aspects of their worldview – for example, for religious or cultural reasons. The source, scope, and strength of people's views on the ethical significance of species boundaries is an empirical matter, as is whether it differs regarding microbials, plants and animals, or regarding chimeras and hybrids. Studies of people's attitudes toward transgenics, while not adequate for sorting out all these subtleties, indicate that quite a lot of people are generally discomforted by them and are opposed to their creation.[51] The fact that many people have a negative evaluative attitude toward the creation of interspecific individuals (or a positive attitude toward species purity), and that they often do so for reasons flowing from their worldviews or value commitments, implies that species boundaries have subjective final value.

As discussed earlier, subjective valuing is not beyond critical assessment, so the fact that some people value species purity does not imply that it should carry normative weight. If, contrary to what was argued earlier, there were no such thing as species, then valuing species boundaries would be not only baseless, but in a way senseless. However, since species and species boundaries do exist, this is not the case. Moreover, while all the arguments in favor of the normative significance of species boundaries were found wanting, so too were all the arguments against the normative significance of species boundaries. This implies that while the valuing lacks an objective basis, it is not irrational in the sense of being contrary to established facts or reasons.

---

[51]   OTA (1987); Program on International Policy Attitudes (2003); RAE (2009); Hart Research Associates (2010).

There may be internal consistency problems in some cases. For example, some people might accept and make use of transgenic individuals regularly or find them permissible in some contexts, even while they are opposed to them in principle or in the abstract. Or it may be that some people are opposed to them because they have false beliefs about what they are and how they are created. However, in other cases, the disvaluing of transgenics is internally consistent and informed. For example, many people who are opposed to genetically modified crops actively attempt to avoid using and consuming transgenics, and their opposition to them is often based on a clear understanding of the technologies.[52] Thus, the subjective final value that many people place on species boundaries can be part of reasonable comprehensive doctrines (or worldviews) that include conceptions of what is valuable, meaningful, and ethical.

In liberal democratic societies, which recognize that a plurality of reasonable conceptions of the good are possible, all such views are to be respected in public policies.[53] This is accomplished through state neutrality with respect to them. Policies should not be enacted in order to privilege some comprehensive doctrines or conceptions of the good over others – for example, to make it more difficult to live according to some and easier to live according to others. That is, there should be *neutrality of intent* in public policy. Moreover, the basis for public policy should not be the values of some subset of reasonable comprehensive doctrines, but rather considerations for which there is overlapping consensus among reasonable comprehensive doctrines. That is, there should be *neutrality of justification* in public policy. In addition, the impacts of public policy should not, as far as is reasonably possible, have the outcome of making it more difficult to live according to a reasonable comprehensive doctrine. That is, there should be (as far as possible) *neutrality of effect* in public policy.[54] Therefore, people's commitment to the value of species boundaries has normative significance in policy contexts in that public policy should not be made on bases that are contrary to the reasonable comprehensive doctrines from which it flows and, as far as is reasonably possible, should not make it more difficult to live in accordance with it.

---

[52] Verhoog (2003); Sandler and Kay (2006).   [53] Rawls (1971, 1996).
[54] Brighouse (1995, 2000); Steiffer and Hedemann (2005); Basl (2010b).

For example, positive labeling of food containing genetically modified crops should be required, so that those who find the foods objectionable are able to live according to their comprehensive doctrines without undue burden.[55] However, a ban on genetically modified crops and foods is not justified, since there are reasonable comprehensive doctrines on which transgenic individuals are not ethically problematic and that are inconsistent with the final value of species boundaries. Moreover, there are other values, such as justice, autonomy, and public welfare, which are relevant to public policy regarding genetically modified crops and are either basic liberal commitments (e.g., autonomy) or have overlapping consensus among reasonable comprehensive doctrines (e.g., human welfare). For these reasons, the subjective final value of species boundaries is not determinative in policy contexts, even as it functions as a constraint on the bases for public policy (through neutrality of intent and justification) and shapes the goals of public policy (through neutrality of effect).

Individuals and private actors need not be committed to neutrality. Nevertheless, respect and tolerance toward the worldviews and values of others is appropriate. If something is offensive to other people, that is a reason, all other things being equal, not to do it. Moreover, all other things being equal, one should not denigrate other people's comprehensive doctrines or make it unduly difficult to live according to them. With respect to the subjective final value of species boundaries, this implies that people should not be disparaged for valuing species boundaries and that it should not function as a barrier to their social participation (e.g., in events around food). It does not require refraining from conducting transgenic research or using chimeras and hybrids for biomedical, agricultural, or conservation purposes; and it does not have implications for private activities. However, in public contexts people ought to be sensitive to the subjective final values and associated commitments of others, not dismiss them as foolish or irrational (particularly when they are part of reasonable comprehensive doctrines), and try to accommodate them where reasonably possible. This is not onerous. Respect toward and tolerance of the view that species boundaries have final subjective value is in this way no more demanding (and probably less so) than is respecting the commitment not to use animal products or the commitment to pray five times a day. Therefore, while the subjective

---

[55] Thompson (2002); Streiffer and Rubel (2004); Streiffer and Hedemann (2005).

final value of species boundaries has some normative significance, even in nonpolicy contexts, it is not determinative of or restrictive on the activities of others. The demands or requests made by those who embrace the value of species boundaries should reflect this, particularly since denying the normative significance of species boundaries can also be part of reasonable comprehensive doctrines that need to be respected.

6.10   Conclusion

The issue addressed in this chapter was whether nonhuman species boundaries have normative significance and, if so, what it amounts to. I have argued that there is not an objective basis for their ethical significance. Nevertheless, the view that species boundaries are ethically significant can be part of reasonable comprehensive doctrines or worldviews. Therefore, the view needs to be respected in both policy and nonpolicy domains. However, such respect does not require refraining from researching, using, or benefiting from transgenic individuals, whether in biomedical, agricultural, or conservation contexts. There may be good justifications for opposing or even prohibiting particular transgenic research programs or applications. However, these would flow from nonintrinsic concerns – for example, concerns about justice or consequences – which will vary among research programs and applications. For this reason, differential assessment of the creation and use of nonhuman transgenics is necessary. Some research programs and applications involving transgenics are ecologically sensitive, compassionate, and just, while others are reckless, short-sighted, and trivial. But there is nothing objectively intrinsically wrong with them.

7   *Homo sapiens* in particular

The focus of the previous chapter was whether non-*Homo sapiens* species boundaries have any ethical significance, particularly with respect to the creation of nonhuman transgenics. The conclusion reached was that there is no objective basis for the ethical significance of nonhuman species boundaries, though the fact that many people value species purity does have some normative implications in both policy and nonpolicy contexts.

Many of the same technologies that are used to create transgenic non-humans can also be used to engineer part-human transgenics. As discussed in Chapter 6, part-human chimeras are already being created for biomedical research purposes. Human stem cells have been introduced into mice, rats, primates, and fowl in order to study the development, migration, and fate of cells and tissue *in vivo*. The hope is that once these behaviors are sufficiently characterized and understood they can then be predicted and controlled, enabling therapeutics for everything from degenerative diseases to lost limbs. Introduction of human genes into nonhuman genomes is also commonplace in biomedical research. For example, house mice, which have a high level of genetic similarity with humans, are often used as animal models for human diseases. When a disease being studied has a genetic risk factor or cause – for example, cancer, sickle cell anemia or schizophrenia – the mice models are often improved (or enabled) by inserting human genetic material that codes for or triggers the disease.[1] Mice have also been enhanced by insertion of human genetic material into their genome. For example, trichromatic mice (mice are usually bichromatic) have been created by replacing a mouse gene with a human gene that encodes for a type of photoreceptor not normally possessed by mice.[2] Human genes have been introduced into nonanimal genomes as well. For example, *E. coli* that

---

[1] Nagel (1998); NIMH (2008).   [2] Smallwood et al. (2003); Jacobs et al. (2007).

synthesize insulin were created by insertion of the human gene for the hormone.[3] As these examples illustrate, there is nothing about human genes or the human genome that prevents them from being engineered using the same techniques now routinely used on nonhuman genes and genomes. As the cost and knowledge constraints on genetic research are reduced, and as the research continues to globalize, part-human genetic hybrids and chimeras are likely to become commonplace.[4]

On a naturalistic understanding of *Homo sapiens*, it is just one evolved species among all the rest. It does not stand outside nature, hold a special place within nature, or have a unique role in the scheme of the universe. Because of this, things should not be any different with respect to the ethical significance of *Homo sapiens* species boundaries or the creation of part-human transgenics than they are for non-*Homo sapiens* species boundaries and transgenics. Therefore, there is not anything objectively intrinsically valuable about *Homo sapiens* species purity or objectionable about creating part-human transgenics. People may be more disturbed by part-human hybrids or chimeras than they are by nonhuman ones.[5] As a result, these may have greater subjective final disvalue. Nevertheless, with respect to the ethical significance of crossing species boundaries or mixing genomic material from different species, the species boundaries of *Homo sapiens* have the same type of normative significance as do the boundaries of other species.

However, there is an additional respect in which the species boundaries of *Homo sapiens* are often taken to be ethically significant: that it defines a unique or special moral community. There are several variations of this view – for example, that being a member of the species *Homo sapiens* is itself a moral status relevant property and that conspecificity is ethically significant. The first half of this chapter addresses whether the species boundary of *Homo sapiens* delineates individuals with a particular moral status, different from that of members of other species.

The second half of this chapter concerns species boundary issues related to technologically enabled human enhancement. Technologies capable of modifying or augmenting human capacities are rapidly increasing in power, and their trajectory suggests that it is not premature to address ethical issues associated with human enhancement and, even, the creation

---

[3] Goeddel et al. (1979).   [4] Carlson (2010).   [5] Robert and Baylis (2003).

of transhumans and posthumans.[6] Transhumans are individuals who have been technologically modified in such a way that they are only partly human. Posthumans are individuals that have been modified such that they are not properly regarded as human at all.[7] In each case, they are people who are not situated fully within *Homo sapiens* species boundaries. In the discourse on the ethics of human enhancement, it is common for both proponents and critics of enhancement to make appeals to human nature in support of their position. Given this, it is necessary to determine whether human nature (and thereby the life form of *Homo sapiens*) is normative, such that it is either intrinsically problematic or intrinsically good to attempt to modify oneself (or one's offspring) in ways that would make one other than purely human. This is the topic of the second part of the chapter.

7.1   *Homo sapiens* and moral status

An entity is morally considerable if it needs to be taken into account in deliberations regarding actions, practices, and policies that might affect it. An entity is directly considerable if it needs to be taken into account because it has inherent worth or some other type of final value. An entity is indirectly considerable if it needs to be taken into account because of its relationship to something that is directly considerable – for example, because it is someone's property. Moral status refers to *how* something is to be taken into account. As discussed earlier, an entity might have inherent worth and, therefore, be due respect, but not be due compassion, because it is not sentient. Or an entity might be due compassion, because it is sentient, but not have rights, because it lacks the requisite autonomy. Or an entity might, for relational reasons, have negative rights (e.g., not to be harmed), but not positive rights (e.g., to have basic goods provided). Morally considerable entities can, therefore, have different (and multiple) types of moral status.

One way in which *Homo sapiens* species boundaries have been thought to be ethically significant is that they delineate entities with a particular sort of moral status: that is, human moral agents need to directly consider members of the species in some way that they do not need to consider non-*Homo sapiens*. There are several distinct, but related, ways in which this is

---

[6] Greely et al. (2008); Bostrom and Sandberg (2009).   [7] Savulescu (2010).

thought to be the case: (1) that members of the species *Homo sapiens* have a particular moral status by virtue of being a member of the species; (2) that human moral agents have special moral obligations to other members of the species *Homo sapiens* by virtue of their being conspecifics; and (3) that members of the species *Homo sapiens* have special moral obligations to the continuance or furtherance of *Homo sapiens* by virtue of its being their species, and this in turn supports special moral consideration toward other members of the species. I discuss each of these in turn.

The view that members of the species *Homo sapiens* have special moral status – for example, human dignity – by virtue of being members of the species (or possessing the nature of the species) is a *species membership* account of moral status.[8] One reason people are attracted to species membership accounts of human moral status is that it is inclusive of all human beings, regardless of their stage of development or capacities. On this view, even if a human being has severe and permanent brain injuries, dementia, or mental disabilities, such that he or she is not able to engage in reciprocal cooperative schemes or cannot be held responsible as a moral agent, he or she still has the same moral status as any other human being.[9] Appeals to the distinctive moral status of humans have been used as a basis for arguing against the development of part-human transgenics and technological transhumans and posthumans on the grounds that the creation of such entities would diminish or violate the dignity of pure humans and that the engineered entities would themselves lack dignity.[10]

However, there are significant difficulties with the view that species membership is necessary and sufficient for having a certain level or type of moral status. Primary among these is that moral status distinctions made on the basis of species membership are arbitrary in the same way as are moral status distinctions made on the basis of skin color or sex, for example.[11]

---

[8] Here is a representative statement of the view: "In sum, human beings constitute a special sort of animal. They differ in kind from other animals because they have a rational nature, a nature characterized by having the basic, natural capacities (possessed by each and every human being from the point at which he or she comes to be) for conceptual thought and deliberation and free choice. By virtue of having such a nature, all human beings are persons; and all persons possess the real dignity that is deserving of full moral respect. Thus, every human being deserves full moral respect" (Lee and George 2008: 430).

[9] Fukuyama (2002); Lee and George (2008).

[10] Fukuyama (2002); Karpowicz et al. (2005); Jotterand (2010).   [11] Singer (1977, 1989).

Differences in skin color and sex among human beings are factual differences. People really do have different colored skin and there really are two different sexes. Moreover, these are explained by genetic differences between people. However, despite their being real biological differences, they are arbitrary and unjustified bases for attributing differential moral status to people. The reason for this is that they do not constitute or track anything ethically significant – for example, moral agency, autonomy, types (or range) of interests, or ability to participate in social (and ecological) relationships. As a result, skin color and sex are not moral status relevant properties.

The same is true of species membership. Members of the species *Homo sapiens* really are biologically different from those who are not members of the species, and there is a genetic explanation for this. But that is not sufficient to establish that it is a nonarbitrary basis for moral status differentiation, any more than it is for skin color or sex. *Homo sapiens* species membership is a justified basis for moral status differentiation only if it constitutes or tracks something morally significant. However, it does neither. There is nothing ethically significant that obtains for all and only members of the species *Homo sapiens*. Some human beings are moral agents, highly autonomous, capable of reciprocal concern, and able to participate in complex cooperative arrangements, but not all are – for example, infants and people who are severely mentally disabled. Moreover, some individuals of some nonhuman species – for example, Bornean orangutans (*Pongo pygmaeus*) and bottlenose dolphins – are more capable of these than are some humans.[12] Similarly, many humans have complex psychological interests in addition to their biological interests, but not all do. Severely mentally disabled people and those with advanced cognitive degenerative diseases are not capable of long-term planning or concerned about the meaning and significance of their lives. Again, some individuals of nonhuman species have equal or greater psychological capacities than do some human beings, and so have comparable or even more complex and diverse interests.[13] Furthermore, it is possible that there could be nonhuman species whose healthy, biologically mature members have interests, agency, and relationships that are comparable to (or exceed) those of healthy, biologically mature members of the species *Homo sapiens* – for example, extraterrestrial species or future terrestrial species. Such beings would,

---

[12] de Waal (2006).   [13] Regan ([1983/1985] 2004); Singer (1977, 1989).

presumably, have the same moral status as healthy, biologically mature members of our species. The mere possibility of this is sufficient to show that membership in *Homo sapiens* is not something that is distinctively ethically significant. Because it neither tracks nor constitutes anything of ethical significance, membership in the species *Homo sapiens* does not confer a distinctive moral status.

In response, proponents of the moral status relevance of *Homo sapiens* membership might argue that the fact that all healthy, fully biologically mature members of *Homo sapiens* have comparable interests and agency justifies treating membership in the species *Homo sapiens* as morally relevant.[14] However, there is no reason why co-membership in a group should confer the moral status associated with properties possessed by some individual members of the group to all group members, including those who lack the relevant properties.[15] It is true that severely mentally disabled people are members of the species *Homo sapiens*, but it is also true that they do not have the autonomy and agency of fully healthy and mature human beings. If there are certain rights that are associated with the autonomy or agency that they lack, why should their being in a biological group with people who have those capacities imply that they should have those rights as well, particularly when they do not have the capacity to exercise them? Moreover, this response, even if it were successful, would establish only that membership in the species *Homo sapiens* is sufficient for a particular moral status, not that it is necessary.[16] It is still possible that there could be nonhuman individuals that have the relevant capacities as well, and there is no reason why they should not possess the same moral status as humans. Thus, even if the extension problem could be solved, membership in the species *Homo sapiens* would still not ground or track a distinctive moral status.

That being a member of *Homo sapiens* is not a moral status relevant property does not imply that humans and nonhumans should be treated the same. In some situations, factual differences between people can be a basis for differential treatment of them, even when they have the same moral status. For example, women, but not men, should receive prenatal health care. The same is true of factual differences between species. For example, humans and bottlenose dolphins might both be due compassion, but it does not follow that we should release people into the open sea and

---

[14] Lee and George (2008).   [15] Norcross (2004); McMahan (2005).   [16] Liao (2010).

give dolphins polio vaccinations. Moreover, it may turn out that all (or nearly all) members of the species *Homo sapiens* have a type of moral status that all members of a different species lack. For example, humans are due compassion, whereas saguaro cacti (*Carnegiea gigantean*) are not. However, the reason for this is not that people are members of the species *Homo sapiens* and saguaro cacti are not, but rather that people are sentient and saguaro cacti are not. It is not people's species membership that explains their differential moral status from individuals of other species (when it is differential).

The difficulties discussed above are sufficiently strong to justify rejecting species membership accounts of moral status. As a result, such accounts cannot be used as a basis for opposing the creation of part-human or transhuman individuals. The alternative to a species membership approach to moral status is a *capacities- and relationships-oriented approach*: that is, individuals have moral status by virtue of the capacities that they possess and their historical relationships with other entities. On this approach, an individual's moral status is based on the sort of things he or she is capable of (and so what can be expected of him or her), the sort of things that are good for him or her (and so the ways in which he or she can be benefited and harmed), the sort of value he or she possesses, and his or her past and present relationships to others. Contrary to what advocates of species membership views sometimes claim, it does not follow from this that an individual who lacks full practical rationality or moral agency has no moral status. Instead, the type of consideration due to an individual is attuned to the capacities that the individual possesses and his or her social (and ecological) situatedness. Compassion, caring, loyalty, and respect toward a severely mentally impaired human being can still be required, even if that person's moral status does not include all the same rights and responsibilities possessed by other human beings.

On a capacities view of moral status, creating transgenics, transhumans, or posthumans does not undermine the moral status (e.g., rights or dignity) of humans, as long as humans have the same capacities and types of relationships that they have always had.[17] Whether transgenics, transhumans,

---

[17] Wilson (2007); Fenton (2008); Buchanan (2009a). There could be challenges related to transhumans and posthumans recognizing the moral status (e.g., rights) of humans (Annas 2005), or with adjudicating conflicts between the rights of humans and those of transhumans or posthumans (Buchanan 2009b), or with establishing justice between humans, transhumans, and posthumans more generally (Wilson 2007). However, these

and posthumans would have the moral status associated with human dignity (or human rights), depends upon the properties that are the basis for the moral status and the properties had by the entities. If the basis for human rights is autonomy, moral agency, or practical rationality, as is often taken to be the case, and posthumans possess these, then they will have those rights. If the basis for positive compassion – that is, not only refraining from causing suffering, but also alleviating it when reasonably possible – is sentience and the capacity for reciprocal concern, and some part-human transgenics possess these, then they will be due positive compassion. Whatever the bases for different varieties of moral status, part-human transgenics and transhumans will have the moral status appropriate to them, given their capacities, relationships, and value.[18] There is, therefore, no intrinsic human dignity, or rights-based problem with engineering part-human individuals, given a capacities-oriented approach to moral status. Human beings will retain their moral status, because they retain their capacities and relationships; and engineered part-humans (transhumans, hybrids, or chimeras) will have the moral status appropriate to them by virtue of their capacities and relationships.

The second way in which the *Homo sapiens* species category is taken to be moral status significant is that we have special obligations to members of our own species by virtue of conspecificity. However, it is not clear why co-membership in a particular biological group should be ethically significant, particularly when there are any number of other ways to divide organisms into groups – for example, living things and mammals. The explanation for why co-membership in the group *Homo sapiens* has special ethical significance would have to appeal to either something about species-level groups in general or something about the features of members of this species-level group (*Homo sapiens*) in particular. The former – that is, there is something moral status significant about co-membership in species-level groups in general – is question begging in the absence of further justification. It

issues are not to do with the moral significance of species boundaries as it pertains to establishing moral status. They are concerned with ensuring that individuals' moral status is appropriately recognized and respected. If the moral status of some individuals (e.g., part-human chimeras) is not recognized or recognizable, then wrongful harms may be likely to occur (Streiffer 2005).

[18] Sandler and Basl (2010). On a capacities-oriented approach to moral status, it is possible that transhumans or posthumans could have a type of moral status that fully biologically mature and healthy nonenhanced humans lack (Sandler 2011).

defends the ethical significance of conspecificity by asserting the ethical significance of species-level joint membership, which is just conspecificity. The latter response – that is, the moral status significance of conspecificity arises from some feature of *Homo sapiens* in particular – raises many of the difficulties associated with the species membership approach to moral status. There is no justification as to why individuals who are members of the species, but lack the moral status relevant capacities and relationships, should have the same moral status as those in the group who possess them. How and why is the status transferred over? After all, it is possible to delineate subgroups of *Homo sapiens*, such that all members of the subgroup have the relevant properties for a type of moral status. Why should those groups not define the boundaries for that type of moral status? Moreover, if there are nonhuman individuals that have all the relevant capacities or relationships, why should they not be afforded the same moral status?

Advocates of the conspecific approach to moral status sometimes appeal to the fact that human beings can enter into cooperative relationships and participate in deliberative decision making with other humans, in ways that they cannot do with nonhuman individuals.[19] The claim is not, and cannot be, that we actually do this, since human beings are very often in conflict and competition with other human beings, or are just indifferent to them. It is, instead, that we are capable of such relationships and interactions. But that capability is grounded in our cognitive and psychological capacities. So this approach to supporting the conspecific account of moral status is ultimately a capacities-based approach. As such, it cannot succeed, since there will be some members of *Homo sapiens* who lacks the relevant capacities, and it is possible that some non-*Homo sapiens* individuals will possess the relevant capacities. This is clearly the case with respect to the capacities of reciprocal cooperation and deliberative decision making. Some human beings (e.g., infants and those with severe mental disabilities) lack the capacities to participate, and it is possible that some nonhumans (e.g., posthumans or transhumans) could participate.

Any attempt to establish the normative significance of conspecificity will confront the difficulties discussed above. It will either not adequately explain why this particular biological group or group level is normatively significant, given all the other possible groupings and levels, or else it will

---

[19] Baxter (1974).

appeal to some features (capacities or relationships) of members of the group *Homo sapiens* that not all members of the group possess and that some non-*Homo sapiens* do (or could) possess. Therefore, it will either be question begging or face the same problems as the species membership approach to moral status.

A third approach to establishing the moral status significance of *Homo sapiens* appeals to the obligations or duties that we have to the species itself, and so derivatively to other humans, by virtue of our being members of the species.[20] However, as discussed in Chapter 2, species have neither inherent worth nor noninterest-based objective final value. Therefore, individual human beings cannot have special moral status derivative upon the objective final-value-based moral status of *Homo sapiens*. Moreover, even if *Homo sapiens* did have (objective final-value-based) moral status, it would not follow that individual human beings have special moral status derivative upon it. That a whole has some moral status does not imply that the parts that comprise it individually do. My cells are not due compassion, even if I am. For these reasons, human beings do not have special moral status derivative upon the objective final value (or moral status) of *Homo sapiens*.

Each of the approaches to establishing that *Homo sapiens* defines a special or unique moral community fails. There is no objective basis for the view. Moreover, although many people believe that human beings have a unique or special moral status by virtue of being members of *Homo sapiens*, it does not follow that *Homo sapiens* species boundaries have subjective value justified moral status significance. This is in contrast to the subjective valuing of species purity, which, as discussed in Chapter 6, does have normative significance. The difference is that, in the case of species purity, there is no (nonoutcome-oriented) objective justification either for or against transgenics, whereas there is an objective fact of the matter concerning the moral status of individuals, and there are objective considerations that undermine the claim that *Homo sapiens* bounds a unique moral community. A capacities-based approach to moral status is the most justified, and on it the belief that human beings have special moral status by virtue of being members of *Homo sapiens* or by virtue of being conspecific is mistaken. It may be that most nonhumans differ in moral status from most humans, but this is not due to their different species membership. Instead, it is an

---

[20] Johnson (2003).

implication of the bases for the types of status involved, as well as the capacities and relationships of the individuals. Subjective valuing that is wrongfully exclusionary (or wrongfully elevating) should not be taken as having ethical significance even in policy contexts. For example, animal cruelty laws should not have an opt-out for those who think animals are not morally considerable, since that view is inconsistent with the compassion due to nonhuman animals by virtue of their inherent worth, which is an objective final value.[21]

Human beings are directly morally considerable, and possess several varieties of moral status. But this is not because of our species membership. It is due to the value and capacities that we have as individuals, as well as our individual activities, relationships, accomplishments, and character.

7.2   Human enhancement technologies

The remainder of this chapter addresses the relationship between human nature, *Homo sapiens* species boundaries, and human enhancement. This section provides an overview of emerging enhancement technologies. The subsequent sections discuss the normative significance of human nature and *Homo sapiens* species boundaries for the ethics of human enhancement.

Augmentation or enhancement of human cognitive, physical, perceptual, and psychological capabilities through technology is, and always has been, ubiquitous. Education technologies, computational devices, nutritional supplements, steroids, pharmaceuticals, communication systems, and optical lenses are each a type of human enhancement technology. Enhancement technologies can be differentiated according to magnitude (i.e., how large or novel the enhancement), reversibility (i.e., how readily the enhancement can be removed or turned off), and internality (i.e., the extent to which the technology integrates with or modifies biological systems). Computers, for example, significantly augment human communication and cognitive abilities: that is, the magnitude of enhancement associated with them is large. However, they are highly reversible, since they are easily turned off, and are external, in that they do not modify the biology of their users. Anabolic steroids, in contrast, provide a more modest enhancement than do computers. But they are less reversible, since the effects of the

---

[21] Basl (2010b).

technology remain some time after the intervention, and they are more internal, since they work by modifying the user's body. An enhancement is more *robust*, the greater its magnitude, irreversibility, and internality. (As the examples above show, these vary independently.) Enhancement technologies that augment a core capacity significantly beyond the range attainable by technologically unassisted human beings (or introduce a capacity not had by technologically unassisted human beings) by altering our biological systems/processes (or introducing some novel system/process) are *robust enhancement technologies*. Such technologies have the potential to create people who are partly nonhuman and, if accomplished on a large enough scale, could alter human nature.

For example, the sort of robust genetic enhancements already accomplished with individuals of other species could be pursued in human beings. Genetically modified mice have been engineered with capacities well beyond those of nongenetically modified mice, with respect to physical capabilities (e.g., strength[22] and endurance[23]), cognitive capabilities (e.g., memory, learning, and problem solving[24]), longevity (up to 65 percent longer lifespan[25]), and perception (e.g., trichromatism). Genetic alteration of behavioral traits has also been accomplished. For example, pair bonding male meadow voles, which normally are not pair bonding, were engineered by inserting the gene responsible for pair bonding behavior in prairie voles (*Microtus ochrogaster*) into their genome. The gene encodes for a receptor for the hormone vasopressin, which is not otherwise present in male meadow voles.[26]

Genetic technologies are not the only potentially robust enhancement technologies in development. Brain–machine interfaces have been accomplished that enable owl and rhesus macaque monkeys to control a robotic arm and a robot's walking by manipulating their brain states.[27] Similar brain–machine interface technologies have been used to enable tetraplegic people to move a cursor, open emails, play video games, and draw figures.[28] These technologies may enable robust computer–brain integration. Nootropics – pharmaceuticals that increase the brain's supply of neurochemicals, increase oxygen supply to the brain, or stimulate nerve growth

---

[22] Lee et al. (2005); Barré et al. (2007).   [23] Wang et al. (2004).
[24] Tang et al. (1999); Routtenberg et al. (2000); Tan et al. (2006).
[25] Longo and Finch (2003); Conti et al. (2006).   [26] Lim et al. (2004).
[27] Carmena et al. (2003); Blakeslee (2008).   [28] Hochberg et al. (2006).

in the brain – are a promising therapeutic for cognitive disabilities and neural degradation. They may also have cognitive enhancement potential. Regenerative medicine, therapeutics employing stem cells to generate new tissue to repair damaged, diseased, and missing organs or new cells to treat degenerative diseases may have longevity enhancement potential, as well as physical and cognitive enhancement potential. Cochlear and retinal implants, therapeutics for deafness and retinal degeneration, could lead to perceptual enhancements as researchers better understand how to build devices that effectively integrate with those systems. Bionic limbs, currently used as replacements for lost limbs, may have the potential to become bionic enhancements. This is not an exhaustive review of advanced therapeutics with robust enhancement potentials, nor is it intended as a set of predictions regarding which technologies will be realized or applied. It is a representative list of possibilities, which collectively suggests that the technological capability for robust human enhancement is not science fiction, but science-in-the-making.

Moreover, many people are eager to use enhancement technologies if they believe that they will improve their abilities, health, longevity, or appearance. The human growth hormone industry, although largely illegal, is estimated to be worth several billion dollars annually; hundreds of thousands, and perhaps millions, of US citizens use anabolic steroids for non-therapeutic reasons each year;[29] 7 percent of college students and 20 percent of research scientists use off-label prescription pharmaceuticals to increase alertness and productivity; and in 2008 there were 10.2 million "aesthetic" or nontherapeutic cosmetic surgery procedures in the United States alone.[30] Robust enhancement technologies will have many enthusiastic adopters.

7.3 The normativity of human nature

There are four distinct ways in which human nature is taken to be normative. The first, is that there are certain things that are contrary to human nature, such that it would be intrinsically problematic for humans to do them: for example, that cloning is unnatural (and so problematic) because

---

[29] United States Sentencing Commission (2006).   [30] Plastic Surgery Research (2010).

human reproduction is sexual;[31] and that homosexuality is unnatural (and so problematic) because homosexual sex cannot result in procreation and the purpose of sex is procreation.[32] On this view, human nature provides the basis for moral guidance (or a law) for human activities.

The second conception of the normativity of human nature is that there are certain things that are expressions of human nature, such that it would be right or good (or at least permissible) that we do them. This conception of the normativity of human nature is prominent in the discourse regarding human enhancement:

> Far from being unnatural, the drive to alter and improve on ourselves is a fundamental part of who we humans are. As a species we've always looked for ways to be faster, stronger, and smarter and to live longer ...
>
> In the end, this search for ways to enhance ourselves is a natural part of being human ... It's wired deep in our genes – a natural outgrowth of our human intelligence, curiosity, and drive. To turn our backs on this power would be to turn our backs on our true nature. Embracing our quest to understand and improve on ourselves doesn't call into question our humanity – it reaffirms it.[33]

The third way in which human nature is sometimes taken to be normative is that, because human nature defines who we are, it would be intrinsically problematic to alter or destroy it. This view is also prominent in discussions regarding human enhancement.[34]

> The most significant threat posed by contemporary biotechnology is the possibility that it will alter human nature and thereby move us into a "posthuman" stage of history. This is important ... because human nature exists, is a meaningful concept, and has provided a stable continuity to our experience as a species ...
>
> We want to protect the full range of our complex evolved natures against attempts at self-modification. We do not want to disrupt either the unity or the continuity of human nature.[35]

These first three conceptions of the normativity of human nature, hereafter the *prescriptive conceptions*, take it to determine ethical norms. In each case, some claimed fact about human nature is thought to have implications for what humans ought to do.

---

[31] President's Council on Bioethics (2002).   [32] Novak (2000).   [33] Naam (2005: 9–10).
[34] Kass (2003); President's Council on Bioethics (2003).   [35] Fukuyama (2002: 7, 172).

The fourth conception involves a weaker relationship between human nature and normativity. On this conception, hereafter the *informational conception*, facts about the kind of creature that human beings are need to inform the content of ethics. One way in which it is frequently thought to do so is that ethical norms and theories should be attuned to human psychology. For example, many hold the view that it must be possible for human beings to be motivated to act according to moral principles.[36] Others argue that if we have strong psychological inclinations to give preference to our friends and family, such that there would be high costs involved in getting people to consider them in ethical deliberations as just another person (counted as one and only one), then ethical norms should not require that we do so. Still others insist that ethical theories need to be fitted to the facts about human reasoning and decision processes.[37]

Another way in which human nature is taken to inform (but not determine) ethical norms is that what makes for a good or flourishing human life depends in part on human nature. Strong social relationships, knowledge, autonomy, and health are part of our good, because we are social, embodied, rational, and cultural beings, for example. Different theories provide different explanations for just what it is about such things as social relationships, knowledge, and autonomy that makes them part of human flourishing – for example, that they promote pleasure and the absence of pain, are conducive to having our desires fulfilled and not frustrated, or are constitutive of flourishing. But on all of these views, the substantive goods that comprise human flourishing are sensitive to the kind of creature or life form that we are.[38]

Assessing the viability of the various normative conceptions of human nature requires specifying what sort of thing human nature is. Neuroscience, behavioral genetics, cognitive science, and evolutionary psychology have been successful in establishing that there is an innate, evolved human nature that substantially explains our form of life. Our nature is in the structure of our brains and bodies, our modes of learning and cognition, our behavioral and emotional dispositions, and our cognitive tendencies.[39]

However, human nature underdetermines individual human (or group) characteristics and behaviors, for several reasons. First, environment is

---

[36] Owen (1991).   [37] Doris (2002); Casebeer (2003); Prinz (2006).   [38] Sandler (2007).
[39] Ehrlich (2000); Pinker (2002); Richerson and Boyd (2005).

relevant to how a particular genotype is expressed or affects phenotype. What a particular gene or gene sequence "does" within a person (or non-human individual) often is dependent upon the internal and external environment. Second, the variation among human traits and behaviors is only partially explained by genetic differences. Environmental factors also explain a significant amount of the variance for most physical, psychological, cognitive, behavioral, and personality traits.[40] Third, although the broad outlines of our form of life are established by our innate human nature, the details are not. Forms of sociability, methods of parenting, ways of taking pleasure, and modes of production, for example, have differed widely among cultures, as well as among individuals within cultures. There are limits on this variation. Some norms, such as prohibition of murder and care for infants, appear in all cultures and seem necessary for a social group to persist or function at all. Nevertheless, the human form of life admits considerable variation in the details of its realization.[41] Fourth, culture is a cause of human behavior that is not reducible to genes and physical environment. Culture is possible for us only because we are capable of certain forms of knowledge and technology creation, transmission, and accumulation; and we are capable of these only because of our innate biologically evolved human nature. However, once culture emerges, it exists independently of our genes and is partially explanatory of many human behaviors and practices.[42] For all of these reasons, human nature does not fully determine what is possible for human beings, let alone what individual human beings can and will do.

Overall, the view of human nature from a naturalistic perspective is that it is the evolved set of traits and dispositions (largely "encoded" in our genetic make-up) that involves the physiological structures, functions, and processes of our brains and bodies, our modes of learning and cognition (e.g., language acquisition, proclivity for teleological explanations, imitation, and social learning), some of our behavioral and emotional predispositions (e.g., sociability, reciprocal altruism, and revenge), and our possibilities and limitations (social, psychological, cognitive, and environmental). In this way, it determines our life form and strongly influences our form of life (but, again, does not fully determine it). Not every member of the species *Homo sapiens* possesses all of the traits and dispositions

---

[40] Pinker (2002).   [41] Brown (1991); Ehrlich (2000).   [42] Richerson and Boyd (2005).

constitutive of human nature, nor do those who possess them all do so in the same way. Human nature is therefore not an "essence" in the classical sense of providing the necessary and sufficient conditions for membership in a category (in this case, the biological category *Homo sapiens*). Membership in the biological category is determined by bare biological features – for example, genetics and lineage.[43] Instead, human nature explains how and why we are different from individuals of other species, and why we tend to go about the world in the ways that we do (in general, not in detail).

This naturalistic conception of human nature cannot support prescriptive norms. On it, "human nature" refers to how our brains are structurally and functionally organized, the innate tendencies and dispositions we have, and our range of physical, cognitive, and psychological possibilities. It does not indicate which tendencies ought to be encouraged or discouraged, which possibilities ought to be pursued or avoided, or by what means these ought to be done. Characterizing innate human nature is a project in description, while deciding among social, ethical, and political norms is a project in prescription. The science of human nature does not determine what ends we ought to promote or how we ought to promote them. Therefore, it does not support any of the prescriptive conceptions of the relationship of human nature to ethics.

However, it can and does support the informational conception of the relationship of human nature to ethics. The prescriptive project needs to take into account the best information about ourselves and our world, since a scientifically informed understanding of human nature may provide support for some prescriptions (and theories) or undermine support for others.[44] This is the case with accounts of human flourishing, for example. We are living, sentient, social, rational animals. As living beings our good involves survival, biological health, and reproduction. As sentient beings our good involves enjoyment and the absence of pain. As social beings our good involves being part of well-functioning social groups and healthy relationships. As rational beings our good involves autonomy, meaningfulness, and the accumulation of knowledge. These

---

[43] As discussed in the Introduction, it is necessary, when thinking of species as exemplifying forms of life, to distinguish the biological grouping criteria that determine which organisms are members of the species from the form of life descriptions that indicate how members of the group standardly go about the world.

[44] Rachels (1990).

are not controversial claims. Most people would agree that, in general and under most circumstances, longevity, health, knowledge, pleasure, and well-functioning social groups are human goods. (And, as discussed above, these claims can be supported by different theoretical accounts of what makes them part of human flourishing.[45])

There is no single correct way of realizing these goods. All human societies care for their young, have forms of recreation, artistic expression, medicine, and innovate and transmit knowledge. But different cultures, subcultures, and individuals do so in different ways. This cultural and individual variation is possible because of human commonalities that substantially differentiate us from individuals of other species.[46] For individuals of other species, because they are less or differently rational, both what constitutes their flourishing and how they realize it are more strongly determined by their biological natures. There is much less (and so much less variable) technological innovation, idea generation, and complex social structuring, as well as transmission and accumulation of these over time. Social learning and social structure play a significant role in the form of life of many species (e.g., meerkats [*Suricata suricatta*] and African elephants), and innovation and tool use has been observed in many species (e.g., chimpanzees and American crows), but these still fall far short of what is distinctive of human culture: the comparatively rapid and widespread accumulation and transmission of knowledge, technology, and social practices.

So, while human nature defines the broad outlines of our form of life, and in so doing provides the basis for a general substantive account of human flourishing, it does not settle the details of how human goods are to be realized or pursued, or their role in the context of different people's lives. What constitutes human flourishing in general is informed by human nature, but it is not determined by it in the particular.[47]

---

[45] One need not realize each of these goods to some maximal or ideal degree in order to live well or flourish. Nor is there a hierarchical ordering of their importance. Certain goods figure more prominently in the lives of some people than in others. A person might flourish or live well in this or that way, or flourish or live well overall, even while some of these goods are not substantially realized in his or her life (Sandler 2007).

[46] Ehrlich (2000); Richerson and Boyd (2005).

[47] Not all realizations of the goods constitutive of human flourishing are equally endorsable. Realizations that are detrimental to accomplishing others, or the same good in the future, are less justified than those with greater fecundity. For example, recreational methamphetamine use may be pleasurable, but it undermines realizing most of the

7.4 Human nature, human enhancement, and human flourishing

As discussed in the last section, some ethicists are opposed to human enhancement because they believe that it would destroy or alter human nature, while others argue that it should be pursued because it expresses human nature. There are both descriptive and prescriptive difficulties with these positions. The prescriptive difficulty is that, for reasons discussed in section 7.3, prescriptive uses of human nature are not tenable. Naturalistic accounts of human nature are strictly descriptive. Therefore, it is not possible to derive from human nature alone a prescription regarding whether we should attempt to modify humans in ways that would alter human nature. Human nature does not support either that it is intrinsically objectionable or intrinsically laudable to create transhuman (or posthuman) individuals or otherwise alter human nature through widespread enhancement.

The descriptive difficulty is that it is within the capacity of human beings both to try to transcend limits/boundaries (as advocates of enhancement emphasize[48]) and to adhere to limits/boundaries (as those opposed to enhancement emphasize[49]). Both are characteristic of human beings. On

other human goods, and is therefore unendorsable. Realizations of the goods can also be unendorsable because they are detrimental to the flourishing of others or are premised on false beliefs. For example, racially motivated hate groups are detrimental to those outside the group, are socially disruptive, and are premised on false beliefs about human biology and the moral significance of skin color and ethnicity. So even (or particularly) when these types of social groups are well functioning, they are not endorsable. These (and other) standards for evaluating possible realizations of human goods do not follow strictly from the science of human nature or the natural sciences more broadly. They involve, for example, nonempirical, normative accounts of what constitutes a morally relevant difference. It is because we are rational that not all realizations of the goods constitutive of human flourishing are equally endorsable. This is another reason that human nature does not determine human flourishing in the particular (Sandler 2007).

[48] "Humans are already replacing parts of their bodies and brains with nonbiological replacements that work better at performing their 'human' functions ... To me, the essence of being human is not our limitations – although we do have many – it's our ability to reach beyond our limitations. We didn't stay on the ground. We didn't even stay on the planet. And we are already not settling for the limitations of our biology" (Kurzweil 2005: 9). See also, Naam (2005).

[49] "A flourishing human life is not a life lived with an ageless body or untroubled soul, but rather a life lived in rhythmed time, mindful of time's limits, appreciative of each season and filled first of all with those intimate human relations that are ours only

the one hand, science and technology involve pushing the boundaries of our knowledge, as well as expanding our capabilities and what we can accomplish both individually and collectively. The capacity for cumulative innovation over generations is enabled by our cognitive, imaginative, psychological, and social capacities (i.e., human nature). On the other hand, custom and law exemplify the need to set and respect limits on what ends we seek, how we pursue acceptable ends, and how we interact with other people and nonhumans. The capacity to determine, identify, and adhere to limits is also enabled by our cognitive, imaginative, psychological, and social capacities (i.e., human nature). In ethics, both the aspirational and the adherence aspects of human nature are operative. Therefore, human nature does not involve a primary tendency toward either transcendence or reconciliation regarding limits and boundaries. They are equally crucial to our form of life. This is, after all, why we can ask whether and how to pursue human enhancement (or posthumanism and transhumanism). We have both transcendent and reconciliation tendencies, within individuals and distributed throughout the species, and we have both transcendent and reconciliation possibilities before us with human enhancement. We can do either while remaining "true" to human nature.

Thus, for both descriptive and normative reasons, human nature is neither supportive of nor opposed to human enhancement. Focusing on what is constitutive of, favored by, or expressive of human nature is not a useful framework for evaluating human enhancement, transhumanism, and posthumanism. It is empirically and conceptually misguided. Posthumanism and transhumanism are neither intrinsically good nor intrinsically problematic by virtue of their "transcending" human nature or the boundaries of *Homo sapiens*.

But what of the informational conception of the relationship between human nature and ethics – that is, the facts about human nature need to inform ethical norms? Can it ground reasons either for or against creating or becoming posthuman (or transhuman)? It cannot. At the core of the

because we are born, age, replace ourselves, decline, and die – and know it ... The pursuit of an ageless body is finally a distraction and a deformation. The pursuit of an untroubled and self-satisfied soul is deadly to desire ... Not the agelessness of the body, nor the contentment of the soul, nor even the list of external achievement and accomplishments of life, but the engaged and energetic being-at-work of what nature uniquely gave to us is what we need to treasure and defend" (Kass 2003: 27–28). See also, President's Council on Bioethics (2003).

informational conception is the recognition that we require an ethic for beings like us in a world like ours. But what is at issue with human enhancement is not what we should do, given the sort of being that we are. What is at issue is what sort of being we ought to try to be.

What is remarkable about robust enhancement technologies is that if they are developed and implemented they could create individuals with different natures from unenhanced humans – for example, different dispositions and physiological and psychological possibilities. If the changes are significant enough, posthuman (or transhuman) flourishing could differ from human flourishing; and posthuman (or transhuman) obligations and responsibilities could differ from human obligations and responsibilities. This is possible precisely because the kind of being would be different and, on the informational account, many ethical norms need to be attuned to an agent's life form. For example, it may be that greater levels of sacrifice for the interests of others can, and should, be expected of individuals with a capacity for empathy and altruism significantly beyond that of unenhanced human beings. Or it may be that intellectual goods will be more important to the flourishing of significantly cognitively enhanced individuals than are bodily goods, in comparison with (unenhanced) human flourishing.

The possibilities described above are speculative. However, they illustrate the fact that, on the informational conception of the relationship between human nature and ethics, human nature does not tell us what sort of being we ought to be, but rather informs what is good (and, possibly, right) for us given the kind of being that we are. There is a difference between (1) what is good (and right) for us, given human nature, and (2) that it is good (or right) for us to have the nature that we do. The informational conception of the relationship between human nature and ethics is embodied in (1), but not (2). On the informational conception, human nature provides material relevant to ethical norms, as long as that is our nature, but it does not provide guidance on what our nature should be. Thus, even on the informational conception, human nature is not normative with respect to transcending the species boundary. There is no basis in human nature for generating a general norm for or against robust enhancement, transhumanism, or posthumanism.

It does not follow from this that human nature is irrelevant to the ethics of human enhancement – that is, to evaluating whether or not to pursue or allow a particular type or mode of enhancement. (The "type" of enhancement refers to the capacity that is augmented or added – for example, memory, problem solving, longevity, strength, endurance, immunity, or concentration. The "mode" of enhancement refers to how the enhancement is accomplished – for example, genetic, pharmacological, or robotic.) Among the considerations germane to whether one ought to undergo enhancement, pursue it for one's children, or advocate it for one's society is whether it would be beneficial or detrimental to become enhanced. As a result, appeals to human and possible posthuman goods are common in the enhancement literature. It has been argued, for example, that cognitive enhancement would open up goods associated with a deeper understanding of the world,[50] that enhancement would diminish goods associated with personal accomplishment[51] and virtue,[52] and that genetically enhancing one's children would undermine goods associated with the parent–child relationship.[53] Identifying constituents of human flourishing that may be amplified, supplemented, undermined, altered, or lost, either in pursuit of some enhancement or in its realization, is crucial to evaluating these arguments. However, these considerations are not related to the ethical or normative significance of human nature or the boundaries of the species *Homo sapiens*. Like the claim that cognitive and psychological enhancements would help to solve social problems (including climate change),[54] the claim that dissemination of enhancement technologies would exacerbate preexisting social injustices,[55] and the claim that transhumans are likely to harm and exploit humans,[56] they are consequential or outcome-oriented concerns.

7.5 Conclusion

The question posed at the outset of this chapter was whether the species category *Homo sapiens* has distinctive ethical significance. It does not. Human nature and the boundaries of *Homo sapiens* have no special normativity. *Homo sapiens* does not delineate a moral community and its members do not have, by virtue of their membership, special or unique moral status. This is so even if people commonly believe that the category is morally

---

[50] Kurzweil (2005); Bostrom (2008).   [51] McKibben (2003); Agar (2010).
[52] Fukuyama (2002); Kass (2003); President's Commission on Bioethics (2003).
[53] Sandel (2007).   [54] Kurzweil (2005); Bostrom and Ord (2006).
[55] Wenz (2005); Garcia and Sandler (2009).   [56] Annas (2005); Agar (2010).

significant and their belief flows from their worldview. Moreover, human nature does not ground either intrinsic objections against or justifications for robust human enhancement. To be made coherent, these must be recast as extrinsic concerns regarding the potential gain or loss of human goods, whereupon it is clear that discriminatory evaluation is needed. Some forms of enhancement might, when introduced into a particular social context, undermine important human goods and promote injustice. Other enhancements (or the same enhancements in different contexts) might instead address aspects of human nature – for example, cognitive biases and capacity for violence – that work against individual and collective flourishing (as evidenced by the fact that we typically aim to overcome or discourage them in ourselves and our children). Not every enhancement will, by virtue of creating transhumans or posthumans, be a change for the worse, but neither will each one be a change for the better.[57]

The discussions in this and the previous chapter have shown that there is nothing intrinsically objectively wrong with creating interspecific organisms, including part-human ones. Whether to proceed with a particular transgenic or human enhancement research program or application depends primarily on extrinsic considerations, such as compassion, prudence, and justice, and, to a lesser extent and only in some cases, on subjective final values.

---

[57] Buchanan (2009b); McConnell (2010).

8 Artifactual species

The previous two chapters considered the ethics of modifying species, both human and nonhuman. The focus was on organisms that fit imperfectly into existing species categories. However, some engineered organisms may not fall even partially into preexisting species categories, either because they are not created from biological materials or because the biological materials that comprise them are so thoroughly recombined and reengineered. Such organisms would not be interspecific. Instead, they would constitute artificially selected, *de novo* species, or *artifactual organisms and species*.

As with transgenics and transhumans, differential extrinsic evaluation of artifactual organism research programs and applications is needed. Some will be hasty, risky, and unnecessary, while others will address significant social and environmental problems in incremental, controlled, and responsible ways.[1] What is distinctive about artifactual organisms and species is the extent to which they are designed and engineered by us – that is, their artifactualness. This chapter concerns whether their artifactualness has any ethical significance. If it does not, then creating novel organisms and species does not raise any unique ethical concerns and, as is the case with transgenics, evaluation of them and public policy regarding them should focus on extrinsic considerations. The next section provides a brief overview of some varieties of artifactual organisms. The subsequent sections address whether "artifactualness" is a value relevant property for the types of value possessed by nonartifactual organisms and species.

8.1 Artifactual organisms

A living thing is artifactual to the extent that it is designed and engineered by humans (or other robust rational agents) using synthetic materials. There

[1] Presidential Commission for the Study of Bioethical Issues (2010).

are degrees of artifactualness, just as there are degrees of naturalness. A genetically engineered mouse is more artifactual (and so less natural) than a wild mouse, but less artifactual than a mouse whose entire genome was synthesized in a laboratory, which is, in turn, less artifactual than a "mouse" constructed of nonbiological material. Thus, there is a natural/artifactual continuum of living things and, thereby, species. Where a living thing or species is located on the continuum is determined by its origin and material composition, and these two factors can vary independently.

At the artifactual end of the continuum are thoroughly engineered entities that do not make use of material (e.g., molecules) or information (e.g., design principles) derived from natural biological organisms. This is the case, for example, with *protocells* – that is, "self-replicating cells assembled from nonliving organic and inorganic matter." One research group has reported that they are near to creating nanoscale protocells that do not contain any biomolecules found in modern living cells. Their goal is to "engineer living-technologies, which will be robust, autonomous, adaptive, and even self-replicating."[2] Another research group is attempting to construct protocells from fatty molecules using nucleic acids as the source code for replication. "Such a system should, given time and the right environment, begin to evolve in a Darwinian fashion, potentially leading to the spontaneous emergence of genomically encoded catalysts and structural molecules."[3] These would be artifactual, evolving life forms that are unrelated to any existing or prior life forms. The aims of protocell research are both practical – for example, production of energy and medicines – and scientific – for example, identifying how life could have emerged.

Protocells are near the artifactual pole of the living entities continuum, but they are not at the limit. Some protocells draw upon design principles from natural biological cells, and, once created, protocells will undergo evolution. As a result, subsequent generations of protocells will, to some extent, be the product of natural evolutionary processes, even as the initial entities and environmental conditions are artifactual. Robust artificial intelligences that are not templated on prior forms or processes are composed of engineered materials (or exist largely virtually), and do not undergo

---

[2] AAAS (2005). See also, Rasmussen et al. (2009).
[3] Szostak Lab (2009). See also, Mansy et al. (2008).

evolution (e.g., because they do not replicate in the requisite ways) would be still more artifactual than protocells. If such entities were to exist, they would be about as artifactual as a living thing could be.

Another type of organism that is potentially nearer the artifactual than the natural pole of the continuum is synthetic organisms, the products of synthetic biology or synthetic genomics. As discussed in Chapter 6, synthetic organisms are thoroughly engineered biological systems that make use of material and design principles taken or derived from natural organisms. They are thus less artifactual than protocells, though more artifactual than hybridized or genetically engineered organisms. Some synthetic organisms are created by intensive genetic engineering, as is the case with the yeast that synthesizes artemisinic acid. Others are created using a biobricks approach, which seeks to develop "a continuously growing collection of genetic parts that can be mixed and matched to build synthetic biology devices and systems." The technical challenges to synthesizing entire functional genomes are steadily being overcome. Already a research group has chemically synthesized the complete DNA of a bacteria species, inserted it into a host cell, and started up the metabolic processes of the organism. Other groups have synthesized chromosomes and proteins not found in natural organisms and inserted them into host cells, which then used them to perform biological functions and sustain growth.[4] As with protocells, the goals of synthetic genomics projects are both practical – for example, creating organism that can "manufacture" vaccines, chemicals and fuels, code information, or supplement our immune system – and scientific – for example, elucidating fundamental "design" principles of life.

Protocells, artificial intelligences, and synthetic organisms are living things that are highly artifactual (albeit to different degrees). These various approaches to engineering artifactual living things are not mutually exclusive. For example, it is possible that a minimal genome could be the host chassis for some organelles or information-coding molecules not derived from natural organisms; or artificial intelligences could be engineered using design principles derived from research on synthetic organisms. Overall, the capacity to engineer a diverse array of highly artifactual organisms is rapidly expanding.[5]

---

[4] Dymond et al. (2011); Fisher et al. (2011).   [5] Carlson (2010).

8.2   Natural value and artifactualness

As discussed in Chapters 2 and 3, a common view among environmental ethicists, environmentalists, and conservation biologists is that natural-ness – that is, independence from humans and continuity with historical evolutionary processes – is valuable.[6] Artifactualness is, by definition, the absence of naturalness. Therefore, artifactual species and organisms will possess little or no natural value. Living organisms that lack natural value are unusual. But is there anything intrinsically problematic or objection-able about creating living organisms that have little or no natural value? Some believe so. Christopher Preston, for example, has argued that their lack of naturalness can be the basis for a deontological objection to them. According to Preston, artifactual organisms "depart from a core principle of Darwinian natural selection – descent with modification – leaving them with no causal connection to historical evolutionary processes."[7] On his view, they differ in this way even from genetically modified organisms, in which only a small amount of genomic material is modified, and the species or form of life that undergoes modification is mostly the product of natural evolutionary processes that stretch back through deep time via a chain of viable organisms connected through descent with modification. In contrast, artifactual organisms are life forms without a natural history, and synthetic species are "biotic kinds *de novo*,"[8] "constructed in [their] entirety according to human plan."[9] As organisms without a natural history, they undermine the distinction between nature and artifact, and, thereby, "the normative foundation of a number of leading positions in environmental ethics [that] rest on a substantial normative commitment to the value of what is bio-logically natural over what is artifactual."[10] Therefore, according to Preston, "if, like Leopold, you are an environmentalist who puts normative stock in the idea of the historical evolutionary process then synthetic biology should be opposed on deontological grounds due to the way it disconnects the biological artifact from this evolutionary history."[11] Preston recognizes that this line of reasoning does not demonstrate that synthetic organisms are ethically problematic and ought to be opposed, since it does not include an argument for natural value, the value of historical evolutionary

---

[6] Elliot (1982); Soulé (1985); Rolston (1989); Katz (1992); Preston (2008).
[7] Preston (2008: 23).   [8] Preston (2008: 35).   [9] Preston (2008: 33).
[10] Preston (2008: 24).   [11] Preston (2008: 36).

processes, or the importance of maintaining a strong nature–artifact distinction. However, if these are highly valuable, then synthetic organisms undermine a primary normative foundation for environmental ethics. This is the "basis for a deontological argument against" them.[12]

There are, however, several difficulties with this argument against the creation of artifactual organisms, even assuming that naturalness is valuable and has normative significance. First, most artifactual organisms and species will have some causal connection with historical evolutionary processes. For instance, the biomaterials that make up synthetic organisms – for example, the DNA components and chasses – would not exist were it not for those processes. It is true that they are extracted from the organisms in which they evolved and are used to form novel organisms according to human design. It is also true that there is not a continuous chain of viable organisms connected through descent with modification at every step of the creation process. Nevertheless, these do not constitute a complete severing from evolutionary history. Because the organisms are comprised of at least some materials that arose from that history, they are possible only because of it. It is a less linear connection to historical evolutionary processes than in the case of wild organisms or even genetically modified organisms. But, given that naturalness is a matter of degree,[13] organisms comprised of parts of organisms that arose through natural historical processes will be natural to some extent. It will be a lesser extent than that of genetically modified organisms, but more than that of protocells.

Moreover, when artifactual organisms reproduce they create a natural history – that is, a historical chain of causally connected organisms. No biological reproduction process reliably produces identical entities. Therefore, over time, there will be differentiated offspring. Some of the trait variations are likely to be relevant to the probability of their possessors' survival and reproduction under the conditions in which they live. So, over time, there is likely to be evolution within the population. This is, in fact, what is intended and observed.[14] Thus, most artifactual organisms – all except perhaps the very early generations – will be the product of descent with modification, in the same sense as natural biological organisms. If having "a causal connection to historical evolutionary processes" is what

[12] Preston (2008: 34).   [13] Preston (2008).   [14] AAAS (2005); Szostak Lab (2009).

is constitutive of (or sufficient for) having a natural history, then these artifactual organisms will have a natural history. It will not be one that stretches back through "deep time" prior to *Homo sapiens*, and the extent to which a population of artifactual organisms' evolutionary history is natural will depend on how intensively its descent and modification are controlled. Nevertheless, many populations of artifactual organisms will be natural to at least some extent.

A second difficulty with the no natural history argument against artifactual organisms and species is that they do not depart from Darwinian natural selection. Darwinism provides an account of how biological complexity and diversity arises from less biological complexity and diversity. It is a descriptive theory, not a normative one, so cannot be violated in a normative sense. This is so even if it is appropriate to attribute natural value to entities that arise from the process. The creation of artifacts – toasters, airplanes, and transistors – does not violate the principles of Darwinism. It just results in entities that do not have natural value. As discussed above, it may be that some artifactual organisms have very little (or no) connection to natural historical processes and so very little (or no) natural value; but that is not a violation of Darwinism. Therefore, the "departure" of artifactual organisms from Darwinian natural selection must not be understood normatively.

However, it is not really possible to depart from Darwinism in a descriptive sense either, any more than it is possible to depart from gravity. There are places or situations where gravity is much less significant than other forces – for example, at the quantum level – but that is not to depart from the core principle of gravity. Similarly, there may be conditions or activities in which Darwinian natural selection processes are less powerful than are cultural evolution or artificial selection, but this is not to depart from the core principles of Darwinism or natural selection. It is only that natural selection is a weaker causal factor in those instances. Furthermore, the creation of artifactual organisms is not entirely independent of or outside Darwinism. Artifactual organisms do not have an evolutionary history in the standard sense associated with most biological organisms. However, human cognitive, psychological, and imaginative capabilities evolved through natural selection and descent with modification, and it is these capabilities that enable the creation of artifactual organisms. Thus, artificial selection – that is, intentional production and selection of organisms and traits – is not contrary to, or historically detached from, Darwinism; it is another selection pressure operative within biological evolution.[15]

A third difficulty with the no natural history argument against artifactual organisms is that even if they lacked natural history and were independent of Darwinian natural selection, this would not challenge environmental ethics that take the normative significance of natural value as foundational. Let us assume, contrary to the arguments above, that artifactual organisms are wholly unnatural – that is, they have no natural history and are entirely independent of Darwinian processes. According to the relevant type of environmental ethics, it would follow that they have no natural value. However, artifacts that lack natural value do not challenge the fundamental nature–artifact distinction on which such ethics depend. If they did, then desk lamps, railroad tracks, and flatware would have undermined the ethics long before artifactual organisms. What is distinctive about artifactual organisms, and according to Preston the source of their potentially distinctive challenge to such ethics, is not merely that they are entirely artifacts, but that they are organisms that are entirely artifacts. However, it is not clear why the fact that they are organisms should make any difference. Why is the implication not simply that they are organisms that lack natural value? Again, this would be unusual. All prior organisms that we are familiar with are organisms with some natural history and so natural value, even if not all equally so (e.g., compare wild organisms, domesticated organisms, and genetically modified organisms). But it is not an ontological, conceptual, nomological, or causal necessity that organisms have a natural history and possess natural value. After all, artifactual organisms are actual (and so possible) organisms that are (*ex hypothesis*) devoid of naturalness and natural value. Moreover, that there can be organisms that lack natural value does not challenge the conceptual validity of the nature–artifact distinction; it depends upon it. Therefore, artifactual organisms do not reduce the natural value of organisms that have a natural history, and they do not undermine environmental ethics that take the normative significance of natural value as foundational.

[15] This is not to claim that artifactual organisms are natural because they are created by members of the species *Homo sapiens*, which is natural. Rather, it is to provide a broader perspective (i.e., beyond the immediate cause and context of their creation) on the relationship between artifactual organisms and Darwinian natural selection.

The foregoing considerations demonstrate that there is no basis in the normative or value commitment to naturalness for a deontological argument or even intrinsic objection against artifactual organisms. They are not contrary to and do not displace natural historical processes, including Darwinian processes. They do not undermine the nature–artifact distinction, any more than do genetically modified crops or domesticated animals (or birds' nests and beaver dams, for that matter). At best, the no natural history argument against artifactual organisms is incomplete, even assuming the normative significance and value afforded naturalness on the sort of environmental ethics at issue. The argument fails to explain adequately why organisms without natural value are intrinsically objectionable. However, it is difficult to see what considerations other than those that have already been discussed might do that justificatory work, so a complete and sound in principle argument against artifactual organisms appears unpromising. Therefore, even if "like Leopold, you are an environmentalist who puts normative stock in the idea of the historical evolutionary process," you ought not oppose artifactual organisms on natural value grounds.

8.3   Inherent worth and artifactualness

Inherent worth is the type of value that something possesses by virtue of having a good of its own or interests that valuers ought to care about for its own sake. It is often the value appealed to in order to ground concern for the well-being (or flourishing or capabilities) of other people and other animals – that is, that they have a welfare or interests that make a claim on moral agents.[16] In Chapter 2, I argued that all natural organisms and some collections of organisms have inherent worth, though how we ought to respond to their worth (i.e., their moral status) can differ dramatically depending upon the sort of capacities they have and our relationships to them. That discussion was restricted to naturally evolved (or largely naturally evolved) organisms and collectives. Here I consider whether artifactualness, or being a member of an artifactual species, is relevant to inherent worth – that is, whether artifactual organisms have the same inherent worth as natural organisms. There are two components to an entity possessing inherent worth: (1) that the entity has a good of its own; and (2) that moral agents

[16] Singer (1977); Nussbaum (2000); Mill (2001).

ought to care about the entity's good. Therefore, if an entity's artifactual-ness precludes it from having a good of its own or constitutes a reason not to care about its good (if it has one), then artifactualness is a value relevant property with respect to inherent worth.

As discussed in Chapter 2, an entity possesses a good of its own if, and only if, it can be benefited or harmed in a way that is not dependent upon another's aims or good. It is possible to make sense of benefit and harm to an entity only if there is something that that entity is striving for or aiming to accomplish – that is, it is teleologically organized or goal-directed. All natural living things have a good of their own, since they are all teleologically organized systems. Their parts, processes, and oper-ations are largely organized in ways and for reasons pertaining to certain ends, such as survival, self-maintenance, and reproduction. As a result, all natural living things can be benefited (or harmed) insofar as their capacity to pursue the ends toward which they are organized and strive are enhanced (or impaired). Thus, for all natural living things, there is a "good for them" and a "bad for them" relative to their biological func-tioning (and, therefore, without reference to the goals, interests, or desires of anything else). Devil facial tumor disease is bad for Tasmanian devils (*Sarcophilus harrisii*), oak wilt is bad for oak trees, and amoxicillin is bad for *Streptococcus pyogenes*, independent of what they do for us or how we feel about them.

The explanation for why nonsentient natural organisms have the good that they do is etiological. The good of the organism is a product of the causal explanations for why its parts and processes exist and/or persist in that life form. The basis for the entity's goal-directedness is that the parts and processes are there because of what they do and the ends they contrib-ute to accomplishing in entities of that type. Those ends (or goal-directedness), in turn, ground what is good and bad for the organism. In the case of naturally evolved nonsentient organisms, the selection etiology or causal explanation for their parts and processes is natural selection. The same is true for the bare biological goods of psychologically complex natu-ral organism, though not for their psychological goods or interests, for which intentional, evaluative, conative, and preferential attitudes play a crucial role.

Artifactual organisms, to the extent that they are artifactual, lack natural selection etiologies. The causal explanation for why they have the form, parts, and processes that they do is, as with other artifacts (e.g., boats and knives), largely explained by human intentions. Nevertheless, they do have a selection etiology. There are "in order that" explanations for why it is that protocells and synthetic organisms have many of the features that they do – for example, they perform certain metabolic processes or maintain organism coherence. Why should the fact that their selection etiologies are largely artificial, rather than natural, be relevant to whether they have a good of their own? Consider an idealized minimal organism, one that has been genomically reduced so that it has only the minimum amount of genes needed for survival, self-repair, and reproduction.[17] Even such a minimal organism has ends (i.e., survival, self-repair, and reproduction) toward which its parts and processes are directed. Moreover, it can be treated in ways that increase or decrease its capacity to pursue or accomplish its ends. If the nutrient source of a minimal organism is withdrawn, the capacity of the organism to pursue its ends is diminished. This is everything that is necessary to ground claims about what is harmful and beneficial for it. Withdrawing the nutrient source is bad for the organism, independent of the effects that it has on others. That the selection process that gave rise to organisms of this type was of a particular sort seems irrelevant. If this is right, then naturalness is not a necessary condition for an entity's having a good of its own.

One response to this might be that the ends of the reduced organism were in fact the product of natural selection. Minimalization of the organism has not created any new ends, but rather knocked some out. Therefore, in this case, artificial selection has not grounded the entity's ends and, thereby, its good. Consider, then, an artifactual organism that is qualitatively identical to a natural organism, but which was entirely artificially synthesized.[18] Suppose, further, that the parts and processes of the artifactual organism were selected for in order to perform the same functions as those in the naturally evolved organism. It would seem, then, that withholding nutrients from the artifactual organism would be bad for it in the same way and for the same reasons that withholding nutrients would be bad for the natural organism – that is, it would impair its ability to pursue its ends in its ways. Thus, it is not the naturalness of natural selection that

---

[17] Hutchison III et al. (1999).   [18] Gibson et al. (2008); Lartigue et al. (2009).

grounds teleological orientation and, thereby, an entity's good; it is the selection.[19]

In the case just considered, the synthesized organism is the same life form as a naturally occurring one. One might argue that the situation is different for organisms that are members of artifactual species – that is, artifactual organisms that do not share a form of life with any natural organisms. For such *de novo* organisms, there is no historical population to serve as a reference class for determining how organisms of their sort make their way in the world or realize their good. Does this difference imply that *de novo* organisms do not have a good of their own? It does not. One reason for this is that it is not really a difference at all. Almost all *de novo* organisms will have a reference class, one that is constituted by its contemporaries and any prior or subsequent generations. *De novo* organisms are members of species; they have a form of life and a life form. They are just artifactual, rather than naturally evolved. Therefore, even if an entity's good is species-dependent, *de novo* organisms will have a good of their own.[20] Another reason is that the etiological approach to grounding an entity's good does not require a reference class. It requires a selection mechanism, and *de novo* organisms are the product of artificial selection.

Still, one might respond, there is a difference between artificial and natural selection that is relevant to whether an entity has a good of its own. The form, parts, and processes of artifactual organisms are selected for people's purposes (or, at least, according to their designs), whereas those of natural organisms are not selected for anyone's or anything's purposes. On this view, an artifactual organism may appear to have a good of its own, but this is precluded by the fact that it is designed or created to perform a

---

[19] One possibly counterintuitive implication of the etiological approach to grounding an entity's good is that two intrinsically identical entities (i.e., two numerically distinct entities with identical internal properties) could have different goods. This would occur if the parts and processes of one were selected for different ends or reasons than the parts or processes of the other. In that case, given the etiological account of an entity's good, they would have different goal-directedness and, therefore, different goods. It is even possible that two entities could be intrinsically identical and one have a good of its own and the other lack a good of its own. This would occur if there were an etiology for the parts and processes of one of the entities, but not for those of the other (i.e., because it was the product of pure randomness or chance). See Basl and Sandler (In press) for an extensive discussion of these implications of the etiological account of teleology and a good of one's own, as well as for a defense of the account in light of them.

[20] Attfield (1987, 1995).

function for someone else. Artifactual organisms may have a good, but it is not a good of their own. However, this response fails, since being selected for some purpose (or according to someone else's designs) does not preclude having a good of one's own. Many living things have been created for use in agriculture, science, and recreation that nevertheless have a good of their own. People selectively bred dogs to be ratters or shepherds, but it seems clear that breaking their legs would be bad for the dogs (in addition to diminishing their utility). The fact that a living thing (or a type of living thing) is selected or created for a purpose by us does not imply that it cannot also have a good of its own.

If an entity is genuinely goal-directed, then things can genuinely be in its interest. What is good and bad for it can be specified in terms of those resources, conditions, and treatments that are conducive to or detrimental to the realization of its goals. The form of selection (i.e., natural or artificial) is not relevant to whether an entity has a good of its own or to what its good is. That there was selection and the basis for it are what matter. It is important not to conflate the explanation for goal-directedness with the subject of goal-directedness or the goal-directedness itself. What is determinative of a nonsentient entity's good (and a psychologically complex entity's biological good) is whether and how they are teleologically organized, not the mechanism by which they came to be that way. The derivativeness of artifactual organisms – that is, that they are the product of human intentions or created to be used by us – does not justify denying that they have a good of their own. The same is true of material composition, the other dimension of artifactualness discussed earlier in this chapter. If the basis for an entity's nonpsychological good is its etiologically grounded teleology, then its material composition (i.e., what it is made of) is not relevant to whether it has a good of its own or the content of its good, except insofar as it relates to etiology.

The focus of the discussion above was the good of nonsentient organisms and the bare biological good of psychologically complex organisms. Artifactualness is not a relevant property with respect to these. Nor is it relevant to the psychological interests of psychologically complex entities. Artifactualness does not preclude an entity from having a psychological good or interests of its own. To claim otherwise would conflate the origins of an entity with the grounds of psychological interests – that is, intentions, desires, emotions, and attitudes. Consider two human beings who have identical capacities, but differ with respect to genesis. One was conceived through natural procreation, the other was created through DNA synthesis and *in vitro* fertilization. The dreams, desires, aspirations, and emotions of the engineered human being are no less his or hers by virtue of his or her artifactual origins. They stand in the same relationship to that human being's conception of his- or herself, his or her life, and his or her well-being as do those of the natural person (as long as they are developed under similar conditions). A human being's origin into the world is not relevant to whether his or her intentions or desires are authentic or autonomous; it is the origins of his or her intentions and desires that matter.

In response, one might argue that if a psychologically complex individual is designed in order to have certain intentions, desires, and emotions, then they are not authentically his or hers and do not constitute or ground interests of his or her own. However, even if this claim is true, it would not follow that artifactualness is relevant to whether an entity has psychological interests or to what those interests are. Instead, it makes a claim about conditions under which some desires or intentions are inauthentic. Such claims are often made regarding acquired intentions and desires as well – for example, that they are formed under oppressive conditions or are manipulated by others. The response is therefore *non sequitur* to the issue of the relationship between artifactualness and psychological interests. As with biological goods, artifactualness is not relevant to whether an entity can have a psychological good of its own or what its good consists in.

As discussed earlier, establishing that artifactual living things (including members of artifactual species) have a good of their own is necessary, but not sufficient, for establishing that artifactualness is not a value relevant property with respect to inherent worth. It must also be shown that artifactualness is not a justified basis for discounting a living thing's good. Is there any reason that we ought to care about natural living things that have a good of their own, but not about artifactual living things that have a good of their own?

Consider, again, an artifactual organism (human or microbial) that is qualitatively identical to a natural organism. If there is a basis for disregarding the good of one but not the other of the organisms, it would have to be a consideration extrinsic to the organisms. However, inherent worth is the type of value that has to do with the features of an entity itself – for example, its complexity, capacities, and interests. It is not based on an entity's relational properties – for example, its utility, the evaluative attitudes of others, or why or how it originated. It is the value that an entity has in and of itself. Because the artifactualness of an artifactual organism, insofar as it concerns its origins, is an extrinsic property, it is not an appropriate basis for disregarding the good of an organism.

The situation is similar with respect to material composition, the other dimension of artifactualness. Material composition is an internal property, but it is not the sort of property that has a bearing on inherent worth. If the internal organization of two living things are similarly complex, such that they have the same capacities, the same range and forms of interests, and the same teleological organization, then their material composition is as irrelevant to their worth as is their surface color. Neither property bears on the capabilities of the entity or how it is able to interact with or experience the world: that is, what its good or interests are, what sort of relationships it is capable of, and how moral agents can impact it. Thus, neither artifactualness in origin nor artifactualness in material composition is a value relevant property with respect to inherent worth.

On a capacities-based account of moral status, two entities with similar capacities have the same inherent worth. Because this is an implication of the type of value, it applies equally to all organisms and entities (nonsentient, sentient nonhuman, and human). Synthetic bacteria have the same inherent worth as naturally occurring bacteria; synthetic plants have the same inherent worth as naturally occurring and evolved plants; sentient artifactual organisms have the same inherent worth as sentient natural biological organism; and rational artifactual entities have the same inherent worth as similarly rational natural biological entities.[21] However, for reasons discussed in Chapter 7, this does not establish what sort of consideration (i.e., moral status) is appropriate to artifactual entities, since an entity's moral status depends not only upon its worth or value, but also on its capacities and relationships, as well as on our form of life – for example, our scale of agency, capabilities, and dependencies and vulnerabilities. For example, it may be that microorganisms, whether natural or artifactual, have inherent worth, but they nevertheless do not merit much if any concern: that is, the responsiveness from moral agents that their worth

---

[21] This conclusion echoes Kant's claim that the final value of human beings is not derived from some "*special property of human nature*" (Kant [1785] 1998, 4:425, original emphasis), but, instead, "applies to all rational beings as such" (Kant [1785] 1998, 4:431).

justifies is insignificant. After all, they have very limited capacities in comparison with other types of living things, and it is not possible to be a human being in the world without relentlessly harming very large numbers of them (e.g., with our immune systems). Moreover, it is not clear how one could even take their good into account, given their size and multitude. We are, in practical terms, not really agents with respect to them. For this reason, even proponents of the view that all living things have inherent worth do not believe that we should be responsive to the good of microorganisms.[22] Similarly, the fact that we must consume living things in order to survive (with some extreme exceptions) implies that respect for plants, whether natural or artifactual, cannot require that we always refrain from killing or using them. It does not follow from this that all killing and using is respectful – some is ecologically insensitive and wanton. But it does illustrate, again, that responsiveness to inherent worth depends upon facts about our form of life.

How we ought to respond to the inherent worth of other organisms, including artifactual ones, also depends heavily upon the facts about them: that is, their capacities. That compassion is appropriate to sentient beings with inherent worth does not imply that it is appropriate to plants, which lack the capacity to suffer. Therefore, that artifactual plants have inherent worth does not imply that they are due the same sorts of consideration as sentient beings or rational beings. It establishes only that they are due the same sort of consideration as comparable natural organisms with inherent worth. That artifactualness is not a value relevant property with respect to inherent worth also does not establish how we ought to treat artifactual organisms in general or any particular artifactual life forms. How an organism is to be treated, even once its moral status is established, depends upon the facts about the organism's form of life.

Again, the claim defended here is just that an entity's artifactualness is not a relevant consideration with respect to inherent worth. If rational natural biological organisms have rights, so too do rational artifactual organisms. If sentient natural biological organisms are due equal consideration of interests, so too are sentient artifactual organisms. If natural biological plants are due respect, so too are artifactual plants. The fact that an organism is a member of an artifactual species or expresses an artifactual form of life is not germane to its inherent worth or to its moral status based upon that worth.

8.4   Subjective value and artifactualness

Subjective value is the type of value that something possesses by virtue of being valued for what it is, rather than for its usefulness. It is distinctive of subjective value that it is created by the (noninstrumental) evaluative attitudes of valuers. Because subjective value is dependent upon the evaluative attitudes of valuers, determining something's subjective value requires identifying the object, form, and strength of people's valuing. Therefore, whether the artifactualness of artifactual living things and species is relevant to their subjective value is largely an empirical issue. It depends upon the actual evaluative attitudes and preferences of valuers and the basis for those attitudes – for example, whether they arise from understanding or false beliefs. There is little data on public knowledge and attitudes regarding artifactual living things in general, let alone data that isolates and measures final valuing of them in particular.[23] Therefore, any comments on the subjective value of artifactual living things are speculative. That said, there are reasons to think that the artifactualness of artifactual living things will be relevant to people's evaluative attitudes toward them.

Individual living things are often valued noninstrumentally – for example, as mascots or for being paradigmatic of a type, as in the case of show dogs. So, too, are particular species – for example, because they have cultural significance or are charismatic. Artifacts are also often valued for what they are. This is the case, for example, with artwork, religious objects, and memorabilia. Thus, neither being an artifact nor being an organism precludes an entity from being valued noninstrumentally. Nor, it would seem, would the combination: that is, being a living artifact. In fact, responses to prior technologies, including prior biotechnologies, suggest that many people will have positive evaluative attitudes toward artifactual living things (and species) precisely because they are artifactual living things (and species). Some people might have a preference for them because the combination ("artifact" and "organism") makes them unusual, novel, and amazing: that is, the "wow" factor often associated with emerging

---

[23] RAE (2009); Hart Research Associates (2010).

technologies.[24] Other people might value them for reasons arising from deep aspects of their worldviews – for example, pertaining to human ingenuity and the role of technological progress in the human form of life[25] – such that artifactual organisms have integral value. This is speculative, but it is consistent with technoprogressive responses to other powerful, emerging technologies, such as nanotechnology and human enhancement technologies.

Many other people are likely to have negative evaluated attitudes regarding artifactual organisms, again, precisely because they are living artifacts. For some, this may be manifest in preferences against them, arising perhaps from their being unusual, unfamiliar, or discomforting: that is, the "yuk" factor.[26] For others, the evaluations might flow from well-integrated aspects of their worldviews – for example, pertaining to the sanctity of life forms and appropriate limits of human power – and be well informed, strong, and stable, and so constitute integral disvaluing. Again, this is speculative. However, it is consistent with bioconservative responses to prior biotechnologies,[27] and is supported by what little empirical research there is on evaluative attitudes toward artifactual living things. For example, the top concern of 25 percent of respondents in one US survey on synthetic biology was that it is "morally wrong to create artificial life."[28]

It seems reasonable to speculate that there will be both positive and negative evaluative attitudes toward artifactual living things, and in each case some that are surface responses and others that express deeper value commitments. However, it is not possible to project the distribution of the responses. Therefore, while it is likely that the artifactualness of artifactual living things will be relevant to their subjective value, in the absence of much more comprehensive and detailed empirical data, it is not clear what the relevance will be.

8.5 Conclusion

The question posed at the start of this chapter was whether artifactualness is a value relevant property for organisms and species. I have argued for the following conclusions: (1) artifactualness is likely to be a value relevant

[24] Kulinowski (2004).   [25] Whitesides (2001); Stock (2002); Naam (2005).
[26] Kulinowski (2004).   [27] Fukuyama (2002); Kass (2003); McKibben (2003).
[28] Hart Research Associates (2010: 14).

property with respect to final subjective value, but it is not possible to determine with any specificity what its relevance will be; (2) artifactualness is a value relevant property with respect to natural value – that is, an entity lacks such value to the extent that it is artifactual – but this is not a reason to oppose creation and use of artifactual organisms and species; and (3) artifactualness is not a value relevant property with respect to inherent worth – that is, an artifactual organism has the same inherent worth as a natural organism with similar capacities.

These conclusions bear on the ethics of creating artifactual organisms and species. For example, if a particular type of artifactual organism has high subjective final value that is a reason in favor of bringing it into existence. However, they have greater significance with respect to how artifactual organisms should be regarded and treated once they exist. That artifactualness is not relevant to inherent worth, a variety of objective final value, implies that artifactual organisms (like natural organisms) are not mere things, and one must ensure that they are considered and treated in accordance with their moral status in both research and postresearch contexts. The practical significance of this depends upon the complexity and capacities of the artifactual organisms. If the only artifactual organisms and species created are comparable with natural microbials, the practical significance will be quite small. However, if robust artificial intelligences are created, the practical implications are much more significant, since the consideration appropriate to natural entities with comparable capacities is much greater. Such entities would be due compassion if they are sentient, or even possess rights if they are rational in the requisite ways.

9   Conclusion

Species are beautiful and wonderful. They are also historical phenomena. They are instantiated at a time and place, they can change over time, and they go extinct. We can influence these events and processes, and increasingly do so as our technological capabilities expand. Therefore, an ethic of species is needed to guide choices regarding preserving, modifying, and creating them. Central to an ethic of species is an account of the value of species and the ethical significance of species boundaries. With respect to these, I have argued:

(1) Some individual species and biodiversity in general have significant instrumental value (present and/or option value), though most individual species do not.

(2) Some individual species and biodiversity in general have considerable preference and integral subjective final value, though most individual species do not.

(3) Species do not have interest-based objective final value (i.e., inherent worth).

(4) Species should not be regarded as possessing natural historical objective final value.

(5) All individual living things, including nonsentient and artifactual ones, have inherent worth, as do some (nonspecies) collectives.

(6) An entity's moral status is underdetermined by its worth, since it depends as well on its capacities and relationships, as well as on features of our form of life.

(7) A capacities-oriented approach is the most justified account of moral status, and on it biological group membership is not among the properties relevant to either inherent worth or moral status.

(8) Species boundaries do not have objective ethical significance.

(9) Species boundaries have subjective ethical significance.

(10) *Homo sapiens* species boundaries do not have any unique or special ethical significance, with respect to either moral status or human modification.

I have also argued that these conclusions have the following implications for the preservation of species under conditions of rapid climatic change, creation of interspecific individuals and novel species, and human enhancement:

(1) The justification for the traditionally predominant species conservation strategies – place-based preservation and ecological restoration – is undermined by global climate change.

(2) The justification for native species prioritization is undermined by global climate change.

(3) Assisted colonization, a prominent emerging species conservation strategy, is only very rarely well justified.

(4) In addition to developing innovative species conservation strategies, global climate change necessitates reconsidering ecosystem management goals.

(5) For less impacted ecological systems, conservation goals must shift away from preservation of particular species and assemblages to promoting adaptive capacity and accommodating ecosystem reconfigurations.

(6) Place-based protections and assisted ecological recovery can play a crucial role in realizing these goals, but expectations for what they can accomplish must be altered and management strategies must be revised – for example, historicity and propping up dwindling populations must be deemphasized.

(7) For highly impacted ecological systems, in which subjective and instrumental values are predominant, intensive species preservation and ecosystem engineering projects can be well justified.

(8) There is nothing objectively intrinsically problematic with creating interspecific individuals (including part-human ones).

(9) The subjective ethical significance of species boundaries needs to be respected in some policy and nonpolicy contexts, but it does not require refraining from researching, using, or benefiting from interspecific individuals.

(10) There is nothing intrinsically problematic with becoming transhuman or posthuman, or with creating such individuals.

(11) There is nothing intrinsically problematic with creating artifactual organisms and *de novo* species.

(12) Evaluation of particular transgenic, artifactual organism, and human enhancement research programs and applications should focus on nonintrinsic considerations – for example, justice, risks, autonomy, flourishing (human and nonhuman), prudence, and compassion – and, to a lesser extent and only in some cases, subjective final values.

(13) Differential assessment of transgenic, artifactual organism, and human modification research programs and applications is, therefore, necessary.

These conclusions, while central to an ethic of species, are not nearly the whole of it. They address the value and normative aspects of species themselves. However, an ethic of species also involves nonspecies-specific ethical considerations to do with risk analysis, distributive and participatory justice, the value of autonomy, and virtues such as compassion and respect, for example. Moreover, evaluation of ecosystem management strategies, transgenic and artifactual life research programs, and methods and modes of human enhancement needs to be done on a differentiated basis. Some may be just, compassionate, and prudent, while others are insensitive, cruel, or unnecessary. The values and general norms defended here ought to inform the particular assessments, but they depend crucially on the details of the concrete cases as well. Ultimately, it is those assessments – which will be made in homes, laboratories, clinics, agencies, legislatures, and the field – that will determine the future of many species, including our own.

References

Agar, N. 2010. *Humanity's End: Why We Should Reject Radical Enhancement.* Cambridge, MA: MIT Press.

Alaska Fish and Wildlife Service 2011. "Final Designation of Polar Bear Critical Habitat." Available at: http://alaska.fws.gov/fisheries/mmm/polarbear/esa.htm#critical_habitat, accessed September 14, 2011.

Almeida-Porada, G., Crapnell, K., Porada, C., Benoit, B., et al. 2005. "In Vivo Haematopoietic Potential of Human Neural Stem Cells," *British Journal of Haematology* 130(2): 276–283.

Alyokhin, A. 2011. "Non-natives: Put Biodiversity at Risk," *Nature* 475: 36.

American Association for the Advancement of Science (AAAS) 2005. "Assembling Life from Scratch." Available at: www.aaas.org/news/releases/2005/1208protocell.shtml, accessed March 9, 2011.

Andam, K. S., Ferraro, P. J., Pfaff, A., Sanchez-Azofeifa, G. A., and Robalino, J. A. 2008. "Measuring the Effectiveness of Protected Area Networks in Reducing Deforestation," *Proceedings of the National Academy of Science* 105: 16089.

Annas, G. 2005. *American Bioethics: Crossing Human Rights and Health Law Boundaries.* Oxford University Press.

Attfield, R. 1987. *A Theory of Value and Obligation.* London: Croom Helm.

1995. *Value, Obligation, and Meta-Ethics.* Amsterdam: Rodopi.

Aubry, K. B., McKelvey, K. S., and Copeland, J. P. 2007. "Distribution and Broadscale Habitat Relations of the Wolverine in the Contiguous United States," *Journal of Wildlife Management* 71: 2147–2158.

Baer, P., Athanasiou, T., Kartha, S., and Kemp-Benedict, E. 2008. *The Right to Develop in a Climate Constrained World: Greenhouse Development Rights Framework.* Berlin: Heinrich-Boll-Stiftung, Christian Aid, EcoEquity and the Stockholm Environment Institute.

Baillie, J. E. M., Bennun, L. A., Brooks, T. M., Butchart, S. H. M., et al. 2004. *A Global Species Assessment.* UK: IUCN. Available at: http://data.iucn.org/dbtw-wpd/html/Red%20List%202004/completed/cover.html, accessed March 13, 2011.

Bálint, M., Domisch, S., Engelhardt, C. H. M., Haase, P., et al. 2011. "Cryptic Biodiversity Loss Linked to Global Climate Change," *Nature Climate Change* 1: 313–318.

Barker, M. J. 2010. "Species Intrinsicalism," *Philosophy of Science* 77(1): 73–91.

Barlow, C. and Martin, P. S. 2004/2005. "Bring *Torreya taxifolia* North – Now," *Wild Earth*. Winter/Spring: 52–56.

Barnosky, A. 2009. *Heatstroke: Nature in an Age of Global Warming*. Washington, DC: Island Press.

Barnosky, A. D., Matzke, N., Tomiya, S., Wogan, G. O. U., et al. 2011. "Has the Earth's Sixth Mass Extinction Already Arrived?" *Nature* 471: 51–57.

Barré, L., Richardson, C., Hirshman, M., Brozinick, J., et al. 2007. "Genetic Model for the Chronic Activation of Skeletal Muscle AMP-Activated Protein Kinas Leads to Glycogen Accumulation," *American Journal of Physiology, Endocrinology and Metabolism* 292: E802–E811.

Basl, J. 2010a. "Restitutive Restoration," *Environmental Ethics* 35(2): 135–147.

2010b. "State Neutrality and the Ethics of Human Enhancement Technologies," *American Journal of Bioethics: Neuroscience* 1(2): 41–48.

Basl, J. and Sandler, R. In press. "Three Puzzles Regarding the Moral Status of Synthetic Organisms," in G. Kaebnick (ed.), *"Artificial Life": Synthetic Biology and the Bounds of Nature*.

Baxter, W. 1974. *People or Penguins: The Case for Optimal Pollution*. New York: Columbia University Press.

Bekoff, M. 2010. "Conservation and Compassion: First Do No Harm," *New Scientist*. Available at: www.newscientist.com/article/mg20727750.100-conservation-and-compassion-first-do-no-harm.html, accessed March 11, 2011.

Benayas, J. M. R., Newton, A. C., Diaz, A., and Bullock, J. M. 2009. "Enhancement of Biodiversity and Ecosystem Services by Ecological Restoration: A Meta-Analysis," *Science* 325: 1121–1124.

Berdik, C. 2008. "Driving Mr. Lynx," *Boston Globe*. Available at: www.boston.com/bostonglobe/ideas/articles/2008/10/12/driving_mr_lynx, accessed March 11, 2009.

Berger, K. M. and Gese, E. M. 2007. "Does Interference Competition with Wolves Limit the Distribution and Abundance of Coyotes?" *Journal of Animal Ecology* 76(6): 1075–1085.

Berkes, F. 2004. "Rethinking Community-Based Conservation," *Conservation Biology* 18: 621–630.

Blackstock, J. J. and Long, J. C. S. 2010. "The Politics of Geoengineering," *Science* 327(5965): 527.

Blain, S., Quéguiner, B., Armand, L., Belvise, S., et al. 2007. "Effect of Natural Iron Fertilization on Carbon Sequestration in the Southern Ocean," *Nature* 446: 1070–1074.

Blakeslee, S. 2008. "Monkey's Thoughts Propel Robot, a Step that May Help Humans," *New York Times*. Available at: www.nytimes.com/2008/01/15/science/15robo.html?_r=1&adxnnl=1&ref=sandrablakeslee&adxnnlx=1300122125-Yl6QVyxaacIHxdytqbK2Fg, accessed March 10, 2011.

Bokinsky, G., Peralta-Yahya, P. P., George, A., Holmes, B. M., et al. 2011. "Synthesis of Three Advanced Biofuels from Ionic Liquid-Pretreated Switchgrass using Engineered *Escherichia coli*," *National Academy of Sciences* 108(50): 19949–19954.

Bosso, C. J. 2005. *Environment Inc. From Grassroots to Beltway*. Lawrence, KS: University Press of Kansas.

Bostrom, N. 2008. "Why I Want to be a Posthuman When I Grow Up," in B. Gordijn and R. Chadwick (eds.), *Medical Enhancement and Posthumanity*. Oxford University Press, pp. 107–137.

Bostrom, N. and Ord, T. 2006. "The Reversal Test: Eliminating Status Quo Bias in Applied Ethics," *Ethics* 116: 656–679.

Bostrom, N. and Sandberg, A. 2009. "Cognitive Enhancement: Methods, Ethics, and Regulatory Challenges," *Science and Engineering Ethics* 15: 311–341.

Bovenkerk, B., Brom, F. W. A., and van den Bergh, B. J. 2002. "Brave New Birds: The Use of 'Animal Integrity' in Animal Ethics," *Hastings Center Report* 32: 16–22.

Boyd, R. and Richerson, P. J. 2005. *Not by Genes Alone: How Culture Transformed Human Evolution*. University of Chicago Press.

Brighouse, H. 1995. "Neutrality, Publicity, and State Funding of the Arts," *Philosophy and Public Affairs* 24(1): 35–63.

2000. *Social Choice and Social Justice*. Oxford University Press.

Brodie, J. F. and Post, E. 2010. "Nonlinear Responses of Wolverine Populations to Declining Winter Snowpack," *Population Ecology* 50: 279–287.

Brodie, J. F., Post, E., and Laurance, W. 2010. "How to Conserve the Tropics as They Warm," *Nature* 468: 634.

Brown, D. E. 1991. *Human Universals*. New York: McGraw-Hill.

Brustle, O., Choudhary, K., Karram, K., Huttner, A., et al. 1998. "Chimeric Brains Generated by Intraventricular Transplantation of Fetal Human Brain Cells into Embryonic Rats," *Nature Biotechnology* 16(11): 1040–1044.

Buchanan, A. 2009a. "Human Nature and Enhancement," *Bioethics* 23(3): 141–150.

2009b. "Moral Status and Human Enhancement," *Philosophy and Public Affairs* 37(4): 346–381.

Burrows, M. T., Schoeman, D. S., Buckley, L. B., Moore, P., et al. 2011. "The Pace of Shifting Climate in Marine and Terrestrial Ecosystems," *Science* 334(6056): 652–655.

Cafaro, P. 2001a. "The Naturalist's Virtues," *Philosophy in the Contemporary World* 8 (2): 85–99.

2001b. "Thoreau, Leopold, and Carson: Toward an Environmental Virtue Ethics," *Environmental Ethics* 23: 1–17.

Cahen, H. 1988. "Against the Moral Considerability of Ecosystems," *Environmental Ethics* 10(3): 196–216.

Callicott, B. 1989. *In Defense of the Land Ethic: Essays in Environmental Philosophy.* Albany, NY: State University of New York Press.

1992. "Rolston on Intrinsic Value: A Deconstruction," *Environmental Ethics* 14: 129–143.

2001. "The Land Ethic," in D. Jamieson (ed.), *A Companion to Environmental Philosophy.* Oxford: Blackwell, pp. 204–217.

2002. "Choosing Appropriate Temporal and Spatial Scales for Ecological Restoration," *Journal of Bioscience* 27: 409–420.

2006. "Explicit and Implicit Values," in J. Scott, D. Goble, and F. Davis (eds.), *The Endangered Species Act at Thirty: Conserving Biodiversity in Human-Dominated Landscapes*, vol. II. Washington, DC: Island Press, pp. 36–48.

Callicott, B., Crowder, L. B., and Mumford, K. 1999. "Current Normative Conceptions in Conservation," *Conservation Biology* 13(1): 22–35.

Callicott, B. and Grove-Fanning, W. 2009. "Should Endangered Species Have Standing? Toward Legal Rights for Listed Species," *Social Philosophy and Policy* 26(2): 317–352.

Camacho, A. E., Doremus, H., McLachlan, J. S., and Minteer, B. A. 2010. "Reassessing Conservation Goals in a Changing Climate," *Issues in Science and Technology* 26: 21–26.

Caney, S. 2008. "Human Rights, Climate Change and Discounting," *Environmental Politics* 17(4): 536–555.

2010. "Climate Change, Human Rights, and Moral Thresholds," in S. Gardner, S. Caney, D. Jamieson, and H. Shue (eds.), *Climate Ethics.* Oxford University Press, pp. 163–177.

Carlson, R. 2010. *Biology is Technology: The Promise, Peril, and New Business of Engineering Life.* Cambridge, MA: Harvard University Press.

2011. "Biodesic 2011 Bioeconomy Update," *Biodesic.* Available at: www.biodesic. com/library/Biodesic_2011_Bioeconomy_Update.pdf, accessed January 10, 2012.

Carmena, J. M., Lebedev, M. A., Crist, R. E., O'Doherty, J. E., et al. 2003. "Learning to Control a Brain–Machine Interface for Reaching and Grasping by Primates," *PLoS Biology* 1(2): 42.

Caro, T. 2007. "The Pleistocene Rewilding Gambit," *Trends in Ecology and Evolution* 22(6): 281–283.

Caro, T., Darwin, J., Forrester, T., Ledoux-Bloom, C., and Wells, C. 2011. "Conservation in the Anthropocene," *Conservation Biology*. DOI: 10.1111/j.1523-1739.2011.01752.x.

Carroll, S. P. 2011. "Conciliation Biology: The Eco-Evolutionary Management of Permanently Invaded Biotic Systems," *Evolutionary Applications* 4: 184–199.

Carson, R. 1956. *The Sense of Wonder*. New York: Harper & Row.

Carter, A. 2004. "Projectivism and the Last Man Argument," *American Philosophical Quarterly* 41(1): 51–62.

Casebeer, W. D. 2003. *Natural Ethical Facts: Evolution, Connectionism, and Moral Cognition*. Cambridge, MA: MIT Press.

Center for International Earth Science Information Network (CIESIN) 2005. "The Last of the Wild, Version Two." Available at: http://sedac.ciesin.columbia.edu/wildareas, accessed March 10, 2011.

Chapron, G. 2005. "Rewilding: Other Projects Help Carnivores Stay Wild," *Nature* 437: 318.

Chapron, G. and Samelius, G. 2008. "Where Species Go, Legal Protections Must Follow," *Science* 322(5904): 1049–1050.

Chen, I-C., Hill, J. K., Ohlemüller, R., Roy, D. B., and Thomas, C. D. 2011. "Rapid Range Shifts of Species Associated with High Levels of Climate Warming," *Science* 333(6045): 1024–1026.

Chu, S. 2009. "Carbon Capture and Sequestration," *Science* 325: 1599.

Climate Interactive 2011. "Possibilities for the Global Climate Deal." Available at: http://climateinteractive.org/scoreboard/scoreboard-science-and-data/graphs-possibilities-for-the-global-climate-deal, accessed January 5, 2012.

Cole, D. N. and Yung, L. 2010. *Beyond Naturalness: Rethinking Park and Wilderness Stewardship in an Era of Rapid Change*. Washington, DC: Island Press.

Conti, B., Sanchez-Alavez, M., Winsky-Sommerer, R., Morale, M. C., et al. 2006. "Transgenic Mice with a Reduced Core Body Temperature Have an Increased Life Span," *Science* 314(5800): 825–828.

Crane, J. 2004. "On the Metaphysics of Species," *Philosophy of Science* 71(2): 156–173.

Crane, J. and Sandler, R. 2011. "Species Concepts and Natural Goodness," in J. K. Campbell, M. O'Rourke, and M. Slater (eds.), *Carving Nature at its Joints: Themes in Contemporary Philosophy*, vol. 8, Cambridge, MA: MIT Press, pp. 289–311.

Crist, E. 2010. "Cloning in Restorative Perspective," in M. Hall (ed.), *Restoration and History: The Search for a Usable Environmental Past*. New York: Rutgers University Press, pp. 284–292.

Cronon, W. 1995. *Uncommon Ground: Rethinking the Human Place in Nature*. New York: W. W. Norton.

Cronquist, A. 1978. "Once Again, What is a Species?" *Biosystematics in Agriculture: Beltsville Symposia in Agricultural Research* 2: 3–20.

Curtis, P. D. and Sullivan, K. L. 2001. "Wildlife Damage Management Fact Sheet Series: White-tailed Deer." Available at: http://wildlifecontrol.info/pubs/Documents/Deer/Deer_factsheet.pdf, accessed November 16, 2011.

Davidson, I. and Simkanin, C. 2008. "Skeptical of Assisted Colonization," *Science* 321(5887): 345–346.

Davis, M. A. 2009. *Invasion Biology*. Oxford University Press.

Davis, M. A., Chew, M. K., Hobbs, R. J., Lugo, A. E., et al. 2011. "Don't Judge Species on Their Origins," *Nature* 474: 153–154.

de Vries, R. 2006. "Genetic Engineering and the Integrity of Animals," *Journal of Agriculture and Environmental Ethics* 19(5): 469–493.

de Waal, F. 2006. *Primates and Philosophers: How Morality Evolved*. Princeton University Press.

Department of the Environment, Food, and Rural Affairs (DEFRA) 2004. "Margaret Beckett [Secretary of State for the Environment, Food, and Rural Affairs] Outlines Precautionary Approach to GM Crops." Available at: www.defra.gov.uk/news/2004/040309a.htm, accessed March 10, 2011.

Derocher, A. E., Lunn, N. J., and Stirling, I. 2004. "Polar Bears in a Warming Climate," *Integrative and Comparative Biology* 44(2): 163–176.

Dinerstein, E. and Irvin, W. R. 2005. "Rewilding: No Need for Exotics as Natives Return," *Nature* 437(7058): 476.

Dondorp, A. M., Nosten, F., Yi, P., Das, D., et al. 2009. "Artemisinin Resistance in *Plasmodium falciparum* Malaria," *New England Journal of Medicine* 361: 455–467.

Donlan, J., Berger, J., Bock, C., Bock, J., et al. 2006. "Pleistocene Rewilding: An Optimistic Agenda for Twenty-First Century Conservation," *The American Naturalist* 168: 660–681.

Donlan, J., Greene, H. W., Berger, J., Bock, C. E., et al. 2005. "Re-Wilding North America," *Nature* 436: 913–914.

Doris, J. M. 2002. *Lack of Character: Personality and Moral Behavior*. Cambridge University Press.

Dowie, M. 2009. *Conservation Refugees: The Hundred-Year Conflict between Global Conservation and Native Peoples*. Cambridge, MA: MIT Press.

Dumas, P., Hourcade, J.C., and Fabert, B.P. 2010. "Do We Need a Zero Pure Time Preference or the Risk of Climate Catastrophes to Justify a 2°C Global Warming Target?" Policy Research Working Paper, World Bank. Available at: www.wds.worldbank.org/servlet/WDSContentServer/WDSP/IB/2010/07/30/000158349_20100730104858/Rendered/PDF/WPS5392.pdf, accessed March 7, 2011.

Dymond, J.S., Richardson, S.M., Coombes, C.E., Babatz, T., et al. 2011. "Synthetic Chromosome Arms Function in Yeast and Generate Phenotypic Diversity by Design," *Nature* 477: 471–476.

Ehrenfeld, D. 1988. "Why Put a Value on Biodiversity?" in E.O. Wilson (ed.), *Biodiversity*. Washington, DC: National Academy Press, pp. 212–216.

  2006. "Transgenics and Vertebrate Cloning as Tools for Species Conservation," *Conservation Biology* 20(3): 723–732.

Ehrlich, P. 2000. *Human Natures*. Washington, DC: Island Press.

Ehrlich, P. and Ehrlich, A. 1981. *Extinction: The Causes and Consequences of the Disappearance of Species*. New York: Ballantine Books.

Elliot, R. 1982. "Faking Nature," *Inquiry* 25(1): 81–93.

  1992. "Intrinsic Value, Environmental Obligation, and Naturalness," *The Monist* 75: 138–160.

Ellis, E.C. and Ramankutty, N. 2008. "Putting People in the Map: Anthropogenic Biomes of the World," *Frontiers in Ecology and the Environment* 6(8): 439–447.

Emerson, R.W. 2000. "Art," in B. Atkinson (ed.), *The Essential Writings of Ralph Waldo Emerson*. New York: Modern Library, pp. 274–283.

Erb, L.P., Ray, C., and Guralnick, R. 2011. "On the Generality of a Climate-Mediated Shift in the Distribution of the American Pika (*Ochotona princeps*)," *Ecology* 92: 1730–1735.

Ereshefsky, M. 1998. "Species Pluralism and Anti-Realism," *Philosophy of Science* 65(1): 103–120.

Evans, J.C. 2005. *With Respect for Nature: Living as Part of the Natural World*. Albany, NY: State University of New York Press.

Fecht, S. 2011a. "UK Geoengineering Tests Delayed until Spring," *Scientific American*. Available at: http://blogs.scientificamerican.com/observations/2011/10/07/geoengineering-tests delayed-until-spring, accessed December 19, 2011.

  2011b. "UK Researchers to Test 'Artificial Volcano' for Geoengineering the Climate," *Scientific American*. Available at: www.scientificamerican.com/article.cfm?id=uk-researchers-to-test-artificial-volcano-for-geoengineering-the-climate, accessed December 19, 2011.

Feinberg, J. 1974. "The Rights of Animals and Future Generations," in W. Blackstone (ed.), *Philosophy and Environmental Crisis*. Athens, GA: University of Georgia Press, pp. 43–68.

Feit, C. 2002. "Genetically Modified Food and Jewish Law (Halakhah)," in M. Ruse and D. Castle (eds.), *Genetically Modified Foods*. Amherst, NY: Prometheus, pp. 123–129.

Fenton, E. 2008. "Genetic Enhancement – A Threat to Human Rights?" *Bioethics* 22(1): 1–7.

Fish and Wildlife Service (FWS) 2009. "Frequently Asked Questions About Invasive Species." Available at: www.fws.gov/invasives/faq.html#q7, accessed December 19, 2011.

   2010a. "Endangered and Threatened Wildlife and Plants; 12-Month Finding on a Petition to List the American Pika as Threatened or Endangered," *Federal Register*. Docket No. FWS-R6-ES-2009–0021. Available at: www.fws.gov/mountain-prairie/species/mammals/americanpika/02052010FRTemp.pdf, accessed January 26, 2012.

   2010b. "Endangered and Threatened Wildlife and Plants; 12-Month Finding on a Petition to List the North American Wolverine as Endangered or Threatened," *Federal Register*. Docket No. FWS-R6-ES-2008-0029. Available at: www.gpo.gov/fdsys/pkg/FR-2010–12–14/pdf/2010–30573.pdf, accessed January 12, 2012.

   2011. "Endangered and Threatened Wildlife and Plants; 12-Month Finding on a Petition to List *Pinus albicaulis* as Endangered or Threatened with Critical Habitat," *Federal Register*. Docket No. FWS-R6-ES-2010-0047. Available at: www.federalregister.gov/articles/2010/12/14/2010-30573/endangered-and-threatened-wildlife-and-plants-12-month-finding-on-a-petition-to-list-the-north, accessed April 19, 2012.

Fisher, M. A., McKinley, K. L., Bradley, L. H., Viola, S. R., and Hecht, M. H. 2011. "*De Novo* Designed Proteins from a Library of Artificial Sequences Function in *Escherichia Coli* and Enable Cell Growth," *PLoS ONE* 6(1): e15364.

Foden, W., Mace, G., Vié, J-C., Angulo, A., et al. 2008. "Species Susceptibility to Climate Change Impacts," in J-C. Vié, C. Hilton-Taylor, and S. N. Stuart (eds.), *The 2008 Review of the IUCN Red List of Threatened Species*. Gland, Switzerland: IUCN, pp. 77–88. Available at: http://training.fws.gov/EC/resources/shc/species_susceptibility_to_climate_change_impacts.pdf, accessed April 19, 2012.

Fox, D. 2007. "When Worlds Collide," *Conservation Magazine*. Available at: www.conservationmagazine.org/articles/v8n1/when-worlds-collide, accessed March 10, 2011.

Fukuyama, F. 2002. *Our Posthuman Future: Consequences of the Biotechnology Revolution*. New York: Picador.

Garcia, T. and Sandler, R. 2009. "Enhancing Justice?" *Nanoethics* 2(3): 277–287.

Gardiner, S. 2006. "A Perfect Moral Storm: Climate Change, Intergenerational Ethics and the Problem of Corruption," *Environmental Values* 15: 397–413.

2010. "Ethics and Climate Change: An Introduction," *Wires Climate Change* 1(1): 54–66.

Gaston, K. J., Jackson, S. E., Cantu-Salazar, L., and Cruz-Pinon, G. 2008. "The Ecological Performance of Protected Areas," *Annual Reviews of Ecology, Evolution, and Systematics* 39: 93–113.

Ghiselin, M. 1997. *Metaphysics and the Origin of Species*. Albany, NY: State University of New York Press.

Gibson, D., Benders, G., Andrews-Pfannkoch, C., Denisova, E., et al. 2008. "Complete Chemical Synthesis, Assembly, and Cloning of a *Mycoplasma genitalium* Genome," *Science* 319(5867): 1215–1220.

Gibson, D., Glass, J. I., Lartigue, C., Noskov, V. N., et al. 2010. "Creation of a Bacterial Cell Controlled by a Chemically Synthesized Genome," *Science* 329: 52–56.

Gillett, N. P., Arora, V. K., Zickfeld K., Marshall, S. J., and Merryfield, W. J. 2011. "Ongoing Climate Change Following a Complete Cessation of Carbon Dioxide," *Nature Geoscience* 4: 83–87.

Gleditsch, J. M. and Carlo, T. A. 2010. "Fruit Quantity of Invasive Shrubs Predicts the Abundance of Common Native Avian Frugivores in Central Pennsylvania," *Diversity and Distributions* 17(2): 244–253.

Goeddel, D. V., Kleid, D. G., Bolivar, F., Heyneker, H. L., et al. 1979. "Expression in *Escherichia coli* of Chemically Synthesized Genes for Human Insulin," *Proceedings of the National Academy of Sciences* 76(1): 106–110.

Goldstein, R. S., Drukker, M., Reubinoff, B. E., and Benvenisty, N. 2002. "Integration and Differentiation of Human Embryonic Stem Cells Transplanted to the Chick Embryo," *Developmental Dynamics* 225(1): 80–86.

Grant, P. R. 1993. "Hybridization of Darwin's Finches on Isla Daphne Major, Galapagos," *Philosophical Transactions: Biological Sciences* 340(1291): 127–139.

Gravel Ortiz, S. 2004. "Beyond Welfare: Animal Integrity, Animal Dignity, and Genetic Engineering," *Ethics and the Environment* 9(1): 94–120.

Greater Yellowstone Coordinating Committee, Whitebark Pine Subcommittee 2011. *Whitebark Pine Strategy*. Available at: http://fedgycc.org/documents/WBPStrategyFINAL5.31.11.pdf, accessed December 19, 2011.

Greely, H., Sahakian, B., Harris, J., Kessler, R.C., et al. 2008. "Towards Responsible Use of Cognitive-Enhancing Drugs by the Healthy," *Nature* 456: 702–705.

Green, R.E., Krause, J., Briggs, A.W., Maricic, T., et al. 2010. "A Draft Sequence of Neanderthal Genome," *Science* 328(5979): 710–722.

Greenpeace 2002. "Genetically Engineered 'Golden Rice' is Fools Gold," in M. Ruse and D. Castle (eds.), *Genetically Modified Foods: Debating Biotechnology*. Amherst, NY: Prometheus, pp. 52–54.

Halpern, B.S., Walbridge, S., Selkoe, K.A., Kappel, C.V., et al. 2008. "A Global Map of Human Impact on Marine Ecosystems," *Science* 319(5865): 948–952.

Hannah, L. 2011. "Climate Change, Connectivity, and Conservation Success," *Conservation Biology* 25(6): 1139–1142.

Hansen, J. 2007. "How Can We Avert Dangerous Climate Change?" *Cornell University Earth Institute*. Available at: http://arxiv.org/abs/0706.3720v1, accessed March 7, 2011.

Hansen, J., Ruedy, R., Sato, M., and Lo, K. 2010. "Global Surface Temperature Change," *Reviews of Geophysics* 48: 1–29.

Hansen, J. and Sato, M. 2007. "Global Warming: East–West Connections," NASA Goddard Institute for Space and Columbia University. Available at: www.columbia.edu/~jeh1/2007/EastWest_20070925.pdf, accessed March 11, 2011.

Hansen, J., Sato, M., Kharecha, P., Beerling, D., et al. 2008. "Target Atmospheric CO_2: Where Should Humanity Aim?" *Open Atmospheric Science Journal* 2: 217–231.

Harris, J., Hobbs, R., Higgs, E., and Aronson, J. 2006. "Ecological Restoration and Global Climate Change," *Restoration Ecology* 14(2): 170–176.

Hart Research Associates 2010. "Awareness and Impressions of Synthetic Biology." Washington, DC: Woodrow Wilson Center for Scholars, Synthetic Biology Project. Available at: www.synbioproject.org/process/assets/files/6456/hart_revised_.pdf?, accessed March 11, 2011.

Hegerl, G.C. and Solomon, S. 2009. "Risks of Climate Engineering," *Science* 325 (5943): 955–956.

Hellmann, J.J. and Pfrende, M.E. 2011. "Future Human Intervention in Ecosystems and the Critical Role for Evolutionary Biology," *Conservation Biology* 25(6): 1143–1147.

Hershner, C. and Havens, K.J. 2008. "Managing Invasive Aquatic Plants in a Changing System: Strategic Consideration of Ecosystem Services," *Conservation Biology* 22(3): 544–550.

Higashide, W., Li, Y., Yang, Y., and Liao, J. C. 2011. "Metabolic Engineering of *Clostridium cellulolyticum* for Isobutanol Production from Cellulose," *Applications of Environmental Microbiology* 77(8): 2727–2733.

Higgs, E. 2003. *Nature by Design: People, Natural Process, and Ecological Restoration.* Cambridge, MA: MIT Press.

Hobbs, R. J., Arico, S., Aronson, J., Baron, J. S., et al. 2006. "Novel Ecosystems: Theoretical and Management Aspects of the New Ecological World Order," *Global Ecology and Biogeography* 15: 1–7.

Hobbs, R. J., Higgs, E., and Harris, J. A. 2009. "Novel Ecosystems: Implications for Conservation and Restoration," *Trends in Ecology and Evolution* 24(11): 599–605.

Hochberg, L. R., Serruya, M. D., Friehs, G. M., Mukand, J. A., et al. 2006. "Neuronal Ensemble Control of Prosthetic Devices by a Human with Tetraplegia," *Nature* 442: 164–171.

Hoegh-Guldberg, O., Hughes, L., McIntyre, S., Lindenmayer, D. B., et al. 2008. "Assisted Colonization and Rapid Climate Change," *Science* 321(5887): 345–346.

Hoerner, J. A. 2006. "Toward a Just Climate Policy," *Race, Poverty and the Environment* 13(1): 11–14. Available at: www.urbanhabitat.org/files/ Andrew.H.Just.Climate.Policy.pdf, accessed March 16, 2011.

Hoffman, M., Hilton-Taylor, C., Angulo, A., Bohm, M., et al. 2010. "The Impact of Conservation on the Status of the World's Vertebrates," *Science* 330(6010): 1503–1509.

Holt, W. V., Pickard, A. R., and Prather, R. S. 2004. "Wildlife Conservation and Reproductive Cloning," *Reproduction* 127: 317–324.

Hooker, B. 2000. *Ideal Code, Real World: A Rule-Consequentialist Theory of Morality.* Oxford University Press.

Hull, D. 1976. "Are Species Really Individuals?" *Systematic Zoology* 25: 174–191. 1978. "A Matter of Individuality," *Philosophy of Science* 45: 335–360.

Hulme, P. E., Pyšek, P., and Duncan, R. P. 2011. "Don't be Fooled by a Name: A Reply to Thompson and Davis," *Trends in Ecology and Evolution* 26(7): 318.

Human Fertilisation and Embryology Authority 2007. *Hybrids and Chimeras: A Report on the Findings of the Consultation.* Available at: www.hfea.gov.uk/docs/ Hybrids_Report.pdf, accessed March 7, 2011.

Hunter, M. L. 1990. *Wildlife, Forests, and Forestry.* Englewood Cliffs, NJ: Prentice Hall.

1991. "Coping with Ignorance: The Coarse Filter Strategy for Maintaining Biodiversity," in K. A. Kohm (ed.), *Balancing on the Edge of Extinction.* Washington, DC: Island Press, pp. 266–281.

2001. *Fundamentals of Conservation Biology*. Oxford: Blackwell.

2007. "Climate Change and Moving Species: Furthering the Debate on Assisted Colonization," *Conservation Biology* 21(5): 1356–1358.

Hunter, M. L., Jacobson Jr., G. L., and Webb III, T. 1988. "Paleoecology and the Coarse-Filter Approach to Maintaining Biological Diversity," *Conservation Biology* 2(4): 375–385.

Hutchison III, C., Peterson, S., Gill, S., Cline, R., et al. 1999. "Global Transposon Mutagenesis and a Minimal Mycoplasma Genome," *Science* 286(5447): 2165–2169.

Intergovernmental Panel on Climate Change (IPCC) 2007a. *Climate Change 2007: Synthesis Report*. Geneva: IPCC.

2007b. *Climate Change 2007: The Physical Science Basis*. Geneva: IPCC.

International Genetically Engineered Machines Competition (iGem) 2010. "Main Page." Available at: http://2010.igem.org/About, accessed March 10, 2011.

International Union for the Conservation of Nature (IUCN) 2011. "IUCN Biodiversity." Available at: www.iucn.org/what/tpas/biodiversity, accessed January 14, 2011.

Jackson, S. T. and Hobbs, R. J. 2009. "Ecological Restoration in Light of Ecological History," *Science* 325(5940): 567–569.

Jacobs, G. H., Williams, G. A., Cahill, H., and Nathans, J. 2007. "Emergence of Novel Color Vision in Mice Engineered to Express a Human Cone Photopigment," *Science* 315(5819): 1723–1725.

James, C. 2010. *Global Status of Commercialized Biotech/GM Crops*. ISAAA Brief No. 42. Ithaca, NY: International Service for the Acquisition of Agri-biotech Applications.

Jamieson, D. 2005. "Adaptation, Mitigation, and Justice," in W. Sinnott-Armstrong and R. B. Howarth (eds.), *Perspectives on Climate Change: Science, Economics, Politics, and Ethics*. Amsterdam: Elsevier, pp. 217–248.

Johnson, L. 1991. *A Morally Deep World*. Cambridge University Press.

2003. "Future Generations and Contemporary Ethics," *Environmental Values* 12: 471–487.

Jotterand, F. 2010. "Human Dignity and Transhumanism: Do Anthro-technological Devices Have Moral Status?" *American Journal of Bioethics* 10 (7): 45–52.

Kagan, S. 1998. "Rethinking Intrinsic Value," *Journal of Ethics* 2: 227–297.

Kant, I. [1785] 1998. *Groundwork for the Metaphysic of Morals*, trans. M. Gregor. Cambridge University Press.

1997. "Duties to Animals and Spirits," in *Lectures on Ethics*, P. Heath and J. B. Schneedwind (eds.), trans. P. Heath. Cambridge University Press, pp. 212–213.

Karpowicz, P., Cohen, C. B., and van der Kooy, D. 2005. "Developing Human-Nonhuman Chimeras in Human Stem Cell Research: Ethical Issues and Boundaries," *Kennedy Institute of Ethics Journal* 15(2): 107–134.

Kass, L. R. 1997. "The Wisdom of Repugnance," *The New Republic* 216(22): 17–26.

2001. "Preventing a Brave New World: Why We should Ban Human Cloning Now," *The New Republic* 224: 30–39.

2002. *Life, Liberty, and the Defense of Dignity: The Challenge for Bioethics*. San Francisco, CA: Encounter Books.

2003. "Ageless Bodies, Happy Souls," *The New Atlantis* 1: 9–28.

Katz, E. 1992. "The Call of the Wild," *Environmental Ethics* 14: 265–273.

2000. "The Big Lie," in W. Throop (ed.), *Environmental Restoration*. Amherst, NY: Humanity, pp. 83–93.

Kawall, J. 2008. "On Behalf of Biocentric Individualism: A Response to Victoria Davion," *Environmental Ethics* 30(1): 69–88.

Keesing, F., Belden, L. K., Daszak, P., Dobson, A., et al. 2010. "Impacts of Biodiversity on the Emergence and Transmission of Infectious Diseases," *Nature* 468: 647–652.

Keim, B. 2008. "Next-Generation Longevity Drug Works Mouse Wonders," *Wired Science*. Available at: www.wired.com/wiredscience/2008/11/next-generation, accessed March 7, 2011.

Keith, D. W. 2001. "Geoengineering," *Nature* 409: 420.

Kelly, B. P., Whiteley, A., and Tallmon, D. 2010. "The Arctic Melting Pot," *Nature* 468: 891.

Kempton, W., Boster, J. S., and Hartley, J. A. 1995. *Environmental Values in American Culture*. Cambridge, MA: MIT Press.

Kitcher, P. 1984. "Species," *Philosophy of Science* 51(2): 308–333.

1987. "Ghostly Whispers: Mayr, Ghiselin, and the 'Philosophers' on the Ontological Status of Species," *Biology and Philosophy* 2: 184–192.

Korsgaard, C. 1983. "Two Distinctions in Goodness," *The Philosophical Review* 92 (2): 169–195.

Kulinowski, K. 2004. "Nanotechnology: From 'Wow' to 'Yuk,'" *Bulletin of Science, Technology and Society* 24: 13–20.

Kurz, W. A., Dymond, C. C., Stinson, G., Rampley, G. J., et al. 2008. "Mountain Pine Beetle and Forest Carbon Feedback to Climate Change," *Nature* 452: 987–990.

Kurzweil, R. 2005. *The Singularity is Near: When Humans Transcend Biology*. New York: Viking.

Lammerts van Bueren, E. T. and Struik, P. C. 2005. "Integrity and Rights of Plants: Ethical Notions in Organic Plant Breeding and Propagation," *Journal of Agricultural and Environmental Ethics* 18: 479–493.

Lammerts van Bueren, E. T., Struik, P. C., Tiemens-Hulscher, M., and Jacobsen, E. 2003. "The Concepts of Intrinsic Value and Integrity of Plants in Organic Plant Breeding and Propagation," *Crop Science* 43: 1922–1929.

Lancet, The 2010. "Another Step towards Preventing Artemisinin Resistance," *The Lancet* 375(9719): 956.

Lanza, R. P., Cibelli, J. B., Diaz, F., Moraes, C. T., et al. 2000. "Cloning of an Endangered Species (*Bos gaurus*) Using Interspecies Nuclear Transfer," *Cloning* 2(2): 79–90.

Lartigue, C., Vashee, S., Algire, M., Chuang, R., et al. 2009. "Creating Bacterial Strains from Genomes that have been Cloned and Engineered in Yeast," *Science* 325(5948): 1693–1696.

Lawler, J. J. and Olden, J. D. 2011. "Reframing the Debate over Assisted Colonization," *Frontiers in Ecology and the Environment* 9: 569–574.

Lee, P. and George, R. P. 2008. "The Nature and Basis of Human Dignity," in *Human Dignity and Bioethics: Essays Commissioned by the President's Council on Bioethics*. Washington, DC: The President's Council on Bioethics, pp. 409–434.

Lee, S. J., Reed, L. A., Davies, M. V., Girgenrath, S., et al. 2005. "Regulation of Muscle Growth by Multiple Ligands Signaling Through Activin Type II Receptors," *Proceedings of the National Academy of Sciences* 102(50): 18117–18122.

Leopold, A. [1949] 1968. *A Sand County Almanac*. Oxford University Press.

Lerdau, M. and Wickham, J. D. 2011. "Non-Natives: Four Risk Factors," *Nature* 475: 36–37.

Lerman, S. B. and Warren, P. S. 2011. "The Conservation Value of Residential Yards: Linking Birds and People," *Ecological Applications* 21: 1327–1339.

Liao, M. 2010. "The Basis of Human Moral Status," *Journal of Moral Philosophy* 7: 159–179.

Light, A. 2000. "Restoration or Domination?: A Reply to Katz," in W. Throop (ed.), *Environmental Restoration: Ethics, Theory, and Practice*. Amherst, NY: Humanity, pp. 95–112.

Lim, M. M., Wang, Z., Olazabal, D. E., Ren, X., et al. 2004. "Enhanced Partner Preference in a Promiscuous Species by Manipulating the Expression of a Single Gene," *Nature* 429: 754–757.

Logan, J. A. 2007. "Climate Change Induced Invasions by Native and Exotic Pests," in K. W. Gottschalk (ed.), *Proceedings of the 17th US Department of Agriculture Interagency Research Forum on Gypsy Moth and Other Invasive Species 2006*. Newtown Square, PA: US Department of Agriculture, Forest Service, Northern Research Station, pp. 8–13.

Logan, J., Macfarlane, W., and Willcox, L. 2010. "Whitebark Pine Vulnerability to Climate-driven Mountain Pine Beetle Disturbance in the Greater Yellowstone," *Ecological Applications* 20(4): 895–902.

Logan, J. A. and Powell, J. A. 2001. "Ghost Forests, Global Warming, and the Mountain Pine Beetle," *American Entomology* 47: 160–173.

Logan, J. A., Régenère, J., Gray, D. R., and Munson, A. S. 2007. "Risk Assessment in the Face of a Changing Environment: Gypsy Moth and Climate Change in Utah," *Ecological Applications* 17(1): 101–117.

Lomborg, B. 2001. *The Skeptical Environmentalist: Measuring the Real State of the World*. Cambridge University Press.

2007. *Cool It: The Skeptical Environmentalists Guide to Global Warming*. New York: Knopf.

Long Island Sound Study 2011. "Sentinel Monitoring for Climate Change in the Long Island Sound Ecosystem." Available at: http://longislandsoundstudy. net/research-monitoring/sentinel-monitoring, accessed December 19, 2011.

Longo, V. D. and Finch, C. E. 2003. "Evolutionary Medicine: From Dwarf Model Systems to Healthy Centenarians?" *Science* 299(5611): 1342–1346.

Lövei, G. L., Lewinsohn, T. M., and Biological Invasions in Megadiverse Regions Network 2011. "Megadiverse Developing Countries Face Huge Risks from Invasives," *Trends in Ecology and Evolution* 27(1): 2–3.

Macdonald, D., Baker, S., Gelling, M., and Harrington, L. 2010. "Animal Welfare in Conservation: Working Towards a Common Goal," Wildlife Conservation Research Unit. Available at: http://compassionateconservation.org/ Presentation%20-%20David%20Macdonald.pdf, accessed March 10, 2011.

Macfarlane, W., Logan, J., and Kern, W. 2010. *Using the Landscape Assessment System (LAS) to Assess Mountain Pine Beetle-caused Mortality of Whitebark Pine, Greater Yellowstone Ecosystem, 2009*. Jackson, WY: Greater Yellowstone Coordinating Committee, Whitebark Pine Subcommittee.

Maclaurin, J. and Sterelny, K. 2008. *What is Biodiversity?* University of Chicago Press.

Maestra, F. T., Quero, J. L., Gotelli, N. J., Escudero, A., et al. 2012. "Plant Species Richness and Ecosystem Multifunctionality in Global Drylands," *Science* 335 (6065): 214–218.

Magurran, A. E. and Dornelas, M. 2010. "Biological Diversity in a Changing World," *Philosophical Transactions of the Royal Society B* 365(1558): 3593–3597.

Maher, B. 2008. "Poll Results: Look Who's Doping," *Nature* 452: 674–675.

Maier, D. 2012. *What's so Good about Biodiversity?* Amsterdam: Springer.

Mansy, S., Schrum, P., Krishnamurthy, M., Tobé, S., et al. 2008. "Template-Directed Synthesis of a Genetic Polymer in a Model Protocell," *Nature* 454: 122–125.

Marris, E. 2008. "Moving on Assisted Migration," *Nature Reports Climate Change*. Available at: www.nature.com/climate/2008/0809/full/climate.2008.86.html, accessed March 10, 2011.

  2009. "Forestry: Planting the Forest of the Future," *Nature* 459: 906–908.

  2010. "Transgenic Fish go Large," *Nature* 467: 259.

Mayr, E. and Ashlock, P. D. 1991. *Principles of Systematic Zoology*, 2nd edn. New York: McGraw-Hill.

McCabe, S. E., Knight, J. R., Teter, C. J., and Wechsler, H. 2005. "Non-Medical Use of Prescription Stimulants Among US College Students: Prevalence and Correlates From a National Survey," *Addiction* 100(1): 96–106.

McClanahan, T. R., Cinner, J. E., Maina, J., Graham, N. A. J., et al. 2008. "Conservation Action in a Changing Climate," *Conservation Letters* 1: 53–59.

McConnell, T. 2010. "Genetic Enhancement, Human Nature, and Rights," *Journal of Medicine and Philosophy* 35: 415–428.

McDonald-Madden, E., Runge, M. C., Possingham, H. P., and Martin, T. G. 2011. "Optimal Timing for Managed Relocation of Species Faced with Climate Change," *Nature Climate Change* 1: 261–265.

McGrath, B. 2007. "Muscle Memory: The Next Generation of Bionic Prostheses," *The New Yorker*: 40–45.

McKibben, B. 2000. *The End of Nature*. New York: Random House.

  2003. *Enough: Staying Human in an Engineered Age*. New York: Henry Holt.

  2010. *Eaarth: Making a Life on a Tough New Planet*. New York: Henry Holt.

McLachlan, J. S., Hellmann, J. J., and Schwartz, M. W. 2007. "A Framework for Debate of Assisted Migration in an Era of Climate Change," *Conservation Biology* 21: 297–302.

McLane, S. and Aitken, S. In press. "Whitebark Pine (*Pinus albicaulis*) Assisted Migration Potential: Testing Establishment North of the Species Range," *Ecological Applications*. DOI: http://dx.doi.org/10.1890/11-0329.1.

McMahan, J. 2005. "Our Fellow Creatures," *Journal of Ethics* 9: 353–380.

Meinecke-Tillmann, S. and Meinecke, B. 1984. "Experimental Chimaeras – Removal of Reproductive Barrier Between Sheep and Goat," *Nature* 307: 637–638.

Mill, J. S. 1904. "On Nature," in *Nature, The Utility of Religion and Theism*. London: Watts & Co., pp. 7–33.

2001. *Utilitarianism*. Indianapolis, IN: Hackett.

Millennium Ecosystem Assessment 2005. *Ecosystem and Human Well-Being: Synthesis*. Washington, DC: Island Press.

Minteer, B. and Collins, J. 2010. "Move It or Lose It? The Ecological Ethics of Relocating Species under Climate Change," *Ecological Applications* 20: 1801–1804.

Molnar, P. K., Derocher, A. E., Klanjscek, T., and Lewis, M. A. 2011. "Predicting Climate Change Impacts on Polar Bear Litter Size," *Nature Communications* 8 (2): 186.

Morelle, R. 2010. "Iberian Lynx: Radical Moves for World's Rarest Cat," *BBC*. Available at: www.bbc.co.uk/news/science-environment-11586279, accessed October 7, 2010.

Mueller, J. and Hellmann, M. 2008. "An Assessment of Invasion Risk from Assisted Migration," *Conservation Biology* 22: 562–567.

Myskja, B. K. 2006. "The Moral Difference Between Intragenic and Transgenic Modification of Plants," *Journal of Agricultural and Environmental Ethics* 19: 225–238.

Naam, R. 2005. *More than Human: Embracing the Promise of Biological Enhancement*. New York: Broadway Books.

Nagel, R. L. 1998. "A Knockout of a Transgenic Mouse-Animal Model of Sickle Cell Anemia," *New England Journal of Medicine* 339: 194–195.

Nathanson, S. 1993. *Patriotism, Morality and Peace*. Lanham, MD: Rowman & Littlefield.

National Academy of Sciences (NAS) 1987. *Introduction of Recombinant DNA-Engineered Organisms into the Environment: Key Issues*. Washington, DC: National Academy of Science.

National Institute of Mental Health (NIMH) 2008. "Mice Expressing Human Gene Bred to Help Unravel Mental Disorders." Available at: www.nimh.nih.gov/science-news/2008/mice-expressing-human-genes-bred-to-help-unravel-mental-disorders.shtml, accessed March 7, 2011.

National Oceanic and Atmospheric Administration (NOAA) 2011. "NOAA's 1981–2010 Climate Normals." Available at: www.ncdc.noaa.gov/oa/climate/normals/usnormals.html, accessed January 10, 2012.

National Oceanic and Atmospheric Administration (NOAA) Coral Reef Protection Program 2011. "Climate Change." Available at: http://coralreef.noaa.gov/threats/climate, accessed December 19, 2011.

National Park Service (NPS) 2010. *National Park Service Climate Change Response Strategy*. Fort Collins, CO: National Park Service Climate Change Response Program.

National Snow and Ice Data Center 2011. "Arctic Sea Ice at Minimum Extent." Available at: http://nsidc.org/arcticseaicenews, accessed September 14, 2011.

Naylor, R. L., Goldburg, R. J., Primavera, J. H., Kautsky, N., et al. 2000. "Effect of Aquaculture on World Fish Supplies," *Nature* 405: 1017–1024.

New, M. 2011. "Four Degrees and Beyond: The Potential for a Global Temperature Increase of Four Degrees and its Implications," *Philosophical Transactions of the Royal Society A* 369: 4–5.

New Zealand Ministry for the Environment 2004. *Genetic Modification: The New Zealand Approach*. Wellington: New Zealand Ministry for the Environment.

Norcross, A. 2004. "Puppies, Pigs, and People: Eating Meat and Marginal Cases," *Philosophical Perspectives* 8: 230–245.

Nordhaus, W. 2007a. "Critical Assumptions in the *Stern Review* on Climate Change," *Science* 317: 201–202.

2007b. "The *Stern Review* on the Economics of Climate Change," *Journal of Economic Literature* 45: 686–702.

Norton, B. 1990. *Why Preserve Natural Value?* Princeton University Press.

1992. "Epistemology and Environmental Values," *Monist* 75(2): 208–226.

2005. *Sustainability: A Philosophy of Adaptive Ecosystem Management*. University of Chicago Press.

Novak, D. 2000. *Covenantal Right: A Study in Jewish Political Theory*. Princeton University Press.

Nussbaum, M. C. 2000. *Women and Human Development: The Capabilities Approach*. New York: Cambridge University Press.

O'Neill, J. 1992. "The Varieties of Intrinsic Value," *The Monist* 75(2): 119–137.

1993. *Ecology, Policy, and Politics: Human Well-Being and the Natural World*. London: Routledge.

Office of Technology Assessment (OTA) 1987. *New Developments in Biotechnology – Background Paper: Public Perceptions of Biotechnology*. OTA-BP-BA-45. Washington, DC: US Government Printing Office.

Okasha, S. 2007. *Evolution and the Levels of Selection*. Oxford University Press.

Okutsu, T., Shikina, S., Kanno, M., Takeuchi, Y., and Yoshizaki, G. 2007. "Production of Trout Offspring from Triploid Salmon Parents," *Science* 317 (5844): 1517.

Olshansky, S. J. and Perls, T. T. 2008. "New Developments in the Illegal Provision of Growth Hormone for 'Anti-Aging' and Bodybuilding," *Journal of the American Medical Association* 299(23): 2792–2794.

Ortiz, R. 2008. "Crop Genetic Engineering under Global Climate Change," *Annals of Arid Zone* 47(3–4): 1–12.

Ourednick, V., Ourednick, J., Flax, J. D., Zawada, W. M., et al. 2001. "Segregation of Human Neutral Stem Cells in the Developing Primate Forebrain," *Science* 293: 1820–1824.

Owen, F. 1991. *Varieties of Moral Personality*. Cambridge, MA: Harvard University Press.

Palmer, C. 2011a. "Does Nature Matter? The Place of the Non-Human in the Ethics of Climate Change," in D. G. Arnold (ed.), *The Ethics of Global Climate Change*. Cambridge University Press, pp. 272–291.

   2011b. "Animal Disenhancement and the Non-Identity Problem: A Response to Thompson," *Nanoethics* 5(1): 43–48.

Parfit, D. 1982. "Future Generations: Further Problems," *Philosophy and Public Affairs* 11(2): 113–172.

   1983. "Energy Policy and the Further Future: The Identify Problem," in D. MacLean and P. G. Brown (eds.), *Energy and the Future*. Totowa, NJ: Rowman & Littlefield, pp. 166–179.

   1984. *Reasons and Persons*. Oxford: Clarendon Press.

Paterson, J. S., Araujo, M. B., Berry, P. M., Piper, J. M., and Rounsevell, M. D. A. 2008. "Mitigation, Adaptation and the Threat to Biodiversity," *Conservation Biology* 22(5): 1352–1355.

Perry, J. 2002. "Genetically Modified Crops," in M. Ruse and D. Castle (eds.), *Genetically Modified Foods*. Amherst, NY: Prometheus, pp. 115–122.

Pew Research Center 2011. "Fewer are Angry at Government, but Discontent Remains High: Overview," Washington, DC: Pew Research Center. Available at: http://people-press.org/report/711, accessed March 10, 2011.

Pimentel, D., Zuniga, R., and Morrison, D. 2005. "Update on the Environmental and Economic Costs Associated with Alien-Invasive Species in the United States," *Ecological Economics* 52(3): 273–288.

Pinchot, G. 1914. *The Training of a Forester*. Philadelphia, PA: J. B. Lippincott.

Pinker, S. 2002. *The Blank Slate: The Modern Denial of Human Nature*. New York: Penguin.

Plastic Surgery Research 2010. "Cosmetic Plastic Surgery Research: Statistics and Trends for 2001–2008," Plastic Surgery Research.info. Available at: www.cosmeticplasticsurgerystatistics.com/statistics.html#2008-NEWS, accessed March 11, 2011.

Plumwood, V. 2002. *Environmental Culture and the Ecological Crisis of Reason*. London: Routledge.

Posner, E. A. and Sunstein, C. R. 2007. "Climate Change Justice," *Georgetown Law Journal* 96: 1565–1612.

Pounds, J. A. and Crump, M. L. 1994. "Amphibian Declines and Climate Disturbance: The Case of the Golden Toad and the Harlequin Frog," *Conservation Biology* 8(1): 72–85.

Pounds, J. A., Bustamante, M. R., Coloma, L. A., Consuegra, J. A., et al. 2006. "Widespread Amphibian Extinctions from Epidemic Disease Driven by Global Warming," *Nature* 439: 161–167.

President's Council on Bioethics 2002. *Human Cloning and Human Dignity: An Ethical Inquiry*. Washington, DC: President's Council on Bioethics.

  2003. *Beyond Therapy*. Washington, DC: President's Council on Bioethics.

Presidential Commission for the Study of Bioethical Issues 2010. *New Directions: The Ethics of Synthetic Biology and Emerging Technologies*. Washington, DC: Presidential Commission for the Study of Bioethical Issues.

Preston, C. J. 2008. "Synthetic Biology: Drawing a Line in Darwin's Sand," *Environmental Values* 17: 23–39.

Preston, C. 2012. "Rethinking the Unthinkable," in C. Preston (ed.), *Engineering the Climate: The Ethics of Solar Radiation Management*. Lanham, MD: Lexington Books.

Prinz, J. 2006. "The Emotional Basis of Moral Judgments," *Philosophical Explorations* 9(1): 29–43.

Program on International Policy Attitudes 2003. "Americans and the World: Public Opinion on International Affairs: Biotechnology." WorldPublic Opinion.org. Available at: www.americans-world.org/digest/global_issues/biotechnology/bio_summary.cfm, accessed March 11, 2011.

Rachels, J. 1990. *Created from Animals: The Moral Implications of Darwinism*. Oxford University Press.

Raffensperger, C. 2002. "Learning to Speak Ethics in Technological Debates," in B. Bailey and M. Lappe (eds.), *Engineering the Farm: Ethical and Social Aspects of Agricultural Biotechnology*. Washington, DC: Island Press, pp. 125–133.

Rands, M. R. W., Adams, W. M., Bennun, L., Butchart, S. H. M., et al. 2010. "Biodiversity Conservation: Challenges Beyond 2010," *Science* 329(5997): 1298–1303.

Rasmussen, S., Bedau, M. A., Chen, L., Deamer, D., et al. (eds.) 2009. *Protocells: Bridging Nonliving and Living Matter*. Cambridge University Press.

Rawinski, T. J. 2008. "Impacts of White-Tailed Deer Overabundance in Forest Ecosystems: An Overview," *Forest Service, US Department of Agriculture*. Available at: http://na.fs.fed.us/fhp/special_interests/white_tailed_deer.pdf, accessed December 19, 2011.

Rawls, J. 1971. *A Theory of Justice*. Cambridge, MA: Harvard University Press.

1996. *Political Liberalism*. New York: Columbia University Press.

Regan, T. [1983/1985] 2004. *The Case for Animal Rights*. Berkeley, CA: University of California Press.

Regehr, E. V., Hunter, C. M., Caswell, H., Amstrup, S. C., and Stirling, I. 2010. "Survival and Breeding of Polar Bears in the Southern Beaufort Sea in Relation to Sea Ice," *Journal of Animal Ecology* 79: 117–127.

Registry of Standard Biological Parts 2010. "Main Page." Available at: http://partsregistry.org/Main_Page, accessed March 7, 2011.

Reichman, J., Watrud, L. S., Lee, E. H., Burdick, C. A., et al. 2006. "Establishment of Transgenic Herbicide-Resistant Creeping Bentgrass (*Agrostis stolonifera* L.) in Non-Agronomic Habitats," *Molecular Ecology* 15: 4243–4255.

Rewilding Europe 2011. "Home." Available at: http://rewildingeurope.com, accessed December 19, 2011.

Ricciardi, A. and Simberloff, D. 2009. "Assisted Colonization is not a Viable Conservation Strategy," *Trends in Ecology and Evolution* 24: 248–253.

Richardson, D. M., Hellmann, J. J., McLachlan, J., Sax, D. F., et al. 2009. "Multidimensional Evaluation of Managed Relocation," *Proceedings of the National Academy of Science* 106: 9721–9724.

Rifkin, J. 1985. *Declaration of a Heretic*. Boston, MA: Routledge & Kegan Paul.

Ro, D., Paradise, E., Ouellet, M., Fisher, K., et al. 2006. "Production of the Antimalarial Drug Precursor Artemisinic Acid in Engineered Yeast," *Nature* 440: 940–943.

Robert, J. S. and Baylis, F. 2003. "Crossing Species Boundaries," *American Journal of Bioethics* 3(3): 1–13.

Robock, A., Bunzl, M., Kravitz, B., and Stenchikov, G. L. 2010. "A Test for Geoengineering?" *Science* 327(5965): 530–531.

Robock, A., Marguardt, A., Kravitz, B., and Stenchikov, G. 2009. "Benefits, Risks, and Costs of Stratospheric Geoengineering," *Geophysical Research Letters* 36: L19703. DOI: 10.1029/2009GL039209.

Rode, K. D., Amstrup, S. C., and Regehr, E. V. 2010. "Reduced Body Size and Cub Recruitment in Polar Bears Associated with Sea Ice Decline," *Ecological Applications* 20: 768–782.

Rollins, B. E. 1995. *The Frankenstein Syndrome: Ethical and Social Issues in the Genetic Engineering of Animals*. New York: Cambridge University Press.

1998. "On *Telos* and Genetic Engineering," in A. Holland and A. Johnson (eds.), *Animal Biotechnology and Ethics*. New York: Chapman & Hall, pp. 156–171.

Rolston III, H. 1982. "Are Values in Nature Subjective or Objective?" *Environmental Ethics* 4: 125–151.

1986. *Philosophy Gone Wild: Essays in Environmental Ethics.* Amherst, NY: Prometheus.

1989. "Duties to Endangered Species," in *Philosophy Gone Wild.* Amherst, NY: Prometheus, pp. 206–222.

1995. "Duties to Endangered Species," *Encyclopedia of Environmental Biology* 1: 517–528.

2001. "Biodiversity," in D. Jamieson (ed.), *A Companion to Environmental Philosophy.* Oxford: Blackwell, pp. 402–415.

2003. "Value in Nature and the Nature of Values," in A. Light and H. Rolston III (eds.), *Environmental Ethics.* Malden, MA: Blackwell, pp. 143–153.

Root, T. L. and Schneider, S. H. 2006. "Conservation and Climate Change: The Challenge Ahead," *Conservation Biology* 20(3): 706–708.

Rosenzweig, M. 2003. *Win-Win Ecology: How Earth's Species can Survive in the Midst of Human Enterprise.* Oxford University Press.

Rossant, J. and Frels, W. I. 1980. "Interspecific Chimeras in Mammals: Successful Production of Live Chimeras Between *Mus musculus* and *Mus caroli*," *Science* 208(4442): 419–421.

Routtenberg, A., Cantallops, I., Zaffuto, S., Serrano, P., and Namgung, U. 2000. "Enhanced Learning after Genetic Overexpression of a Brain Growth Protein," *Proceedings of the National Academy of Sciences* 97(13): 7657–7662.

Royal Academy of Engineering (RAE) 2009. "Synthetic Biology: Public Dialogue on Synthetic Biology." London: Royal Academy of Engineering. Available at: www.raeng.org.uk/news/publications/list/reports/Syn_bio_dialogue_report. pdf, accessed January 26, 2012.

Royal Society 2009a. "Geoengineering the Climate: Science, Governance, and Uncertainty." Available at: http://royalsociety.org/geoengineering-the-climate, accessed March 11, 2011.

2009b. "Reaping the Benefits: Science and the Sustainable Intensification of Global Agriculture." Available at: http://royalsociety.org/uploadedFiles/ Royal_Society_Content/policy/publications/2009/4294967719.pdf, accessed January 5, 2012.

Rubenstein, D. R., Rubenstein, D. I., Sherman, P. W., and Gavi, T. A. 2006. "Pleistocene Park: Does Rewilding North America Represent Sound Conservation in the 21st Century?" *Biological Conservation* 132: 232–238.

Russell, A. W. and Sparrow, R. 2008. "The Case for Regulating Intragenic GMOs," *Journal of Agricultural and Environmental Ethics* 21: 153–181.

Rutgers, B. and Heeger, R. 1999. "Inherent Worth and Respect for Animal Integrity," in M. Dol, M. Fentener van Vliessingen, S. Kasanmoentalib,

T. Visser, and H. Zwart (eds.), *Recognizing the Intrinsic Values of Animals*. Assen: Van Gorcum, pp. 41–51.

Ryder, O. A. 2002. "Cloning Advances and Challenges for Conservation," *Trends in Biotechnology* 20(6): 231–232.

Ryder, O. A., McLaren, A., Brenner, S., Zhang, Y-P., and Benirschke, K. 2000. "DNA Banks for Endangered Animal Species," *Science* 288(5464): 275–277.

Saeidi, N., Wong, C. K., Lo, T-M., Nguyen, H. X., et al. 2011. "Engineering Microbes to Sense and Eradicate *Pseudomonas aeruginosa*, a Human Pathogen," *Molecular Systems Biology* 7: 521. DOI: 10.1038/msb.2011.55.

Sagoff, M. 1982. "At the Shrine of Our Lady of Fatima or Why Political Questions are not all Economic," *Arizona Law Review* 23: 1281–1298.

  1988. *The Economy of the Earth: Philosophy, Law, and the Environment*. New York: Cambridge University Press.

Sahasrabudhe, S. and Motter, A. E. 2011. "Rescuing Ecosystems from Extinction Cascades through Compensatory Perturbations," *Nature Communications* 2: 1–8.

Salazar, C., Baxter, S. W., Pardo-Diaz, C., Wu, G., et al. 2010. "Genetic Evidence for Hybrid Trait Speciation in *Heliconius* Butterflies," *PLoS Genet* 6(4): e1000930.

Sandel, M. J. 2007. *The Case Against Perfection: Ethics in the Age of Genetic Engineering*. Cambridge, MA: Harvard University Press.

Sandler, R. 2007. *Character and Environment. A Virtue-Oriented Approach to Environmental Ethics*. New York: Columbia University Press.

  2011. "Enhancing Moral Status?" National Humanities Center. Available at: http://onthehuman.org/2011/05/enhancing-moral-status, accessed December 19, 2011.

  2012a. "Global Warming and Virtues of Ecological Restoration," in Thompson and Bendik-Keymer (eds.), *The Virtues of the Future: Climate Change and the Challenge of Restoring Humanity*. pp. 63–79.

  2012b. "Solar Radiation Management and Nonhuman Species," in C. Preston (ed.), *Engineering the Climate: The Ethics of Solar Radiation Management*. Lanham, MD: Lexington.

  In press. "The Ethics of Mitigation," in M. Di Paola and G. Pellegino (eds.), *The Ethics and Politics of Climate Change*. London: Routledge.

Sandler, R. and Basl, J. 2010. "Transhumanism, Human Dignity, and Moral Status," *American Journal of Bioethics* 10(7): 63–66.

Sandler, R. and Cafaro, P. 2005. *Environmental Virtue Ethics*. Lanham, MD: Rowman & Littlefield.

Sandler, R. and Crane, J. 2006. "On the Moral Considerability of *Homo sapiens* and Other Species," *Environmental Values* 15: 69–84.

Sandler, R. and Kay, W. D. 2006. "The GMO-Nanotech (Dis)Analogy?" *Bulletin of Science, Technology, and Society* 26: 57–62.

Sandler, R. and Pezzullo, P. C. (eds.) 2007. *Environmental Justice and Environmentalism: The Social Justice Challenge to the Environmental Movement.* Cambridge, MA: MIT Press.

Sandøe, P. and Christensen, S. B. 2008. *The Ethics of Animal Use.* Oxford: Wiley-Blackwell.

Sandøe, P., Nielsen, B. L., Christensen, S. B., and Sørensen, P. 1999. "Staying Good while Playing God – The Ethics of Breeding Farm Animals," *Animal Welfare* 8: 313–328.

Sarkar, S. 2005. *Biodiversity and Environmental Philosophy: An Introduction.* Cambridge University Press.

Savulescu, J. 2010. "The Human Prejudice and the Moral Status of Enhanced Beings: What Do We Owe the Gods?" in J. Savulescu and N. Bostrom (eds.), *Human Enhancement.* Oxford University Press, pp. 211–247.

Sax, D. F. and Gaines, S. D. 2008. "Species Invasion and Extinction: The Future of Native Biodiversity on Islands," *Proceedings of the National Academy of Sciences* 105: 11490–11497.

Schafer-Landau, R. 2003. *Moral Realism: A Defence.* Oxford University Press.

Schlaepfer, M. A. 2005. "Rewilding: A Bold Plan that Needs Native Megafauna," *Nature* 437(7061): 951.

Schlaepfer, M. A., Sax, D. V., and Olden, J. D. 2011. "The Potential Conservation Value of Non-Native Species," *Conservation Biology* 25(3): 428–437.

Schliebe, S., Evans, T., Johnson, H., Roy, M., et al. 2006. "Range-wide Status Review of the Polar Bear (*Ursus maritimus*)." Anchorage, AK: US Fish and Wildlife Service.

Schouten, H. J., Krens, F. A., and Jacobsen, E. 2006a. "Cisgenic Plants are Similar to Traditionally Bred Plants," *EMBO Reports* 7(7): 750–753.

2006b. "Do Cisgenic Plants Warrant Less Stringent Oversight?" *Nature Biotechnology* 24(7): 753.

Schrag, D. P. 2007. "Preparing to Capture Carbon," *Science* 315: 812.

Schwartz, M. 2004/2005. "Conservationists Should Not Move *Torreya taxifolia*," *Wild Earth* Winter/Spring: 73–79.

Schwille, P. 2011. "Bottom-Up Synthetic Biology: Engineering in a Tinkerer's World," *Science* 333(6047): 1252–1254.

Scott, D. 2005. "The Magic Bullet Criticism of Agricultural Biotechnology," *Agriculture and Environmental Ethics* 18(3): 259–267.

Sharma, S., Vander Zanden, M. J., Magnuson, J. J., and Lyons, J. 2011. "Comparing Climate Change and Species Invasions as Drivers of Coldwater Fish Population Extirpations," *PLoS ONE* 6(8): e22906.

Shepard, P. M. and Corbin-Mark, C. 2009. "Climate Justice," *Environmental Justice* 2 (4): 163–166.

Shindler, B. and Cheek, K. A. 1999. "Integrating Citizens in Adaptive Management: A Propositional Analysis," *Conservation Ecology* 3(1): 9–23.

Shirey, P. D. and Lamberti, G. A. 2009. "Assisted Colonization Under the US Endangered Species Act," *Conservation Letters* 3: 45–52.

Simberloff, D. 2011. "Non-natives: 141 Scientists Object," *Nature* 475: 36.

Simberloff, D., Souza, L., Nuñez, M. A., Barrios-Garcia, M. N., et al. In press. "The Natives are Restless, but not Often and Mostly when Disturbed," *Ecology*. DOI: 10.1890/11–1232.1

Sinervo, B., Mendez-de-la-Cruz, F., Miles, D. B., Heulin, B., et al. 2010. "Erosion of Lizard Diversity by Climate Change and Altered Thermal Niches," *Science* 328(5980): 894–899.

Singer, P. 1977. *Animal Liberation*. London: Paladin.

1989. "All Animals are Equal," in T. Regan and P. Singer (eds.), *Animal Rights and Human Obligations*. Upper Saddle River, NJ: Prentice Hall, pp. 148–162.

Smallwood, P., Olveczky, B., Williams, G., Jacobs, G., et al. 2003. "Genetically Engineered Mice with an Additional Class of Cone Photoreceptors: Implications for the Evolution of Color Vision," *Proceedings of the National Academy of Sciences* 100: 11706–11711.

Smith, C. 2005. "Rewilding: Reintroductions could Reduce Biodiversity," *Nature* 437: 318.

Smith, D. S., Asche, F., Guttormsen, A. G., and Wiener, J. B. 2010. "Genetically Modified Salmon and Full Impact Assessment," *Science* 330(6007): 1052–1053.

Smith, T. B., Kark, S., Schneider, C. J., Wayne, R. K., and Moritz, C. 2001. "Biodiversity Hotspots and Beyond: The Need for Preserving Environmental Transitions," *Trends in Ecology and Evolution* 16(8): 431.

Smithsonian Institution 2001. "Passenger Pigeon," *Encyclopedia Smithsonian*. Available at: www.si.edu/encyclopedia_Si/nmnh/passpig.htm, accessed September 14, 2011.

Sober, E. 1986. "Philosophical Problems for Environmentalism," in B. Norton (ed.), *The Preservation of Species*. Princeton University Press, pp. 173–194.

Sober, E. and Wilson, D. S. 1998. *Unto Others: The Evolution and Psychology of Unselfish Behavior*. Cambridge, MA: Harvard University Press.

Sogge, M. K., Sferra, S. J., and Paxton, E. H. 2008. "Tamarix as Habitat for Birds: Implications for Riparian Restoration in the Southwestern United States," *Restoration Ecology* 16: 146–154.

Sokal, R. and Crovello, T. 1970. "The Biological Species Concept: A Critical Evaluation," *American Naturalist* 104: 127–153.

Soulé, M. E. 1985. "What is Conservation Biology?" *Bioscience* 35(11): 727–734.

Southgate, C., Hunt, C., and Horrell, D. 2008. "Ascesis and Assisted Migration: Responses to the Effects of Climate Change on Animal Species," *European Journal of Science and Theology* 4: 99–111.

Spratt, D. and Sutton, P. 2008. *Climate "Code Red": The Case for Sustainability Emergency.* Melbourne, Australia: Friends of the Earth.

Stamos, D. N. 2003. *The Species Problem.* Lanham, MD: Lexington Books.

Sterba, J. 1995. "A Biocentrist Fights Back," *Environmental Ethics* 17(4): 361–376.
    2001. *Three Challenges to Ethics: Environmentalism, Feminism, and Multiculturalism.* Oxford University Press.

Stern, N. 2006. *The Stern Review of the Economics of Climate Change.* Cambridge University Press.

Stirling, I. and Derocher, A. E. 2007. "Melting Under Pressure: The Real Scoop on Climate Warming and Polar Bears," *The Wildlife Professional* 1(3): 24–27, 43.

Stirling, I. and Parkinson, C. L. 2006. "Possible Effects of Climate Warming on Selected Populations of Polar Bears (*Ursus maritimus*) in the Canadian Arctic," *Arctic* 59(3): 261–275.

Stirling, I., Lunn, N. J., Iacozza, J., Elliott, C., and Obbard, M. 2004. "Polar Bear Distribution and Abundance on the Southwestern Hudson Bay Coast during Open Water Season, in Relation to Population Trends and Annual Ice Patterns," *Arctic* 57(1): 15–26.

Stock, G. 2002. *Redesigning Humans.* Boston, MA: Houghton Mifflin Harcourt.

Stone, C. 1972. "Should Trees Have Standing?" *Southern California Law Review* 45: 450–501.

Stone, R. 2010. "Home Home Outside the Range," *Science* 329: 1592–1594.

Strain, D. 2011. "8.7 Million: A New Estimate for All the Complex Species on Earth," *Science* 333(6046): 1083.

Streiffer, R. 2003. "In Defense of the Moral Relevance of Species Boundaries," *American Journal of Bioethics* 3(3): 37–38.
    2005. "At the Edge of Humanity: Human Stem Cells, Chimera, and Moral Status," *Kennedy Institute of Ethics Journal* 15(4): 347–370.

Streiffer, R. and Hedemann, T. 2005. "The Political Import of Intrinsic Objections to Genetically Engineered Food," *Journal of Agricultural and Environmental Ethics* 18: 191–210.

Streiffer, R. and Rubel, A. 2004. "Democratic Principles and Mandatory Labeling of Genetically Engineered Foods," *Public Affairs Quarterly* 18(3): 223–248.

Stringer, L. C., Dougill, A. J., Fraser, E., Hubacek, K., et al. 2006. "Unpacking 'Participation' in the Adaptive Management of Social–Ecological Systems: A Critical Review," *Ecology and Society* 11(2): 39.

Strong, A., Chisholm, S., Miller, C., and Cullen, J. 2009. "Ocean Fertilization: Time to Move On," *Nature* 461: 347–348.

Sutherland, W. J., Clout, M., Cote, I. M., Daszak, P., et al. 2010. "A Horizon Scan of Global Conservation Issues for 2010," *Trends in Ecology and Evolution* 25(1): 1–7.

Swenson, W., Wilson, D. S., and Elias, R. 2000. "Artificial Ecosystem Selection," *Proceedings of the National Academy of Sciences* 97(16): 9110–9114.

Sylvan, R. 1973. "Is There a Need for a New, an Environmental Ethic?" *Proceedings of the Fifteenth World Congress of Philosophy* 1: 205–210.

Szostak Lab 2009. "Home." Szostak Lab. Available at: http://genetics.mgh.harvard.edu/szostakweb/index.html, accessed March 7, 2011.

Tan, D. P., Liu, Q. Y., Koshiya, N., Gu, H., and Alkon, D. 2006. "Enhancement of Long-Term Memory Retention and Short-Term Synaptic Plasticity in cbl-b null Mice," *Proceedings of the National Academy of Sciences* 103(13): 5125–5130.

Tan, J., Pu, Z., Ryberg, W. A., and Jiang, L. 2011. "Species Phylogenetic Relatedness, Priority Effects, and Ecosystem Functioning," *Ecology*. DOI: http://dx.doi.org/10.1890/11-1557.1.

Tang, Y. P., Shimizu, J., Dube, G. R., Rampon, C., et al. 1999. "Genetic Enhancement of Learning and Memory in Mice," *Nature* 401: 63–69.

Taylor, P. 1986. *Respect for Nature: A Theory of Environmental Ethics*. Princeton University Press.

Taylor, S. W., Carroll, A. L., Alfaro, R. I., and Safranyik, L. 2006. "Pine Beetle Outbreak Dynamics in Western Canada," in L. Safranyik and B. Wilson (eds.), *The Mountain Pine Beetle: A Synthesis of Biology, Management and Impacts on Lodgepole Pine*. Victoria: Natural Resources Canada, Canadian Forest Service, pp. 67–94.

Thomas, C. D. 2011. "Translocation of Species, Climate Change, and the End of Trying to Recreate Past Ecological Communities," *Trends in Ecology and Evolution* 26(5): 216–221.

Thomas, C. D., Cameron, A., Green, R. E., Bakkenes, M., et al. 2004. "Extinction Risk from Climate Change," *Nature* 427: 145–148.

Thompson, A. 2010. "Radical Hope for Living Well in a Warmer World," *Journal of Agriculture and Environmental Ethics* 23(1): 43–45.

Thompson, A. and Bendik-Keymer, J. (eds.) 2012. *The Virtues of the Future: Climate Change and the Challenge of Restoring Humanity*. Cambridge, MA: MIT Press.

Thompson, K. and Davis, M. A. 2011. "Why Research on Traits of Invasive Plants Tells us Very Little," *Trends in Ecology and Evolution* 26(4): 155–156.

Thompson, P. 2002. "Why Food Biotechnology Needs an Opt Out," in B. Bailey and M. Lappe (eds.), *Engineering the Farm: Ethical and Social Aspects of Agricultural Biotechnology*. Washington, DC: Island Press, pp. 27–44.

2008. "The Opposite of Human Enhancement: Nanotechnology and the Blind Chicken Problem," *Nanoethics* 2: 305–316.

Throop, W. 2012. "Environmental Virtues and the Aims of Restoration," in Thompson and Bendik-Keymer (eds.), *The Virtues of the Future: Climate Change and the Challenge of Restoring Humanity*, pp. 47–62.

Turnbaugh, P. J., Ley, R. E., Hamady, M., Fraser-Liggett, C. M., et al. 2007. "The Human Microbiome Project," *Nature* 449: 804–810.

Turner, W. R., Bradley, B. A., Estes, L. D., Hole, D. G., et al. 2010. "Climate Change: Helping Nature Survive the Human Response," *Conservation Letters* 3(5): 304–312.

Turner, W. R., Oppenheimer, M., and Wilcove, D. S. 2009. "A Force to Fight Global Warming," *Nature* 462: 278–279.

United Nations 1992a. Rio Declaration on Environment and Development. Available at: www.unesco.org/education/information/nfsunesco/pdf/RIO_E.PDF, accessed April 19, 2012.

1992b. Convention on Biological Diversity. Available at: www.cbd.int/doc/legal/cbd-en.pdf, accessed March 11, 2011.

United Nations Environmental Programme (UNEP) 2009. *Climate Change Science Compendium 2009*. New York: UNEP.

United Nations Food and Agriculture Organization (UNFAO) 2004. "The State of Food and Agricultural Biotechnology: Meeting the Needs of the Poor?" *FAO Agriculture Series No. 35*. Rome: UNFAO.

United States Climate Change Science Program 2008. *Preliminary Review of Adaptation Options for Climate-Sensitive Ecosystems and Resources*. Washington, DC: Environmental Protection Agency. Available at: www.climatescience.gov/Library/sap/sap4-4/final-report, accessed March 10, 2011.

United States Congress 1973. Endangered Species Act (*as Amended through December 2004*). 109th Congress, First Session. Washington, DC.

United States Department of Agriculture (USDA) 2011. "Adoption of Genetically Engineered Crops in the US." Available at: www.ers.usda.gov/Data/BiotechCrops, accessed January 5, 2012.

United States Energy Information Administration 2010. "Energy and the Environment Explained." Available at: www.eia.gov/energyexplained/index.cfm?page=environment_home, accessed March 8, 2011.

United States Global Change Research Program 2009. *Global Climate Change Impacts in the United States*, T. R. Karl, J. M. Melillo, and T. C. Peterson (eds.). New York: Cambridge University Press.

United States Sentencing Commission, Steroids Working Group 2006. *Steroid Report*. Washington, DC: United States Sentencing Commission.

University of Chicago Medical Center 2007. "'Interspecies' Rodent Created Using Embryonic Stem Cells," *Science Daily*. Available at: www.sciencedaily.com/releases/2007/10/071019093241.htm, accessed March 11, 2011.

University of Michigan Health System 2008. "Stress May Lead Students to Use Stimulants," *Science Daily*. Available at: www.sciencedaily.com/releases/2008/04/080407195349.htm, accessed March 10, 2011.

Urban, M. C., Tewksbury, J. J., and Sheldon, K. S. 2012. "On a Collision Course: Competition and Dispersal Differences Create No-analog Communities and Cause Extinctions During Climate Change," *Proceedings of the Royal Society B*. DOI: 10.1098/rspb.2011.2367.

van Kleunen, M., Dawson, W., and Dostal, P. 2011. "Research on Invasive-plant Traits Tells Us a Lot," *Trends in Ecology and Evolution* 26(7): 317.

van Valen, L. 1976. "Ecological Species, Multispecies, and Oaks," *Taxon* 25(2/3): 233–239.

van Wensveen, L. 1999. *Dirty Virtues*. New York: Humanity Books.

Varner, G. 1998. *In Nature's Interests? Interests, Animal Rights and Environmental Ethics*. New York: Oxford University Press.

Vatican 2009. "Transgenic Plants for Food Security in the Context of Development," PAS Study Week, Vatican City. Available at: www.task-force.org/web/Vatican-PAS-Statement-FPT-PDF/PAS-Statement-English-FPT.pdf, accessed June 15, 2012.

Verhoog, H. 2003. "Naturalness and the Genetic Modification of Animals," *Trends in Biotechnology* 21(7): 294–297.

Verhoog, H., Matze, M., Lammerts van Bueren, E. T., and Baars, T. 2003. "The Role of the Concept of the Natural (Naturalness) in Organic Farming," *Journal of Agricultural and Environmental Ethics* 16: 29–49.

Vié, J-C., Hilton-Taylor, C., and Stuart, S. N. (eds.) 2009. *Wildlife in a Changing World: An Analysis of the 2008 IUCN Red List of Threatened Species*. Gland, Switzerland: IUCN.

Vilà, M. and Hulme, P. E. 2011. "Jurassic Park? No Thanks," *Trends in Ecology and Evolution* 26(10): 496–497.

Vince, G. 2011. "Embracing Invasives," *Science* 331(6023): 1383–1384.

Vitt, P., Havens, K., Kramer, A. T., Sollenberger, D., and Yates, E. 2010. "Assisted Migration of Plants: Changes in Latitudes, Changes in Attitudes," *Biological Conservation* 143(1): 18–27.

Vogel, S. 2002. "Environmental Philosophy after the End of Nature," *Environmental Ethics* 24(1): 23–39.

Wang, Y., Zhang, C., Yu, R. T., Cho, H. K., et al. 2004. "Regulation of Muscle Fiber Type and Running Endurance by PPAR8," *PLoS Biology* 2(10): 294.

Wapner, P. 2010. *Living Through the End of Nature: The Future of American Environmentalism.* Cambridge, MA: MIT Press.

Watrud, L. S., Lee, E. H., Fairbrother, A., Burdick, C., et al. 2004. "Evidence for Landscape-Level, Pollen-Mediated Gene Flow from Genetically Modified Creeping Bentgrass with CP4 EPSPS as a Marker," *Proceedings of the National Academy of Science* 101(40): 14533–14538.

Webber, B. L., Scott, J. K., and Didham, R. K. 2011. "Translocation or Bust! A New Acclimatization Agenda for the 21st century?" *Trends in Ecology and Evolution* 26(10): 495–496.

Wenz, P. 2005. "Engineering Genetic Injustice," *Bioethics* 19(1): 1–11.

Whitesides, G. 2001. "The Once and Future Nanomachine," *Scientific American.* Available at: www.ruf.rice.edu/~rau/phys600/whitesides.htm, accessed March 11, 2011.

Wigley, T. M. L. 2006. "A Combined Mitigation/Geoengineering Approach to Climate Stabilization," *Science* 314(5798): 452–454.

Wilcove, D. S., Rothstein, D., Bubow, J., Phillips, A., and Losos, E. 1998. "Quantifying Threats to Imperiled Species in the United States," *Bioscience* 48(8): 607–615.

Wiley, E. O. 1978. "The Evolutionary Species Concept Reconsidered," *Systematic Zoology* 27(1): 17–26.

Williams, F., Eschen, R., Harris, A., Djeddour, D., et al. 2010. "The Economic Cost of Invasive Non-Native Species on Great Britain," *CABI.* Available at: http://secure.fera.defra.gov.uk/nonnativespecies, accessed December 19, 2011.

Willis, S. G., Hill, J. K., Thomas, C. D., Roy, D. B., et al. 2008. "Assisted Colonization in a Changing Climate: A Test-Study Using Two UK Butterflies," *Conservation Letters* 2: 45–51.

Wilson, D. S. and Swenson, W. 2003. "Community Genetics and Community Selection," *Ecology* 84: 586–588.

Wilson, E. O. [1999] 2010. *The Diversity of Life.* New York: W. W. Norton.

Wilson, J. 2007. "Transhumanism and Moral Equality," *Bioethics* 21(8): 419–425.

World Bank 2008. *World Bank Development Indicators*. Available at: http://books. google.com/books?id=O67oDJW01pwC&printsec=frontcover&source=gbs_ ge_summary_r&cad=0#v=onepage&q&f=false, accessed January 26, 2012.

World Health Organization (WHO) 2010. "Malaria: Fact Sheet." Available at: www.who.int/mediacentre/factsheets/fs094/en, accessed March 10, 2011.

Worm, B., Barbier, E.B., Beaumont, N., Duffy, J.E., et al. 2006. "Impacts of Biodiversity Loss on Ocean Ecosystem Services," *Science* 314(5800): 787–790.

Wouters, A. 2005. "The Function Debate in Philosophy," *Acta Biotheoretica* 53(2): 123–151.

Yule, J. 2002. "Cloning the Extinct: Restoration as Ecological Prostheses," *Common Ground* 1(2): 6–9.

Zeebe, R.E. and Archer, D. 2005. "Feasibility of Ocean Fertilization and its Impact on Future Atmospheric CO_2 Levels," *Geophysical Research Letters* 32: L09703. DOI: 10.1029/2005GL022449.

Zimmer, C. 2007. "A Radical Step to Preserve a Species: Assisted Migration," *New York Times*. Available at: www.nytimes.com/2007/01/23/science/23migrate. html?pagewanted=1, accessed March 11, 2011.

Zimov, S. 2005. "Pleistocene Park: Return of the Mammoth's Ecosystem," *Science* 308: 796–798.

Index